THE CATHOLIC UNIVERSITY OF AMERICA
CANON LAW STUDIES
No. 239

CONTRACTS BETWEEN BISHOPS AND RELIGIOUS CONGREGATIONS

A HISTORICAL SYNOPSIS AND A COMMENTARY

BY

REV. TIMOTHY LYNCH, M.S.SS.T., J.C.L.
Priest of the Congregation of the Missionary Servants of the Most Holy Trinity

A DISSERTATION

Submitted to the Faculty of the School of Canon Law of the Catholic University of America in Partial Fulfillment of the Requirements for the Degree of Doctor of Canon Law

THE CATHOLIC UNIVERSITY OF AMERICA PRESS
WASHINGTON, D. C.
1946

Nihil Obstat:

HIERONYMUS D. HANNAN, A.M., S.T.D., LL.B., J.C.D.,
Censor Deputatus.

Washingtonii, D. C., die 31, iulii, 1946.

Imprimatur:

✠ MICHAEL J. CURLEY, D.D.,
Archiepiscopus Baltimorensis-Washingtonensis.

Washingtonii, D. C., die 31 iulii, 1946.

Printed by
THE PAULIST PRESS
401 West 59th Street
New York 19, N. Y.

51

MARIAE MATRI

SPONSAE IMMACULATAE

SPIRITUS SANCTI

TABLE OF CONTENTS

CHAPTER IV

CHAPTER V

CHAPTER VI

CHAPTER VII

PART II

CHAPTER VIII

FOREWORD

As long as man has lived in society with his fellow man, he has made pacts and agreements. From these pacts and verbal agreements, as civilization progressed, the system of contracts developed. The agricultural mode of life in early times did not need contracts as did the future generation of bankers and merchants. It was with the rise of trade between people of the same nation and with people of other nations that contracts received the stimulus and approached the importance in law which marks them today.

It was in Roman Law that the modern law of contracts was chiefly developed. With the advent of Christianity, little change was wrought in the Roman Law system of contracts. Emphasis was placed upon the moral issues involved, although contract as it existed in Roman Law had already achieved a high moral as well as technical development. It is for this reason that the law of contract is that part of Roman Law which has survived in modern legal systems with the least alteration.

For this reason, also, it was deemed necessary in this work to show the development of the various types of contracts in Roman Law, especially since the concept of the individual contracts so developed has been accepted by Canon Law. The material selected from the *Decretum Gratiani* and from the Decretals was chosen with an eye towards bringing out the relations of bishops and religious congregations in contracting with each other.

A contract is generally defined as an agreement of two or more persons about the same thing, producing an obligation arising from commutative justice. A bilateral contract produces this obligation in both contracting parties. The portion of this treatise dealing with the development of contracts is restricted almost exclusively to bilateral contracts, since this is the type usually employed in agreements between bishops and religious congregations. Unilateral contracts are touched upon only incidentally and by way of demonstration of the evolution of bilateral contracts in Roman Law.

The effect of conciliar legislation on the contractual power of both bishops and religious is discussed. An endeavor in made to indicate the application of previous church legislation to contracts between these parties. The relation of religious institutes to this problem is treated in the order of their historical development. Particular attention is paid to the solemnities necessary for the formulation of a contract and the application of these solemnities to different types of religious institutes.

With the advent of the Code of Canon Law, the great innovation brought about by the general adoption of the civil law of each territory in regard to contracts demands special analysis. The lack of case law in the ecclesiastical forum is supplied to some degree by the introduction of conclusions from civil law decisions which are compatible with canonical jurisprudence. The Canon Law provision canonizing the civil law regarding contractual matters has not yet reached that full stage of development which can only be achieved by numerous declarations on individual matters by the Holy See. Pending authentic interpretations modifying the scope of the adoption of civil contractual law, a literal interpretation of Canon 1529 as contained in the Code and as accepted by canonists will be applied to the contracts under discussion in this work.

The canonical principles expressed are applicable to all types of contracts between bishops and religious congregations. However, it has been deemed advisable to emphasize those contracts which concern the assignment of parishes to religious congregations. In addition to their practical importance, the basic juridical problems involved demand special elucidation. With a proper safeguarding of the rights of both parties, an attempt will be made to propose suggestions which serve the interest of both law and equity. By the interaction of both, the fulfillment of the desire of the I Council of Carthage (348): *"Pax servetur, pacta custodiantur,"* [1] will be considerably facilitated. As a practical aid, an Appendix containing forms for various types of contracts now in use is included.

The writer wishes to express his gratitude to his religious superiors for the opportunity of graduate study in Canon Law. A special word of gratitude is due to the Reverend Eugene A. Dooley,

[1] Bruns, *Canones Apostolorum et Conciliorum Veterum Saeculorum IV-VII* (2 vols., Berolini, 1839), I, 116.

O. M. I., J. C. D. of Newburgh, New York and to the Reverend Michael Harding, O. F. M., of Holy Name College, Brookland, D. C. for their kindness and valuable suggestions. Profound appreciation is due to the members of the Faculty of the School of Canon Law of the Catholic University for their cordial and generous assistance, to the Discaled Carmelite Fathers of Carmelite College, Brookland, D. C., and to all others whose suggestions and encouragement have made this work possible. Lastly, the writer wishes to express his gratitude to his brothers, the Missionary Servants of the Most Holy Trinity and to his sisters, the Missionary Servants of the Most Blessed Trinity whose prayers, encouragement and kindly help contributed much towards the completion of this work.

Part I

Historical Synopsis

CHAPTER I

BILATERAL CONTRACTS IN ROMAN LAW

Gaius (second century) describes contracts as one of the modes of creating an obligation.[1] Before the time of Gaius, Labeo in the early first century of the Christian era had given the definition of contract as something above and beyond obligation, which the Greeks called συνάλλαγμα (bilateral), such as buying and selling, renting and hiring, and partnership.[2] Ulpian (+229) remarked that some agreements of the *ius gentium* allowed judicial actions, and some allowed judicial exceptions only. Those which allowed actions had the proper name of contract; such are sale, renting, partnership, deposit, and other similar contracts.[3] Civil obligations arose from the synallagmatic or bilateral contract according to Celsus (+ca. 130).[4]

In the earliest times, an agreement was made through the use of an oath (*iurisiurandum* or *Iovis iurandum*), by which means men called upon Jupiter to witness their good faith. This method disappeared with the rise of other forms of binding agreements. The use of this oath was still retained in the *Digest* in the single case in which freedmen agreed to give due service to their patrons.[5] Gaius

[1] Gaius. *Institutiones* (ed. Johannes Baviera in *Fontes Iuris Romanae Antejustiniani*, Florentiae, 1909), III, 88. Hereafter cited Gaius.

[2] *Corpus Iuris Civilis* (3 vols., Vol. I, ed. stereotypa quinta decima, *Institutiones*, quas recognovit Paulus Krueger, *Digesta* quae recognovit Theodorus Mommsen, retractavit Paulus Krueger, Berolini: Apud Weidmannos, 1928), D. (50, 16) 19. Hereinafter cited I. and D.

[3] D. (2, 14) (7, 1).

[4] D. (2, 14) (7, 1).

[5] D. (38, 1) 7.

refers to this oath in his *Institutiones.*[6] The penal sanction invoked against violators of the oath in the early times was most severe. Divine protection was withdrawn and the delinquent was at the mercy of any man who chose to slay him.

Another early form of agreement was known as *sponsio*. It developed from the original ceremony of pouring out wine (σπονδή, σπένδειν) for the sake of lending a sacred character to the contract. Later this evolved as the verbal contract known to Gaius.[7] In early times the pouring out of wine signified that blood would be spilt if the agreement were broken. Gaius admitted the possibility of the Greek origin of *sponsio,* but he stated that the word *spondeo* was so peculiarly Roman that it could not be rendered in Greek.[8]

Sponsio was used by the Romans also in connection with *Sponsalia* or betrothal. It seems that at one time this contract could be sued upon, but the employment of this legal action was later revoked, for in the words of Paulus (late 2nd—early 3rd century) it tended to immorality to hold a marriage, existing or future, to be dependent on a penal bond.[9]

Gaius questioned those who would allow *sponsio* to be used by aliens, even in making treaties of peace. This indicates that, even at the time of Gaius, this contract had departed far from the original wine-pouring contract for making peace treaties, whence the contract itself derived its name.

ARTICLE 1. THE CONTRACT OF *Nexum*

There is much dispute about the contract of *nexum.* That it designated a contract is known from the very derivation of the word. That it was made *per aes et libram* is known from Gaius.[10] The use of the scale and copper coin was a favorite Roman method of making binding agreements. Leage distinguishes it from *Mancipatio,* which

[6] (3.83).

[7] (3.93).

[8] *Loc. cit.*

[9] *Corpus Iuris Civilis* (Vol. II, ed. stereotypa nona, *Codex Iustinianus,* quem recognovit et retractavit Paulus Krueger, Berolini: Apud Weidmannos, 1915), C. (1, 3) 56. Hereinafter cited C.

[10] (3.173).

was also made *per aes et libram*, "but whereas *mancipatio* was a sale, the *nexum* was probably a money loan." [11]

The *Twelve Tables* remedied some of the abuses which had arisen from the use of *nexum* by placing emphasis on the words rather than on the act of weighing the copper pieces. Hence the Table states: "*Cum nexum faciet mancipiumque uti lingua nuncupassit ita ius esto*", i. e., that the language used in the nexal loan was to be adhered to strictly. It seems that the contract of *nexum* followed the same form as *solutio* described by Gaius. *Nexum* was abolished by the *Lex Poetelia* (313 B. C.) because of the severity of its sanction, which was the "*manus iniectio*" (execution on the body of the debtor) by which the creditor could enslave the debtor if the terms of the contract were not carried out.[12]

Article 2. *Dotis Dictio*

Ulpian enumerated three ways of bestowing a dowry—*dotis dictio, dotis promissio*, and *dotis datio*.[13] The Theodosian Code indicates that the *dotis dictio* was borrowed from the ancient law.[14] Gaius limited the ability to contract an obligation in the giving of a dowry by means of a *dotis dictio* to the bride, to her father, and to her debtors.[15] A dowry had to be provided by the bride's father under penalty of ignominy.[16]

The form was an oral declaration on the part of the one giving the dowry, spoken in the presence of the bridegroom. In this declaration the amount of property to be bestowed was set forth. The property could be movable or immovable.[17] This contract was

[11] Leage, *Roman Private Law* (second edition by C. H. Ziegler, London: Macmillan & Co., reprinted in 1942), p. 293.

[12] Muirhead (1855-1940) summed up the admission of most authors about the *nexum* when he wrote: "Nexum has been the subject of many disquisitions, and opinions about it are conflicting."—*The Institutes of Gaius and the Rules of Ulpian* (Edinburgh, 1904), fn. to Gaius (3.89), p. 208.

[13] Muirhead, *op. cit.*, Ulpian (6.2).

[14] *Codices Gregorianus, Hermogenianus, Theodosianus* (edidit Gustavus Haenel, prostant Bonnae; Apud Adolphum Marcum, 1942), C. Th. (3.123).

[15] (3.96).

[16] D. (24.3) 1.

[17] Gaius (3.96).

undoubtedly protected with a legal sanction, since Gaius spoke of the one who gave the dowry as being bound lawfully by the *dotis dictio.*[18] *Dotis dictio* as a contract had become obsolete by Justinian's time (527-565).

The prevalent custom recognized by law in Justinian's time was to bind the giver of the dowry by a simple stipulation, a verbal contract by which the dowry was promised in the event that the marriage took place. This was known as the *dotis promissio.* If the dowry was handed over immediately, it was understood that it would be returned in the event that the marriage did not take place. This contract was known as the *dotis datio. Dotis promissio* and *dotis datio* were of much later origin than *dotis dictio,* which was one of the earliest of binding contracts.[19]

ARTICLE 3. *Mancipatio*

Mancipatio was described by Gaius as a fictitious sale. He explained that it had to be made in the presence of five witnesses and of an officer holding a scale (*libripens*).[20] It was used as a means of transferring the ownership of a slave. Gaius indicated the form to be used in the making of this transfer.[21] Ulpian restricted its use to *res mancipi* which explains how this class of goods received its name.[22] The *Twelve Tables* contained the provision that when anyone contracted concerning property or sold it by making a verbal statement, this agreement was to have the force of law.[23]

ARTICLE 4. CONCLUSIONS CONCERNING THE EARLY ROMAN FORMS OF CONTRACT

All the contracts so far treated had serious limitations: (1) They were restricted in use to Roman citizens; (2) the contracting

[18] *Loc. cit.*

[19] Amos, *Roman Civil Law* (London, 1883), p. 288.

[20] (1.113).

[21] (1.119).

[22] (19.3). Land, houses or permanent buildings in Italy, slaves and domesticated animals were all considered *res mancipi.*

[23] "Cum nexum faciet mancipiumque uti lingua nuncupassit ita ius esto."

parties had to be present in order to make the agreement binding; (3) the contractual form was intensely formalistic, and this formalism was essential for the validity of the contract; and (4) remedies at law in the event of a breach of contract were of a vague and indefinite character.

By the end of the Republic these defects were remedied. *Stipulatio* was introduced. It was similar to *sponsio,* but differed in the important feature that it was available to aliens as well as to Roman citizens.[24] Stipulatory contracts were made actionable by the *Lex Silia.*[25] Next came the contract of suretyship called *fideipromissio.* The form to be used in the making of this contract is indicated by Gaius.[26] He explained that *fideipromissores* as well as *sponsores* were employed frequently to obtain greater security for a contract.[27]

Before a true contract could arise in Roman Law two elements were necessary: (1) The agreement of the contracting parties in the nature of a *pactum,* and (2) some legal reason why the pact should be enforceable in law. This reason was called a *causa.* So rigorous was Roman Law in its formalism that, if no *causa* existed, the pact was considered unenforceable in law, and was known as a *pactum nudum.* Although it allowed no legal sanction for the enforcement of the nude pact, Roman Law did allow the raising of an *exceptio,* which as a defense was based on the natural obligation to fufill the contract.[28]

Article 5. The Written Contract—*Expensilatio*

Expensilatio designated the creation of an obligation in writing by means of a fictitious entry into the creditor's book with the permission of the intended debtor. Gaius furnished two examples of this type of contract: (1) transcription from thing to person, by which a debt due for the sale of some object was entered in the

[24] Gaius (3.93).

[25] Gaius (4.19).

[26] (3.116).

[27] (3.117).

[28] "Nuda pactio obligationem non parit, sed parit exceptionem."—D. (2.14) 74.

ledger as though it were a personal loan,[29] and (2) transcription from person to person, e.g., A owed B 100 *aurei*; B owed C 100 *aurei*. An entry was made in C's ledger to the effect that A owed C 100 *aurei*. B's debt was thus cancelled out. This contract was known in Justinian's time, but Gaius seemed not at all sure that it was binding on aliens.[30] Possibly because of this fact *expensilatio* gave way to the contracts of *chirographum* and *syngrapha*, which were borrowed from the Greeks as their names imply. These contracts were certainly suitable to have a binding force for aliens also.[31]

Article 6. The Contract of Buying and Selling

The consensual contract of *emptio vendito* had in the early period of Roman Law no binding force inasmuch as it was a nude pact. It could, however be made binding by means of the adjoining of a *sponsio* or a *restipulatio*, either of which the law recognized. As this contract was of such frequent occurrence, this situation gave rise to a dangerous state of affairs. With the increase of Roman conquests, contracts of sale between the citizens and the State became frequent. This frequency was founded on the necessity on the part of the State of disposing of slaves, booty, and conquered lands. These contracts were formless, but were invested with a certain amount of solemnity in view of the facts that there was much publicity connected with them and that the State was one of the contracting parties. The *actio empti venditi* was in time established in order to extend the force of the public sale into private law. With the rise of this legal action the bilateral contract of sale achieved legal recognition.

In analyzing the contract of *emptio venditio*, one notes the transition from a unilateral to a bilateral contract. At first there was a union of two stipulations or promises. This union was essential for making the contract actionable in law. In all of these contracts of sale mutual obligations had to be exchanged but, since the law did not at first recognize *emptio venditio* as a legal contract, it was

[29] (3.129).

[30] (3.133).

[31] (3.134).

separated into two unilateral contracts—the promise to pay a certain sum for a specified article, and the promise to deliver the article. It may be in view of the fact that these two contracts existed as unilateral conventions that the name of the contract itself was expressed in two words (and this fact obtained equally in the case of *locatio conductio*), whereas other contracts could be and were described by means of a single word.

Gaius made the distinction between unilateral and bilateral contracts clear when he treated of consensual contracts. He classed all these as bilateral contracts. He mentioned four consensual contracts—*emptio venditio* (sale), *locatio conductio* (hire), *societas* (partnership), and *mandatum* (agency).[32] He continued: "Further, these contracts are bilateral, that is, both parties incur a reciprocal obligation to perform whatever is fair and equal." [33]

Article 7. Innominate Contracts

Gaius classified contracts as real, literal, verbal, and consensual.[34] He omitted mention of the great body of contracts which had no name before the law, and have thus become known as innominate contracts. These were classified by Paulus a century after Gaius. It is this classification which is contained in the *Digest*.[35] From this fact one can conclude that innominate contracts were not recognized until comparatively late in Roman jurisprudence. These innominate contracts were bilateral conventions demanding reciprocal performance. All these contracts were enforceable by civil action.[36] Among these innominate contracts may be classed: *permutatio* or exchange; [37] *transactio* or compromise; [38] and *precarium* or temporary occupancy with the permission of the owner.[39]

[32] (3.135).

[33] "Item in his contractibus alter alteri obligatur de eo quod alterum alteri ex bono et aequo praestare opportet."—(3.137).

[34] (3.89).

[35] D. (19.5) 5: "Aut enim do tibi ut des, aut do ut facias, aut facio ut des, aut facio ut facias."

[36] D. (9.5) 15.

[37] D. (19.4).

[38] D. (2.15).

[39] D. (43.26).

CHAPTER II

MORAL ASPECTS OF THE CONTRACT IN GRATIAN

ROMAN LAW refused to recognize a pact which did not fall within its category of contracts enforceable by judicial action. The pacts which were not clothed in judicial dress were simply called nude pacts. It was concerning these agreements that early Canon Law made its chief departure from the Roman Law of contract. Being more concerned with the morality of the pact than its adherence to legal ritual, the Christian tendency was to recognize pacts even though they were not clothed in legal form, provided only that they had the requisite elements of an honest agreement.

Emperor Leo I (457-474) in 472 did much to remedy this misplaced emphasis on the verbal solemnity by declaring that the intentions of the contracting parties formed the terms of contract.[1] It is true that some words had to be spoken to indicate what the contracting parties intended, but these words did not have to follow the formal pattern demanded in early Roman Law, as in the *sponsio*.[2]

Gratian (+ca. 1157) was more concerned with the moral than the formal aspect of contracts. He cited a canon taken from the VIII Provincial Council of Toledo (653), which declared that it was better to leave a promise unfufilled if, by fufilling it, a crime would result.[3] As a promise which fell in this category, Gratian pointed to the example of Herod (who had promised to give Salome the head of John the Baptist).[4] This prescription was repeated in other canons of Gratian which were likewise taken from the VIII Provincial Council of Toledo.[5] This council dealt with the question of letting contracts go unfulfilled as preferable to incurring the guilt of sin by fulfilling them. The council's leading argument was taken from

[1] C. (8.37) 10.
[2] Gaius (3.93).
[3] C. 1, C. XXII, q. 4.
[4] C. 2, C. XXII, q. 4.
[5] C. 12, 13, C. XXII, q. 4.

St. Ambrose (+397), who relied upon various texts of Scripture to prove his point.[6]

Pope St. Felix III (483-492) in a letter written in 484 enunciated the principle that contracts are to be kept, provided that they are not made contrary to good morals and are in conformity with the laws of the Church.[7] Contracts made contrary to the customs and decrees of the Roman Pontiffs were invalid.[8] Gratian reported the following succinct rule to regulate the making of contracts: "Things done contrary to law are held as not done at all."[9] This *dictum* was borrowed from a Constitution issued by Constantine the Great (306-337) and promulgated in 329.[10]

The Council of Agde (506) forbade bishops to alienate by contract any property which belonged to the Church, or vessels from monasteries, or any other thing from which the poor derived their living, as long as it belonged by law to the Church.[11]

This statute was likewise incorporated in the codification of Justinian, who derived it from the Constitution of Emperor Leo I (457-474). Justinian, in a decree addressed to the Patriarch of Constantinople, ordered that no *res immobilis* was to be sold, given away or in any way alienated from the Church of Constantinople. The buyer of any such property was bound to restore it, and any econome so alienating church property was to be deprived of his office. Justinian permitted the loan of a thing for a while. However, this was to be done in such a manner that adequate compensation was to be given by the borrower. If the borrower was guilty of fraud in any way, the contract was void (*"infirmum contractum et pro non*

[6] St. Ambrose, *De officiis,* Lib. I, cap. 50; Mansi, *Sacrorum Conciliorum Nova et Amplissima Collectio* (53 vols. in 60; Vols. 1-31, Florentiae, Venetiis, Parisiis, 1759-1798; Vols. 31b-53, Parisiis, Leipzig, Arnhem, 1901-1927), X, 1214. Hereinafter cited Mansi.

[7] Jaffé, *Regesta Pontificium Romanorum ab condita Ecclesia ad annum post Christum natum MCXCVIII* (2. ed. by Kaltenbrunner [to the year 590], Ewald [590-882] and Löwenfeld [882-1198], 2 vols. in 1, Lipsiae, 1885-1888), n. 365. Hereinafter cited JK, JE, and JL.

[8] D. X, c. 4 (Felix III, Letter to Zeno Augustus 484)—JK, n. 365.

[9] C. 13, C. XXV, q. 2: "Quae contra leges fiunt, pro infectis habeantur."

[10] C. (1.19) 3.

[11] C. 1, C. X, q. 2.

facto ponit"). Justinian extended this law to the whole Christian world and to all classes of ecclesiastical institutes. He renewed the punishments which the Constitution of Leo had invoked upon violators of this law.[12]

The Emperor Leo I in his *Constitutio Nova* had permitted the sale of a *res mobilis* for the clearing of debt. If this did not suffice, he allowed the mortgage of a *res immobilis,* but not beyond 3 per cent of its value. Later, the IV General Council of Constantinople (869) restricted the sale of church vessels to the single case in which the money so obtained was used for the redemption of captives.[13]

Pope St. Leo I (440-461) in 447 wrote to the bishops of Sicily and forbade them to make transactions concerning church goods unless it was done for the betterment of the Church and with the consent of the clergy. Contracts concerning ecclesiastical goods could not be made without the approval and signatures of the clergy.[14] A similar decree is found in the Council of Agde.[15] However, this decree provided that in case of necessity the bishop did not need this consent of his clergy.

The III Provincial Council of Toledo (589) permitted the alienation of ecclesiastical goods for the benefit of religious.[16] A bishop could with the consent of his chapter give over a parish to a monastery. He could give them what was necessary for their livelihood, provided that no detriment came to the church.[17]

The X Provincial Council of Toledo (656) restricted this right to the bishop in such a manner that he could give no more than one-fiftieth (according to some manuscripts, one-fortieth) of the church's goods to a monastery which he erected.[18] In this case equity was to be served, so that the monastery would receive a fair sum and the church's goods would not be depleted to the extent of

[12] *Corpus Iuris Civilis* (Vol. III, ed. stereotypa quinta, *Novellae,* quas recognovit Rudolfus Schoell, absolvit Guglielmus Kroll, Berolini: Apud Weidmannos, 1928), N. 7. Hereinafter cited N.

[13] C. 12, C. XIII, q. 2.

[14] JK, n. 193.

[15] C. 45—Mansi, VIII, 332.

[16] C. 4—Mansi, IX, 994.

[17] C. 72, C. XII, q. 2.

[18] C. 74, C. XII, q. 2.

causing grave damage. Gratian showed that the practice of making donations in this way actually obtained. He referred to a letter of Pope St. Gregory I (590-604) which granted to a certain Gratiosus a house, which together with all its appurtenances was owned by the Church, for the erection of a congregation of monks.[19]

In Roman Law much of the legislation was concerned with the development of the various types of contracts. Canon Law accepted this great body of contracts as it existed in Roman Law. Certain additions had to be made to meet changing circumstances. The Church looked at contracts from a moral as well as a legal aspect. Rules also had to be made for the governing of contracts between moral persons, such as a diocese and a religious Order. The case of the religious themselves and their legal capacity to make contracts fitted into the Roman legal system. The religious themselves were likened to persons living under a *paterfamilias*. If they were to assume contractual obligations, permission had to be received from their superiors.

Once a contract was made its conditions could not be changed by either party without the consent of the other. Gratian cited a case brought before Pope Pelagius I (555-561), in which a dispute had arisen concerning a contract for the erection of a monastery. The case was brought before the Pope by a Bishop Eleutherius, whose mother had made the contract with a certain Bishop Gardelus. By the terms of the agreement, she was allowed to erect an oratory and to invite monks to reside there, one of whom was to be the priest of the oratory. It was agreed that the offerings given on the day of the dedication, or on the feast-day of the martyrs whose relics were kept in the monastery, were to be divided equally between the monastery and the bishop. Another priest, Marius by name, came in and created trouble for the monks by preventing their priest from saying Mass in the oratory. Moreover, he demanded a pension from them. The Pope declared that only those things which were designated in the original contract could be demanded of the monks, and no new demands were to be made.[20]

[19] C. 75, C. XII, q. 2; JE, n. 1221.

[20] C. 30, C. XVIII, q. 2.

The benefice which a cleric received from the church was given him in accord with the contract of *precarium* or temporary occupancy. So decreed the VII Provincial Council of Toledo (646) in order to make sure that a cleric could not usurp church property by prolonged possession. The contract of *precarium* as it existed in Roman Law was a bilateral contract.[21] A cleric who refused to accept his benefice under the conditions of this contract was to be deprived of his stipend.[22]

[21] D. (43.26).

[22] C. 72, C. XII, q. 2.

CHAPTER III

THE DECRETALS OF GREGORY IX

It is in the Decretals of Gregory IX (1227-1241) that the recognition of nude pacts is discussed at length. This was an important departure from the Roman Law system of contracts. The I Council of Carthage (348) enunciated the principle that pacts were to be binding even though not clothed in official form.[1] This canon of the Council of Carthage is found in the *Prima Compilatio* and in the *Decretum Gratianum*.[2]

A certain Antigonus had made an agreement with Optantius about the division of parishioners. Optantius canvassed among the people who had fallen to Antigonus, and asked them to nominate him as their pastor, thus placing Antigonus in a secondary capacity. Antigonus sought redress against Optantius on the grounds that the latter was violating the agreement. The Fathers at the Council agreed that the pact should be kept. It is this case which is cited in the Decretals as proof that nude pacts were binding.[3] Although this Council was provincial (some authors thought it was general and presided over by the Pope), it later received the approval of Pope Leo IV (847-855).[4]

Gibalini (1592-1671) held that this was not proof that Canon Law allowed a legal action for the enforcement of nude pacts. He cited several authors in favor of his opinion, but admitted that the *sententia communior* was against him. According to Gibalini, Panormitanus, Hostiensis (+1271), Molina (1535-1600), Lessius (1554-

[1] Bruns, *Canones Apostolorum et Conciliorum Veterum Saeculorum IV-VII* (2 vols., Berolini, 1839) I, 116. Hereinafter cited Bruns.

[2] C. 8, C. XX, q. 1; c. 23, C. XXII, q. 4; c. 30, C. XVIII, q. 2.

[3] C. 1, X, *de pactis*, I, 35.

[4] Pirhing, *Jus Canonicum Novo Methodo Explicatum* (5 vols. in 4, Dilingiae, 1674-1678), Lib. I, tit. 35, n. 9. Hereinafter cited Pirhing; Fagnanus, *Commentarium in Quinque Libros Decretalium* (Venetiis, 1709), Lib. I, tit. 35, nn. 1, 65. Hereinafter cited *Commentarium*.

1623), and Lugo (1583-1660) held the *sententia communior.* Gibalini contended that the statement: *"Pax servetur, pacta custodiantur,"* in the I Council of Carthage, was but a repetition of what had been held by the Praetor in Roman Law.[5]

More modern authorities were also divided on this question. Pirhing (1606-1679) affirmed that Canon Law allowed a legal action for the enforcement of nude pacts.[6] Schmalzgrueber (1663-1735) taught that nude pacts did not admit a judicial action in Canon Law. He maintained that the case considered in the Council of Carthage was a legitimate pact, not a nude one.[7]

The gloss to the decree of the I Council of Carthage points to the Praetor's statement as contained in the *Digest.*[8] The author of the edict *Pacta Conventa* was C. Cassius Longius (116 B. C.). He merely stated that in the future the Praetor would examine pacts when disputes arose, and give a decision according to his own discretion. It was customary for the Praetor to depart from the formalism of the law and to settle questions equitably. He simply gave an opinion on the subject, whereas the I Council of Carthage decreed that in the future pacts were to be kept as long as they were otherwise honorable, even though they were only nude pacts. So binding were pacts of this type in Canon Law that one could be compelled to fulfill them under pain of incurring ecclesiastical censures, namely, excommunication, suspension or interdict.[9] On the other hand, agreements made contrary to the law, that is, deceitfully or in other evil ways, or agreements which proved detrimental to one's eternal salvation, were not to be kept.[10]

The fact that deceit nullified a contract was further stressed by Pope Innocent III (1198-1216) in his settlement of a dispute con-

[5] Gibalini, *De Universa Rerum Humanarum Negotiatione* (2 vols., Lugduni, 1863) I, 483.

[6] Pirhing, Lib. I, tit. 35, n. 36.

[7] Schmalzgrueber, *Ius Ecclesiasticum Universum* (5 vols. in 12, Romae, 1843-1845), Lib. III, tit. 35, n. 7. Hereinafter cited Schmalzgrueber.

[8] D. (2.14) (7, 7): "Ait praetor: 'Pacta conventa, quae neque dolo malo, neque adversus leges plebis scita senatus consulta decreta edicta principum, neque quo fraus cui eorum fiat, facta erunt, servabo.'"

[9] C. 20, X, *de verborum significatione,* V, 40.

[10] Glossa ad *"pacta custodiantur"* in c. 1, X, *de pactis,* I, 35.

cerning benefices. L. and G. had agreed to exchange benefices. G. kept his part of the contract, but L. gave G.'s benefice to a relative. Then L. refused to resign from his original benefice as he had agreed to do. G. appealed to his bishop. After prolonged litigation L. appealed to the Holy See, but failed to appear in defense of his case. Pope Innocent III took cognizance of the fact that there should have been no exchange of benefices in the first place without the necessary permissions. He also declared that G. was to be reinstated in his original benefice.[11] The glossator pointed out the following rules to be noted: "Laws come to the aid of the deceived and not of the deceivers." "Fraud and deceit ought to protect no one." "An action arises from a nude pact."[12]

In proof of the rule that a nude pact could give rise to a judicial action, the IV Provincial Council of Toledo (633) was cited. The case there treated concerned the promise of a bishop to pay a man for a certain work. Afterwards the bishop refused to keep his part of the agreement. The Council declared that the plaintiff could bring the bishop before the provincial council for his failure to fulfill his promise.[13]

Restrictions were often placed upon contracts to exclude the ever-present specter of simony and to prevent unworthy men from assuming ecclesiastical offices. Pope Alexander III (1159-1181) in a letter to the Bishops of Exeter and Worcester declared that a contract was invalid because certain clerics had agreed to resign a benefice in favor of monks for a monetary compensation. Even though the compensation was to be made as just payment for expenses, the Pope refused to approve the contract. He suggested that the monks provide the clerics with another benefice. The monks refused to do this. The Pope then declared the contract by which the clerics had resigned their benefice (even though the money received was not a price for the benefice, but compensation for work done) was simoniacal and invalid.[14]

Pope Alexander III decreed that when the church had been

[11] C. 8, X, *de rerum permutatione*, III, 19.

[12] Glossa ad "*cum universum*" in c. 8, X, *de rerum permutatione*, III, 19.

[13] Bruns, I, 233.

[14] C. 4, X, *de pactis*, I, 35.

enormously damaged through a contract of sale, a petition for *restitutio in integrum* could be entered for the repairing of the damages sustained. However, a buyer who had made his gains in good faith through any contract was not to be deprived of his profits.[15] The *laesio enormis* of Roman Law was described in two rescripts of Diocletian (284-305). If a thing was sold for less than half its real value, the vendor could rescind the contract unless the vendee gave an additional amount to make the price a fair one.[16]

Pope Gregory IX (1227-1241) also allowed a *restitutio in integrum* when a guardian had sold the goods of a minor without the requisite solemnities of the contract. The petition had to be made within a year and a day from the time of the contract. Even if the solemnities were carried out, but the minor's better interests were hurt, restitution was to be made.[17] The *glossa* on the word *"constitutus"* stated that the same rules applied to the Church in an identical case. This bears out the fact that the Church as a moral person was held as a minor in the law.[18]

Pope Innocent III in the IV General Council of the Lateran (1215) ruled that contracts could not be made which were prejudicial to the parochial rights of another church. Moreover, any revenue received on the occasion of the violation of another church's parochial rights was to be restored to the church which had a right to it.[19] A very practical case of this sort arose in connection with the matter of ecclesiastical burials. It was true of course that the faithful could freely choose to receive burial in a place outside the territory of their own parish.[20] However, their choice could not be made a matter of contract. If they were urged to make a contract to be buried in another church by the clerics of that church, the contract was held to be invalid. A person who had made such a contract was to receive burial at his proper parish church notwithstanding the agreement he had been urged to make.

[15] C. 1, X, *de in integrum restitutione,* I, 41.

[16] C. (4.44), 2, 8.

[17] C. 8, X, *de in integrum restitutione,* I, 41.

[18] C. 1, X, *de in integrum restitutione,* I, 41.

[19] C. 7, X, *de pactis,* I, 35.

[20] C. 1, X, *de sepulturis,* III, 28.

Finally, Pope Gregory IX stressed a moral principle regarding the matter of any contract. It must not be evil nor must it lead to sin. It must conform to the laws and to good morals. It must not concern spiritual things. A contract whereby a person's pension would be augmented if he resigned a benefice in favor of some other person was declared invalid by Pope Alexander III in a letter to the Archbishop of Canterbury and his suffragans. Any person who made such a contract was to be deprived of his benefice and clerical rank.[21] A contract could not be made concerning evil or impossible things.[22] In the *Rules of Law* it was stated that no one could be obliged to perform the impossible.[23] Whatever was not considered as possible in law was reputed to be impossible.[24]

[21] C. 6, X, *de pactis*, I, 35.
[22] C. 8, X, *de pactis*, I, 35.
[23] Reg. 6, R. J., in VI°—"Nemo potest ad impossibile obligari."
[24] Glossa ad *"Quod potest"* in c. 15, C. XXII, q. 2.

CHAPTER IV

FROM GREGORY IX TO THE COUNCIL OF TRENT

CANON LAW extended the inability to make contracts to religious inasmuch as it was deemed that they had relinquished their will in virtue of their vow of obedience.[1]

Of great importance relative to matters of contracts made by religious institutes is the Constitution issued by Pope Boniface VIII (1294-1303) in 1296, which revoked a privilege given to the Franciscans by Pope Alexander IV (1254-1261). According to this earlier papal concession, contracts made by the Franciscans (even though made by the Guardians of their Monasteries), if contrary to the statutes and customs of the Order and made without the consent of the General or Provincial, were considered as voidable. This grant included also those contracts which were made by individual members of the Order and by individual houses with prelates, rectors and clerics of churches. If these contracts were made without the permission of the General or Provincial and his chapter, and later proved prejudicial to the Order, they were considered as rescissible.[2]

Now, Pope Boniface VIII decreed as follows: "Inasmuch as it has happened that the Friars Preachers and Friars Minors and other Mendicants have made pacts and agreements concerning parochial rights and other matters with prelates, chapters, rectors and others in places where they have houses, and either they or their predecessors, having made these agreements, now refuse to keep them under the pretext that they were made without the permission of their General or Provincial chapters, We now decree that the pacts made by Priors or Guardians, or approved by the council and assent of their convents (as long as these pacts are licit and honorable), must be observed perpetually, even though the Masters or Ministers or Priors General or Provincial have not given their consent, and even

[1] C. 2, *de testamentis et ultimis voluntatibus*, III, 11, in VI°; c. 5, *de sepulturis*, III, 12, in VI°.

[2] C. 3, *de pactis*, I, 18, in VI°.

if they have not been approved by the Provincial or General Chapters or by the Holy See in those things which need such permission." [3]

Ioannes Andreae (1272-1348) in his gloss to this papally enacted canon explained that this legislation was brought about by disputes over parochial rights, especially the rights regarding burial. For the peaceful settlement of the quarrels which arose, pacts were made between the religious superiors and the local pastors. In various instances, however, the religious later repudiated these pacts for the reason that they lacked the confirmation of the proper authority.[4]

This Constitution of Boniface VIII was revoked by Pope Sixtus IV (1471-1484) through his renewal of the original concession to the Franciscans. Sixtus IV ruled that rectors of inferior collegiate churches could not undertake alienations or contracts regarding the rights or immovable goods of their churches unless they had the permission of the bishop. Similarly the Prior of a conventual church needed the permission of the General, or at least, of the Provincial.

Pope Boniface VIII likewise ruled that monks were bound to the terms of a contract whereby they agreed to renounce the privilege of burying the subjects of a parish, even though these subjects had freely chosen the church of the monks as the place of their burial. The religious were allowed to make this contract, for in so doing they conformed to the common law concerning the proper place of burial as established by Pope Leo III (795-816).[5]

Pope Boniface VIII forbade the making of a contract whereby a person gave up his right to be buried at his parish church by choosing the church of the religious instead. If, despite this decree, a person was buried at the church of the religious, the offering received on such an occasion was to be restored to the parish church. The restitution was to be made within ten days under pain of interdict.[6]

[3] Potthast, *Regesta Pontificum Romanorum inde ab anno post Christum natum 1198 ad annum 1304* (2 vols., Berolini, 1874-1875), n. 24447. Hereinafter cited Potthast. The translation is the writer's.

[4] Glossa ad v. *"quia ex eo"* in c. 3, *de pactis,* I, 18, in VI°.

[5] JE, n. 5795.

[6] C. 1, *de sepulturis,* III, 12, in VI°.

Pope Leo X in the Constitution *Dum intra* (December 19, 1516), issued in the eleventh session of the V General Council of the Lateran (1512-1517), settled the question of the rights of religious to rescind a contract made without the necessary permission of the General or Provincial. He declared that these contracts had to be kept, pending the revocation by the next general or provincial chapter. But this chapter had to be held within a reasonable space of time after the making of the agreement.[7]

[7] Mansi, XXXII, 972.

CHAPTER V

CONTRACTUAL POWER OF BISHOPS FROM THE COUNCIL OF TRENT TO THE CODE OF CANON LAW

ARTICLE 1. DERIVATION OF THIS POWER

IT was a general rule, admitted by all commentators, that all persons could make contracts unless they were specifically excluded by nature, by law or by the canons.[1] By nature, bishops were not denied contractual power, since the natural law had reference to those who were incapable of entering into contracts inasmuch as they lacked the ability to give the consent which was essential to the formulation of a contract.[2] By positive law, likewise, bishops were not forbidden to enter into contracts, although of course their contractual power had been limited somewhat by positive legislation enacted by Pope Clement V (1305-1314).[3]

In commenting on this Clementine decretal, authors pointed out that the bishop was limited by virtue of the fact that he had to consult his chapter in many cases. In contracts affecting the union of one church with another, not only was the consent of the chapter necessary, but the matter had to be discussed with other interested parties whose rights might be affected by this act. Such parties were the local pastors and also those having the right of patronage.[4]

In addition to these requirements for the union of a church to a religious institute, the permission of the Holy See was required. Furthermore, the bishop was absolutely forbidden to unite a church with the goods designated as a means for his personal sustenance (*mensa episcopalis*). Even with the permission of the chapter, this

[1] Schmalzgrueber, Lib. I, tit. 35, n. 8.

[2] Cf. definition of Contract—"consensu duorum vel plurium . . ." Wernz, *Ius Decretalium ad Usum Praelectionum in Scholis Textus Canonici sive Iuris Decretalium* (2. ed., 6 vols., Romae-Prati, 1906-1913), III, n. 230. Hereinafter cited *Ius Decretalium.*

[3] C. 2, *de rebus ecclesiae alienandis vel non,* III, 13, in Clem.

[4] Pirhing, Lib. III, tit. 8, n. 49.

act was unlawful, and any such contract was invalid. Not even a custom of long standing could be alleged as permitting such a union.[5]

Article 2. Alienation

Alienation, in the wide sense comprehends every act or disposition by which direct dominion, as a *ius in re* or as a *ius ad rem* was transferred. Contracts through which the status of a church would be rendered less favorable were also included in the notion of alienation. Wernz (1842-1914) included the contracts of sale, of renting, of mortgage, of donation, of exchange, and also others in the notion of alienation.[6] Such is also the opinion of other authors, both medieval and modern.[7]

In the investigation of the bishop's power to make contracts, it is of great importance to study and to know the legislation concerning alienation. The Council of Trent (1545-1563) enacted little new legislation concerning alienation, but it affirmed the former laws which had fallen into desuetude. Principal among these laws, and vital for the consideration of the subject here being discussed, was the Constitution *Ambitiosae* of Pope Paul II (1464-1471), issued by him on March 1, 1468.[8]

This Constitution was the basis upon which future laws concerning alienation rested. Its provisions were renewed on several occa-

[5] Pirhing, *loc. cit.*

[6] *Ius Decretalium*, III, n. 154.

[7] Cf. Schmalzgreuber, *loc. cit.;* Pirhing, *loc. cit.;* Vermeersch-Creusen, *Epitome Iuris Canonici cum Commentariis ad Scholas et ad Usum Privatum* (3 vols., Vol. I, ed. quarta, 1929, Vol. II, ed. tertia, 1927, Vol. III, ed. tertia, 1928, Mechliniae-Romae: H. Dessain), II, n. 851 (hereinafter cited *Epitome*); Ayrinhac, *Administrative Legislation in the New Code of Canon Law* (New York: Longmans, Green & Co., 1930), p. 239 (hereinafter cited *Administrative Legislation*); Coronata, *Institutiones Iuris Canonici ad Usum Utriusque Cleri et Scholarum* (5 vols., Taurini: Ex Officina Libraria Marietti, 1933-1939, Vols. I-II, 2. ed., 1939), II, n. 1070 (hereinafter cited *Institutiones*); Augustine, *A Commentary on the New Code of Canon Law* (8 vols., Vol. II, 4. ed., 1923, Vol. III, 4. ed., 1929, Vol. VI, 2. ed., 1923. St. Louis: B. Herder Book Co.), VI, 593 (hereinafter cited *Commentary*).

[8] C. un., *de rebus ecclesiae non alienandis*, III, 4, in Extravag. com.

sions by papal pronouncements after the Council of Trent, and it was again renewed in recent times by Pope Pius IX (1846-1878) in the Constitution *Apostolicae Sedis.*[9]

The Constitution *Ambitiosae* forbade the alienation of immovable goods as well as of precious movable goods. Alienation, in the words of this Constitution, included any contract by which dominion was transferred or diminished. The giving away of such goods, their mortgaging, the renting of them beyond three years, and emphyteusis were thus prohibited. This enactment indicated the necessary requisites for entering into any contract by which ecclesiastical property could be alienated. Such alienation had to serve the evident utility of the church. It had to be made in reference to goods which could not be used by the church at the time when the contract was made.

The penalties for the violation of these provisions were severe. The contract itself was rendered void. Both the alienator and the beneficiary of the alienation incurred the extreme penalty of excommunication. Abbots and bishops were punished by means of special penalties for the violation of this Constitution. They were put under a personal interdict, by which they were prohibited from entrance into church. Moreover, if they persisted in their contumacy for six months, they were suspended from the administration of both spiritualities and temporalities. Inferior prelates were deprived of any benefices and offices they held, and it was left to the discretion of the local ordinary to make provision for replacing them with worthy successors. If, however, the benefice was reserved to the Holy See, the Pope was to provide a successor for the benefice.

Violations of the principles stressed in the Constitution *Ambitiosae* nevertheless occurred. Accordingly, on July 14, 1555, Pope Paul IV (1555-1559) issued the Constitution *Iniunctum nobis,* which renewed the former law and stressed the fact that it applied not only to the Roman Church, but to churches in all the provinces as well. It allowed exceptions only in the cases wherein the law expressly per-

[9] *Codicis Iuris Canonici Fontes, cura Emi Petri Card. Gasparri editi* (9 vols., Romae [postea Civitate Vaticana]: Typis Polyglottis Vaticanis, 1923-1939). (Vols. VII-IX ed. cura et studio Emi Iustiniani Card. Serédi), n. 552. Hereinafter cited *Fontes.*

mitted them. The penalties invoked by the former law were renewed. All were bound to these provisions, no matter what their rank, state, or dignity. All contracts made contrary to law in the past were invalidated. All who were beneficiaries of such invalid contracts were bound to return the goods to the rightful owner, and were compelled through the use of penal sanctions and fines to make this restitution.[10]

The Council of Trent confirmed the former legislation by censuring clerics and laymen even though they were of royal or imperial dignity. It condemned all those who converted a benefice into their own private use, or prevented the rightful incumbent from the lawful exercise of his rights. Transgressors had to return the benefice to the rightful possessor before seeking absolution, which they could obtain only from the Pope himself. If one having the right of patronage was guilty of a violation of this law, he lost that right for the future. Furthermore, a cleric could be suspended from the exercise of orders even after he had obtained a papal absolution, if such a step was deemed necessary.[11]

Article 3. Reasons for Entering Into Contracts

The papal Constitution *Ambitiosae* enumerated the principal requirements to be fulfilled before any contract could be made relative to the alienation of ecclesiastical goods. Contracts had to serve the evident utility of the church.[12] This basic reason and others discussed by commentators and countenanced by the usage and practice (*praxis*) of the Roman Curia applied to contracts entered into by bishops. Reiffenstuel (1642-1703) enumerated the following causes: (1) The necessity of the church; (2) the utility of the church; (3) reasons of piety.[13]

The utility of the church had to be manifest according to Barbosa (1589-1649). It was not sufficient that the church did not suffer

[10] *Fontes*, n. 88.

[11] Conc. Trident., sess. XXII, *de ref.*, c. 11.

[12] C. un., *de rebus ecclesiae non alienandis*, III, 4, in Extravag. com.

[13] Reiffenstuel, *Jus Canonicum Universum, editio novissima cui accessit Tractatus de Regulis Juris* (6 vols., Romae, 1831-1834), Lib. III, tit. 13, n. 2. Hereinafter cited Reiffenstuel.

hurt or harm through the transaction. It was required that the church's position be improved.[14] Reasons of piety offered a sufficient cause for alienation, for example, when the money which accrued from the transaction was used for the redemption of captives or for building a church or a cemetery.[15]

Besides the three cases mentioned above, Barbosa mentioned a fourth case in which the bishop could alienate ecclesiastical goods, namely, when the following conditions concurred: (1) when the matter concerned was of little value; (2) when the goods alienated were of no great utility to the church; and (3) when there was present a necessity or a utility for the alienation.[16] The same opinion was held by Fagnanus (1598-1678).[17] Barbosa's addition, however, seemed to be superfluous, since the conditions he proposed were all comprehended by the phrase, "utility of the church," as asserted by Reiffenstuel.[18]

Article 4. Solemnities Required for Contracts

Certain solemnities were required before a bishop could enter into a contract affecting the dominion of immovable or precious movable goods belonging to the church. The bishop had to consult his chapter to determine whether a sufficient cause was present for entering into the contract. Consent of the entire chapter was to be sought. If unanimous consent could not be obtained, consent of the majority sufficed.

This consent had to be manifested in writing. Permission of the Holy See was necessary for entering into the contract. In two cases the consent of the patron was also necessary; namely, if the patron did not entirely relinquish the dominion over the goods in question, or if he had made this a condition upon giving the property to the church and the bishop had accepted this condition.[19]

[14] Barbosa, *Iuris Ecclesiastici Universi Libri Tres* (3 vols., Lugduni, 1650), Lib. III, c. 30, n. 17.

[15] Reiffenstuel, *loc. cit.*

[16] Barbosa, *loc. cit.*

[17] *Commentarium,* Lib. III, tit. 13, c. 5, n. 7.

[18] Lib. III, tit. 13, n. 2.

[19] Pirhing, Lib. III, tit. 2, n. 29; Lib. III, tit. 13, n. 62.

Custom permitted a notary to attest the fact that the chapter concurred in the bishop's decision. The seal of the chapter stamped on the document, or also the signature of the head of the chapter, sufficed by customary usage for the fulfillment of this provision.[20]

When the bishop was a party to the contract and it concerned immovable goods, the approval of the Holy See was also necessary. According to Reiffenstuel, custom excused from complying with this provision where the Constitution *Ambitiosae* was not followed in all its rigor. This custom was alleged for places distant from the Holy See. Germany, in particular, was mentioned.[21] This concession on the part of various authors is difficult to understand in the face of the constant insistence upon the necessity of complying with this requirement by the Popes and by the Roman Congregations from Paul II (1464-1471) to Pius IX (1846-1878).[22]

The rigorous demands of the Constitution *Ambitiosae*, as also of the Council of Trent which reënacted its provisions, seemed to conflict with an earlier canon of the Council of Agde (506). By virtue of that canon, bishops were permitted to alienate small plots of land and vineyards which were of no great value, and which were far removed from the church which owned them. In cases of necessity the bishops could freely make contracts concerning these properties, even though they had not obtained the consent of their chapters.[23]

Most authors were willing to concede that this permission still remained intact after the enactment of the papal Constitution *Ambitiosae*, and also after the legislation of the Council of Trent.[24] According to Fagnanus (1598-1678), who based his teaching on the replies of the Sacred Congregation of the Council, the concession granted by the Council of Agde still remained.[25]

[20] Reiffenstuel, Lib. III, tit. 13, n. 27.

[21] Reiffenstuel, *ibid.*, n. 32.

[22] Paulus IV, const. *Iniunctum nobis*, 14 iul. 1555—*Fontes*, n. 88; Pius IX, const. *Apostolicae Sedis*, 12 oct. 1869—*Fontes*, n. 552; *decretum* S. C. C., 7 sept. 1624—*Fontes*, n. 2453; S. C. C., *Mediolanen.*, 14 mart. 1682—*Fontes*, n. 2862.

[23] C. 53, C. XIII, q. 2.

[24] Pirhing, *loc. cit.*; Reiffenstuel, *loc. cit.*

[25] S. C. C., *Trivican.*, 11 ian. 1596; S. C. C., *Messanen.*, 14 dec. 1613—as reported by Fagnanus, *Commentarium*, Lib. III, tit. 13, c. 5, nn. 25, 26.

The Sacred Congregation of Bishops and Regulars issued a decree which confirmed the decisions of the Sacred Congregation of the Council. On January 16, 1653, the first mentioned Congregation stated that the faculty of permitting alienations according to the chapter "*Terrulas*" (the canon of the Council of Agde which is being discussed here) belonged to bishops and abbots *nullius*.[26]

Article 5. Insistence on the Solemnities of Contract

It is evident from an investigation of the decisions of the various Congregations and from the pronouncements of the Popes that ecclesiastical legislation always demanded that the solemnities of contracts be fulfilled. Despite the omissions on the part of individuals, the constant tenor of these decrees insists upon the fulfillment of the provisions of the Constitution *Ambitiosae*, which formed the keystone of future legislation on contracts and alienation.[27] Its provisions, as reinforced by the decree of the Sacred Congregation of the Council issued by order of Pope Urban VIII (1623-1644) on September 7, 1624,[28] and confirmed by the Constitution *Apostolicae Sedis* of Pope Pius IX of October 12, 1869,[29] are repeated in all the cases of this nature brought to the attention of the Sacred Congregation of Bishops and Regulars during these centuries.

To the Bishop of Rimini the Sacred Congregation of Bishops and Regulars declared on January 7, 1579, that a contract involving the perpetual alienation of a cemetery and other church goods was invalid. Both for the past and the future, the bishop needed the permission of the Holy See to make a contract of this kind concerning these properties.[30] In a contract concerning the lease of ecclesiastical property in the city of Rome,[31] the same Congregation

[26] *Collectanea in Usum Secretariae Sacrae Congregationis Episcoporum et Regularium*, cura A. Bizzarri Archiepiscopi Phillipensis Secretarii edita (Romae: Ex Typographia Polyglotta, S. C. de Propaganda Fide, 1885), p. 298. Hereinafter cited Bizzarri, *Collectanea*.

[27] C. un., *de rebus ecclesiae non alienandis*, III, 4, in Extravag. com.

[28] *Fontes*, n. 2453.

[29] *Fontes*, n. 552.

[30] *Fontes*, n. 1348.

[31] S. C. Ep. et Reg., 20 dec. 1844—Bizzarri, *Collectanea*, p. 537.

questioned the utility of the contract, and repeated the norm that positive proof of the utility must be given before a contract of this kind can be made by the Church authorities.[32]

If not all who had a voice in the matter concurred in the decision to enter into the contract, the Holy See was reluctant to give its *beneplacitum*. This traditional caution may have been based upon a reluctance to compromise the acquired rights of others, but it also seems consonant with the desire to have full assurance that there was a real necessity for, or utility in, the contract. This tendency was manifest in a decision given by the Sacred Congregation of the Council regarding the alienation of property left for the support of twin canonries in a collegiate church. One of the canons refused consent to this contract, although all the other interested parties agreed that it would be beneficial for the church. The Sacred Congregation refused permission persistently, and it was not until the case had been proposed for consideration the fourth time that the requested permission was granted.[33]

In April, 1792, a college at Ancona requested permission for the sale of ecclesiastical property. This body alleged both necessity and utility for the contract. The usefulness consisted in the probable hope of increasing the income of the college; the necessity was based on the danger of fire because of the wooden steps and partitions in the structure. One faction of the college opposed the contract, and the *beneplacitum* was withheld until it was satisfactorily proved to the Sacred Congregation of the Council that evident utility and necessity were truly present.[34]

The Constitution *Apostolicae Sedis*, promulgated by Pope Pius IX on October 12, 1869, condemned the abuses prevalent at that time regarding the contracts of alienation of church property. It declared that the provisions of the Constitution *Ambitiosae* were still in force, and pronounced an excommunication *latae sententiae nemini*

[32] De Luca (*Theatrum Veritatis et Justitiae* [15 vols. in 8, Coloniae Agrippinae, 1706], XII, pars 3, *de alienationibus*), disc. 1, n. 44: "debet enim esse utilitas certa . . . adeo ut Ecclesia plus percipiat alienando, quam retinendo, unde non sufficiat quod non sit in damno, nisi lucrum percipiat."

[33] Fontes, nn. 3816, 3819, 3822, 3824.

[34] *Fontes*, n. 3876.

reservata upon all those who dared to violate the former legislation. This penalty extended also to all those who received ecclesiastical goods without the Apostolic *beneplacitum* and thus became party to the illegal contract.[35]

In reply to a question proposed, the Sacred Congregation of the Holy Office declared on December 20, 1880, that the Constitution *Apostolicae Sedis* was intended to ratify and reaffirm the legislation of the Constitution *Ambitiosae.* Furthermore, it asserted that the penalty for the violation of these provisions would have been incurred even if similar legislation had not preceded Pius IX's Constitution.[36] It admitted that some mitigation of the rigor of the law was made in regard to certain pious places and ecclesiastical institutes erected in times past. Those which had been established under royal protection as approved by the Council of Trent,[37] and given the faculty of administering their goods according to the necessity as determined by the institute itself, retained this permission. In its response, the Congregation of the Holy Office stated that these foundations remained exactly as they were before the promulgation of the Constitution *Apostolicae Sedis.*

Article 6. The Practice of the Roman Curia Concerning Solemnities of Contracts of Alienation

The following were the rules governing the practice of the Roman Curia, as exemplified by various decisions of the Sacred Congregation of the Council, of the Sacred Congregation of Bishops and Regulars, and of the Sacred Roman Rota.

1. Contracts concerning pious places were *ipso iure* null until the *beneplacitum* of the Holy See was obtained in cases wherein the law provided for this approval.

2. The execution of the rescript granting papal approval had to be in writing, even though the contract of its nature did not require a written instrument. Both the Sacred Roman Rota and the

[35] *Fontes,* n. 552.

[36] *Fontes,* n. 1068, ad V.

[37] Cf. Conc. Trident., sess. XXII, *de ref.,* c. 8.

Sacred Congregation of the Council insisted upon this written execution.[38]

3. The contract was null unless a written document attested the execution of the rescript granted by the Holy See. This rescript gave form and strength to the contractual act.

4. If the permission was granted but the execution was not properly effected, the execution had to be supplied.

5. The act did not become perfect until the execution of the rescript had taken place.[39]

6. Before the necessary papal rescript was obtained the contract could still be rescinded.[40]

[38] *In Firmana emphyteusis,* 10 maii 1794—*Thesaurus Resolutionum Sacrae Congregationis Concilii* (167 vols., Romae, 1718-1908), LXXIII, 86. Hereinafter cited *Th. Resol. S. C. C.; in Placentina,* 9 sept. 1786—*Th. Resol. S. C. C.,* LXIV, 201; *in Senogalien. emphyteusis,* 15 sept. 1792—*Th. Resol. S. C. C.,* LXXI, 153; *Sacrae Rotae Romanae Decisiones coram Molines* (5 vols., Romae, 1728) decis. 1034, n. 11.

[39] Petra, *Commentaria ad Constitutiones Apostolicas* (5 vols. in 4, Venetiis, 1729) I, sec. 3, n. 40.

[40] S. R. R., *coram Ubaldo* (1646)—*Sacrae Romanae Rotae Decisiones Recentiores* (Pars I, Francofurti, 1623; Pars II, Aurelii, 1623; Partes III-XIX, Romae, 1645-1703), Pars IV, tom. 2, dec. 372.

CHAPTER VI

CONTRACTUAL POWER OF RELIGIOUS CONGREGATIONS IN GENERAL FROM THE COUNCIL OF TRENT UNTIL THE CODE OF CANON LAW

ARTICLE 1. DERIVATION OF THIS POWER

THE power of a religious congregation to make a contract concerning its possessions is bound up with its power to possess temporal goods. That religious congregations have always possessed temporal goods is a historical fact. This fact finds juridical support in the positive legislation based on the assumption that religious organizations actually had goods in their possession. Posited the right to possess, the right to administer follows. Although the individual members were forbidden the exercise of the rights of possession and could not enter into private contracts, the moral person constituted by the members collectively acted through the members in the administration of the institute's goods. It is upon the moral person that the right to enter into contracts devolved.[1]

The congregation as constituted in this moral person was not forbidden either by nature, or by law, or by the canons to enter into contracts.[2] The Council of Trent took cognizance of the right of religious institutes to formulate contracts when it declared that the administration of their property belonged to the superiors of the institutes.[3] The Council further ordered common possession of immovable goods for all institutes except the Capuchins and the Friars Minor of the Observance.[4]

The superiors' powers to make contracts were limited by the

[1] Ferraris, *Prompta Bibliotheca Canonica, Iuridica, Moralis, Theologica necnon Ascetica, Polemica, Rubricistica, Historica* (8 vols., Romae, 1885-1892); *Supplementum*, ed. Ianuarius Bucceroni (Romae, 1899), s. v., "*Alienatio,*" art. 4, n. 39. Hereinafter cited Ferraris.

[2] Cf. *supra*, p. 21.

[3] Conc. Trident., sess. XXV, *de regularibus*, c. 2.

[4] Conc. Trident., sess. XXV, *de regularibus*, c. 3.

general law of the Church concerning alienation as well as by the particular constitutions of the individual institutes.[5] By these enactments, the contractual powers of superiors were restricted to certain determined cases.

Article 2. Solemnities of Contracts in Religious Congregations

As the administration of the goods of the diocese from earliest times belonged to the bishops, so also the administration of the temporal goods of religious institutes belonged to the superiors of these institutes. Among the powers of administration was the power to formulate contracts.[6] Religious congregations were, therefore, subject to the provisions of the Constitution *Ambitiosae* of Pope Paul II,[7] and, as in the case of bishops, this Constitution formed the basis for the future legislation which restricted the use of the power of religious institutes to make contracts concerning temporal goods.

As has been stated above, this Constitution delineated the elements which had to be present before contracts could be attempted, and recounted the solemnities which were required by law for the validity of contracts. In the case of religious congregations, these elements or considerations were:

(a) the extant necessity with respect to the congregation; or

(b) the well-founded utility for the congregation; or

(c) reasons of piety.

The solemnities required by law were:

(a) the consent of the chapter in writing;

(b) the permission of the superior to enter into the contract; and

(c) the consent of the patron in certain cases.[8]

[5] Ferraris, s. v., "*Alienatio,*" art. 4, n. 39.

[6] Suarez, *Opera Omnia,* ed. nova a Carolo Berton (28 vols., Parisiis: Apud Ludovicum Vives, 1856-1861), Vols. XII-XVI, *De Religione,* tract. 8, lib. 2, c. 26, n. 1.

[7] C. un., *de rebus ecclesiae non alienandis,* III, 4, in Extravag. com.

[8] Cf. *supra,* pp. 24-27.

Article 3. Restriction of Contractual Power

The Constitution *Iniunctum nobis* of Pope Paul IV, issued on July 14, 1555, furnished an extensive interpretation of the Constitution *Ambitiosae,* and its provisions applied likewise to religious congregations.[9]

The general prohibitions of the Council of Trent were also applicable to the goods of religious institutes. Encroachments upon these property rights by others, and unlawful alienations by administrative bodies of religious congregations were severely censured.[10] The Council of Trent legislated concerning the administration of both movable and immovable goods in religious institutes by prohibiting the individual religious from possessing goods in his own name. These possessions were to be incorporated with the goods of the religious house, and to be administered by officials appointed by the superiors.[11]

A restriction of the contractual power of religious congregations was contained in a decree of the Sacred Congregation of the Council issued by order of Pope Urban VIII (1623-1644) on September 7, 1624.[12] Realizing the detrimental effects which might befall religious institutes through an unrestricted power to enter into contracts, the Holy See placed the following limitations upon this power:

(1) For contracts by which the dominion of immovable goods and precious movable goods was transferred, for renting beyond three years, for emphyteusis and for mortgage, the express permission of the Holy See was required.

(2) The provisions and penalties of the papal Constitution *Ambitiosae* remained in force.

(3) Contracts made contrary to the provisions of this Constitution were by the authority of the Holy See declared null and void.

(4) Constitutions and apostolic grants in favor of any Order or persons were revoked.

[9] *Fontes,* n. 88.

[10] Conc. Trident., sess. XXII, *de ref.,* c. 11.

[11] Conc. Trident., sess. XXV, *de regularibus,* c. 3.

[12] *Fontes,* n. 2453.

(5) This decree applied to all religious institutes within the boundaries of Europe. It applied equally to individual houses and monasteries.

(6) Customs, even immemorial ones, contrary to the prescripts of this decree were revoked, as were also all exemptions, privileges, and indults.

Superiors who presumptuously violated these provisions were deprived of all offices they possessed, of their vote and of eligibility for office, and were declared incapable of acquiring these rights in the future.[13] These penalties were incurred *ipso facto*, and could not be mitigated by the General of the institute or the Cardinal Protector.[14]

The Sacred Congregation of the Council was wont to give absolution in the cases in which violations of these provisions occurred in good faith. If the superior firmly believed he was acting for the utility of the Church, and was motivated by the desire to spread the faith and divine cult, the same Congregation was willing to sanate the contract.[15] Immovable goods included also incorporeal rights and things pertaining to the soil, such as trees.[16]

In order to expedite these matters more speedily and to save the poorer institutes added expenses, the papal *beneplacitum* was conferred by the Sacred Congregation of Bishops and Regulars. By this delegation the congregations were spared the necessity of appealing to the Apostolic Datary or to the Secretary of the Briefs in each case. The Sacred Congregation of the Council likewise had the power of bestowing the papal *beneplacitum*.[17]

Although the decree just cited of the Sacred Congregation of the Council as issued by order of Pope Urban VIII appeared to be all-inclusive in its scope, an extensive interpretation was issued on February 27, 1666. By virtue of this interpretative decree, con-

[13] S. C. C., *in Fanen.*, 10 ian. 1784—*Th. Resol. S. C. C.*, LIII, 2.

[14] S. C. C., *in Capuana*, 15 iul. 1848—*Th. Resol. S. C. C.*, CVIII, 284.

[15] S. C. C., *in Fanen.*, 19 apr. 1823—*Th. Resol. S. C. C.*, LXXXIII, 69, 75; S. C. C. *in Pisauren.*, 18 aug. 1827—*Th. Resol. S. C. C.*, LXXXVII, 159.

[16] Vecchiotti, *Institutiones Canonicae* (16. ed., 3 vols., Taurini, 1875) II, 86.

[17] Regulae Generales S. C. Ep. et Reg., n. xvii,—Bizzarri, *Collectanea*, p. 8.

tracts involving loans of money were forbidden, and the restrictions of the decree of 1624 [18] were extended to comprise also such contracts as were entered between two houses of the same institute.[19] Even when the contract concerned superabundant goods of one house made in favor of a poor house of the same province, the Sacred Congregation of the Council declared that the decree of 1624 had to be observed.[20]

The interpretative decree of 1666 applied equally to the congregations whose members took simple vows as well as to Orders which professed solemn vows. The permission of the Holy See was required for contracts entered into by all churches, monasteries, and houses of congregations erected by the local ordinary, and, *a fortiori*, if they were erected by the Holy See. Contrary custom could not be alleged as an excuse for failing to comply with these provisions. Despite any and all contrary customs, such contracts were declared null and void.[21] That these rules were followed is evident from the numerous cases in which the permission of the Sacred Congregation of the Council was requested. That they were sometimes violated through inadvertence is also evident from the sanations granted by the same Congregation.[22]

The Constitution *Apostolicae Sedis* of Pope Pius IX [23] made no exception in favor of religious institutes; all alike were subject to its provisions. Since it renewed the demands of the Constitution *Ambitiosae*, religious superiors who entered into contracts in violation of that Constitution, i. e., if they proceeded without the required papal indult, were subject to excommunication. However, those institutes which and superiors who held personal privileges,

[18] *Fontes*, n. 2453; *supra*, p. 33.

[19] S. C. C., 27 febr. 1666, as reported in *Analecta Juris Pontificii* (26 vols. Romae, 1855-1869; Parisiis, 1872-1891), I (1855), 1139. Hereinafter cited *Analecta J. P.*

[20] S. C. C., *in Lisbonen.*, 29 nov. 1783; S. C. C., 19 mart., 19 apr., 1685; S. C. C., *in Florentina Benopl.*, 27 aug. 1712, as reported in *Analecta J. P.*, I (1855), 1139; *Th. Resol. S. C. C.*, LII, 193.

[21] S. C. C., *in Terracinen.*, 23 ian. 1790—*Th. Resol S. C. C.*, LIX, 6.

[22] *Analecta J. P.*, I (1855), 1143-1145.

[23] *Fontes*, n. 552.

rightly obtained prior to Pius IX's Constitution, were not obliged to relinquish them. On the other hand, all general privileges were revoked by this Constitution.[24]

An important document which in recent times restricted the contractual power of religious institutes was the Instruction *Inter ea,* issued by the Sacred Congregation of Religious on July 30, 1909.[25] Its principal provisions were the following:

(1) Contracts which involved the congregation in debt were not to be entered into directly or indirectly by the Superior General, or by the Provincial or the Local Superior, unless they had previously consulted their respective councils.

(2) Contracts involving a notable debt were defined as:

(a) Contracts involving an expenditure of between 500 and 1,000 francs for individual houses;

(b) 1,000 to 5,000 francs for the Province or quasi-province; and

(c) 5,000 to 10,000 francs for the *Curia Generalis.*

For contracts involving debts over 10,000 francs the *beneplacitum* of the Holy See had to be obtained.

(3) Contracted debts, no matter how small, coalesced. An indult received upon the presentation of a petition which had not listed these debts was invalid.

(4) Those congregations which were without councils to take care of these matters had to establish one within three months.

(5) The vote of the council was secret and definitive. The proceedings of the council had to be written and signed by the superior and each councillor.

(6) The Superior was commanded to give a complete exposition of all debts, no matter in what manner they had been contracted. Nothing of this nature was to be hidden from the other councillors. All these matters were to be examined fully, exactly, sincerely, and faithfully, before the approval of the council was given.

(7) A new foundation was not to be made, nor were changes to be made in existing foundations, unless the assets on hand were sufficient to cover these expenditures. Promises made by benefactors

[24] S. C. C. Off. (*Ratisbonen.*), 22 dec. 1880, ad V—*Fontes,* n. 1068.

[25] *Fontes,* n. 4934.

were considered to be of too precarious a nature to constitute sufficient security for new contracts.

Article 4. Exemption from the Necessity of Obtaining the *Beneplacitum* of the Holy See

Those who acted by necessity of law were excused from requesting the *beneplacitum* of the Holy See as demanded by Pope Urban VIII. This contention was sustained by the Sacred Congregation of the Council, according to Fagnanus (1598-1678).[26] Such a necessity of law arose in the case of the Franciscans who were left pious legacies of immovable goods. Since they were incapable of possessing immovable goods, they were permitted to dispose of them and use the income thus obtained for the upkeep of their churches. The Theatines and all those who professed poverty in common, and thus were incapable of possessing immovable goods, were in a similar way, exempted from the necessity of obtaining the *beneplacitum* of the Holy See before selling these properties.[27]

All Regulars had enjoyed exemption from the necessity of asking for the *beneplacitum* of the Holy See in virtue of concessions granted by Leo X (1513-1521), by Gregory XIII (1572-1585), and by Clement VIII (1592-1605). However, the decree of the Sacred Congregation of the Council, issued by order of Pope Urban VIII in 1624, revoked these privileges. After that decree Regulars not endowed with special privileges were bound to request the papal permission before making contracts concerning immovable and precious movable goods.[28]

The exemption possessed by the Mendicants who were incapable of possessing immovable goods was subject to abuse, as is evidenced in a response of the Sacred Congregation of the Council on March 18, 1719. Since the *syndici* of the Franciscan Order enjoyed the privilege of exemption from requesting the papal *beneplacitum* before entering into contracts, the Holy See was reluctant to rule that they relinquish this privilege. However, grave harm was being done to

[26] *Commentarium,* Lib. III, tit. 13, c. 5, n. 27.

[27] *Analecta J. P.*, I (1855), 1140.

[28] Ferraris, s. v., *"Alienatio,"* art. 4, nn. 28, 29.

the Franciscan Order by the sale of goods for meager prices. These sales were often made in favor of the friends of the *syndici,* and at other times the latter were coerced into making such contracts by powerful persons. In order to remedy this evil state of affairs, the Sacred Congregation of the Council decreed that in the future the movable precious goods which were incorporated in the fixed and permanent assets of the Order could not be made the subject matter of contracts of sale unless the *beneplacitum* of the Holy See was first obtained. Regarding other goods, the *syndici* were forbidden to make any contract, unless the sale was first declared public, and preference was given to the highest bidder.[29]

A further exemption from obtaining the Holy See's permission in contractual matters was stated by Fagnanus.[30] He declared that, during his time as Secretary of the Sacred Congregation *super Statu Regularium,* contracts of Regulars concerning general mortgage were not forbidden by the decrees of the Holy See.

[29] S. C. C., *Ord. S. Francisci,* 18 mart. 1719—*Fontes,* n. 3185.
[30] *Commentarium,* Lib. III, tit. 13, n. 32.

CHAPTER VII

NORMS OF CONTRACTS BETWEEN BISHOPS AND RELIGIOUS CONGREGATIONS FROM THE COUNCIL OF TRENT UNTIL THE CODE OF CANON LAW

Introduction

The nature of the legislation concerning the contractual power of bishops on the one hand and of religious congregations on the other is at times identical, and at times distinct. Since both are subject to ecclesiastical law in contractual relations, it is incumbent upon both to follow the rules established for them whether these rules apply to them jointly or severally. Bishops have concessions in law which are not granted to religious congregations. Some religious institutes may have been granted privileges exempting them from the common law in particular cases. Bishops may be further restricted by decrees of plenary or provincial councils, and religious congregations must follow the rules incorporated in the constitutions which govern them. Further, the subject matter of the contract more often than not will concern ecclesiastical matters which are governed by special laws. Such is the case when the contract refers to the union of a church with a religious institute. In the preceding chapters the contractual powers of bishops and religious congregations have been treated separately. It is the purpose of the present chapter to consider the interrelation of these powers.

Article 1. Exception of Law in Favor of Bishops Forbidden to Religious Congregations

The principal exception to the general law requiring the papal *beneplacitum* for contracts concerning immovable goods was found in a canon of the Council of Agde (506).[1] Both bishops and religious were accustomed to take advantage of this exception, whereby even

[1] C. 63, C. XII, q. 2.

immovable goods of little value could be alienated without a papal indult. Since the phrase, "of little value," was indefinite, it was not surprising that its interpretation should be a source of concern for administrators. The passage of time could readily occasion a change in its interpretation.

A Brief of Pope Clement VIII (1592-1605), issued by the Sacred Congregation of the Council on October 7, 1602, seems to indicate that land which yielded an annual income of forty ducats constituted the limit of ecclesiastical goods of little value.[2] The Sacred Congregation of Bishops and Regulars declared that the custom of the Roman Curia was to regard twenty five gold *scutata* as the maximum which could be alienated without the permission of the Holy See.[3] Ferraris (+ ca. 1763) set the maximum amount at 20 *solidi.*[4] He cited responses of the Sacred Congregation of Bishops and Regulars in support of this view.[5]

With the passage of time the maximum amount increased, as is indicated in the opinion of authors. Authors who wrote in the past century set the sum as high as five hundred francs.[6] Vecchiotti (+ 1870),[7] discussing the opinion of Giraldi (1692-1775), who held for the sum of about forty *scutata,* concluded that the matter was to be left to the judgment of the bishop, since he was qualified to judge the particular circumstances in each case. Wernz (1842-1914) listed various opinions whose authors placed the maximum sum at from twenty-five to one hundred *aurei.*[8]

Although religious institutes had availed themselves of the concession of Pope Clement VIII, it was made clear by a declaration of the Sacred Congregation of Bishops and Regulars on January 16,

[2] Bizzarri, *Collectanea,* p. 241.

[3] S. C. Ep. et Reg., *Faventina,* 22 mart. 1711—Bizzarri, *Collectanea,* p. 298.

[4] Ferraris, s. v., *"Alienatio,"* art. 3, nn. 3, 4.

[5] S. C. Ep. et Reg., *Faventina,* 22 maii 1611; *Messanensi,* 29 nov. 1613; *Barensi,* 12 apr. 1689; *Papiensi,* 15 maii 1710; *Amalphitana,* 8 aug. 1665, as cited by Ferraris, s. v., *"Alienatio,"* art. 3, nn. 3, 4.

[6] Bouix, *Tractatus de Jure Regularium* (2 vols., Parisiis, 1857), II, 291.

[7] *Institutiones Canonicae,* II, 89.

[8] *Ius Decretalium,* III, n. 165.

1653, that what was allowable for bishops was not by the same token allowable for religious institutes.[9]

ARTICLE 2. THE CASE OF NECESSITY

In certain extraordinary cases in which there was danger in delay, and in cases of urgent necessity when recourse to the Holy See was impossible, the rigor of the law concerning contracts by which ecclesiastical goods were alienated was mitigated.[10] This concession could be used by both bishops and religious congregations, and it was admitted in the decisions of the Sacred Congregation for the Propagation of the Faith.[11]

The Council of Trent permitted bishops to unite churches perpetually in such cases without obtaining the *beneplacitum* of the Holy See. In this matter the bishop acted as the delegate of the Holy See. These unions were usually occasioned by the poverty of one of the churches. The bishop was cautioned to effect these unions according to the form prescribed by law, and it was declared that, once made, these unions could not be revoked or infringed upon in any way.[12] Barbosa (1589-1649) furnished an example of the form used in making these unions.[13]

This kind of union could not be made in favor of religious institutes through the union of a church with a monastery of any kind, or with an abbey, or with the collegiate chapter of religious.[14] However, if the union had been made in the past without deceit, and the churches had been held by the religious for forty years, they could remain united with the monastery, the abbey or the collegiate chapter of religious. The bishop was to review each case and give the decision in this matter.[15]

[9] Bizzarri, *Collectanea*, p. 298.

[10] Schmalzgrueber, Lib. III, tit. 13, n. 112.

[11] 27 aug. 1832; 31 mart. 1836—*Collectanea S. Congregationis de Propaganda Fide* (2 vols., Romae; Typographia Polyglotta S. C. de Propaganda Fide, 1907), n. 827, and I, p. 484, nota 1; *Fontes*, nn. 4753 and 4763.

[12] Conc. Trident., sess. XXI, *de ref.*, c. 5.

[13] Barbosa, *Pastoralis Sollicitudo seu de Officio et Potestate Episcopi Descriptio* (3 partes in 2 vols., Lugduni, 1656), II, 508.

[14] Conc. Trident, sess. XXIV, *de ref.*, c. 13.

[15] Conc. Trident., sess. VII, *de ref.*, c. 6.

An exception to the general rule demanding the *beneplacitum* of the Holy See was also made in cases of necessity, and especially in consideration of the benefit of the faithful. A church one day's journey distant from Düsseldorf was given to the Jesuits on condition that one of their members would reside there with the intention of opening a college in that heretical region.[16] The Archbishop of Cologne made this agreement with the Jesuit Fathers who resided in Düsseldorf.

A further condition could be annexed to this contract between the bishop and the religious institute. This is illustrated in the union of a parish church with a college of the Jesuits in Cracow, whereby it was agreed that a secular priest be deputed as the church's vicar. The necessity of the union was brought about by the poverty of the college and by the need for such a college in that area.[17]

An example of urgent necessity was alleged in the case of persecution in China. The Sacred Congregation for the Propagation of the Faith approved the action of the Vicar Apostolic in contracting for the disposal of ecclesiastical goods when the safety of the church was threatened, and when recourse could not be had to obtain the *beneplacitum* of the Holy See.[18]

Article 3. Immemorial Custom

Immemorial custom was not permitted to derogate from the provisions of the law concerning contracts about immovable goods. Despite the restrictions enacted in the Constitution *Ambitiosae* of Paul II [19] and reaffirmed in the Constitution *Iniunctum nobis* of Paul IV,[20] the Archbishop of Milan claimed an immemorial custom as permitting him to contract freely without prior approval of the Holy See. In virtue of the same custom he claimed the right to delegate this power to others who administered church goods. The Archbishop

[16] S. C. C., *in Colonien.*, 20 sept. 1727—*Th. Resol. S. C. C.* IV, 119.

[17] S. C. C., *in Cracovien.*, 30 ian. 1740—*The Resol. S. C. C.* IX, 19.

[18] S. C. de Prop. Fide (C. P. *pro Sin.-Cochinchin.*), 27 aug. 1832—*Fontes*, n. 4753; S. C. de Prop. Fide, litt. (*ad Vic. Ap. Cochinchin.*), 31 mart. 1836—*Fontes*, n. 4763.

[19] C. un., *de rebus ecclesiae non alienandis*, III, 4, in Extravag. com.

[20] *Fontes*, n. 88.

asserted that the Popes were aware of this custom, since in times past St. Charles Borromeo (1538-1584) had written to Popes Pius IV (1559-1565) and Gregory XIII (1572-1585) about its validity. Letters attested these facts and proved the validity and laudability of the custom. St. Charles consulted weekly with a group of theologians and canonists appointed to examine the proposed contracts and to pass on the feasibility of accepting them. Before the contract took place, St. Charles demanded that a decree be issued declaring its evident usefulness for the Church. In 1665, by order of the Sacred Congregation of the Council, this custom was abrogated. According to the report of the Archbishop of Milan in 1682, this caused great difficulties and harm to the Church. Administrators who had formerly been compelled to place the matter before the Archbishop and his commission now acted without his consent. They asserted further that they were excused from applying for the papal *beneplacitum* because of the difficulties of having recourse. The Archbishop declared that a restoration of the former custom would obviate the dangers in this system of formulating contracts.

The Sacred Congregation of the Council did not deem the reasons alleged by the Archbishop of Milan to be sufficiently grave to permit the restoration of a custom which derogated from the general law. In reply the Sacred Congregation stated that the decision of 1665, which had revoked the custom, was to remain in force.[21]

The Constitution *Apostolicae Sedis* of Pius IX also abolished general privileges and contrary customs regarding contracts of alienation, as is evident from a reply of the Sacred Congregation of the Holy Office.[22]

Article 4. Contracts Concerning Erection of Religious Houses

By virtue of the Constitution *Instaurandae* of Pope Innocent X (1644-1655), issued on October 15, 1652, the former papal Constitution of Boniface VIII, *Cum ex eo*, which had prohibited re-

[21] S. C. C., *Mediolanen.*, 14 mart. 1682—*Fontes*, n. 2862.

[22] Pius IX, Const. *Apostolicae Sedis*, 12 oct. 1869—*Fontes*, n. 552; S. C. S. Off. (*Ratisbonen.*), 22 dec. 1880, ad V—*Fontes*, n. 1068.

ligious institutes from establishing foundations of any type without the permission of the Holy See, was revived.[23] Also restored was the Constitution *Quoniam* of Clement VIII (1592-1605).[24] Among the penalties visited upon violators of these Constitutions were *ipso facto* incurred deprivation of office and dignities, the loss of the active and passive voice in elections, and the perpetual incapacity for obtaining any office in the future.[25]

Clement VIII's Constitution *Quoniam* also restricted the power of bishops in the erection of new religious foundations by decreeing that the bishops had to consult the superiors of religious houses already erected in the vicinity where the new foundation was to be established. This consultation was demanded in order that it might first be manifest that the new foundation would not be detrimental to the rights of the houses already established.[26]

Pope Gregory XV (1621-1623) in his Constitution *Cum alias* of August 27, 1622, had also confirmed the provisions of the Constitution *Quoniam,* and it was determined that the term "vicinity" was identifiable with a maximum distance of four thousand paces.[27]

The Council of Trent had declared that the consent of the local ordinary was necessary for the erection of a house by any institute.[28] This episcopal permission was needed in addition to the papal *beneplacitum* required by Boniface VIII's Constitution *Cum ex eo.*[29] Pope Urban VIII confirmed this law of the Council of Trent in his Constitution *Romanus Pontifex* on August 28, 1624.[30]

There ensued no little discussion concerning the scope of these various decrees, but Benedict XIV (1740-1758) declared that both papal and episcopal permission were necessary before a new religious

[23] *Fontes,* n. 233.

[24] 23 iul. 1603—*Fontes,* n. 190.

[25] Innocentius X, const. *Instaurandae,* 15 oct. 1652—*Fontes.* n. 233.

[26] *Fontes,* n. 190.

[27] *Bullarum Diplomatum et Privilegiorum Sanctorum Romanorum Pontificum Taurinensis Editio* (25 vols., Augustae Taurinensis, 1857-1872), XII, 719.

[28] Conc. Trident., sess. XXV, *de regularibus,* c. 3.

[29] C. un. *de excessibus praelatorum et subditorum,* V, 6, in VI.°

[30] *Fontes,* n. 204.

foundation could be attempted.[31] Various decisions of the Roman Rota likewise prove that this was the practice of the Roman Curia, and the Sacred Congregation of Bishops and Regulars plainly declared that these permissions were necessary despite privileges asserted to the contrary.[32] The Constitution *Romanos Pontifices,* issued by Pope Leo XIII (1878-1903) on May 8, 1881, confirmed this practice by demanding that both papal and episcopal permission be obtained before the erection of a religious house.[33]

Sometimes the local ordinary entered into a contract concerning the erection of a religious house by appending certain conditions to his granted permission. In 1621 the Bishop of Piacenza in Italy agreed to let the Augustinian Friars erect a house in his diocese, provided that they assigned twelve members to the house. The Sacred Congregation of Bishops and Regulars declared that the Friars had not violated this agreement by keeping a lesser number in the house before it was completed.[34]

The force of circumstances also effected changes in the contractual agreements between bishops and religious congregations, as is evidenced in a case proposed by a French bishop to the Sacred Congregation of Bishops and Regulars. In 1835 the bishop entered a contract with a group of priests who formed a congregation with a view to having them direct a seminary in his diocese. The bishop gave approval to the congregation and permitted the members to take vows, provided that they would send their constitutions to Rome for papal approbation. Meanwhile, decrees issued by civil authorities in France forbade seminaries to function under the direction of religious congregations. The bishop, in order to permit the priests to direct the seminary, revoked his approval of them as a religious congregation, but permitted them to observe their vows and to perform their community exercises in secret.[35]

[31] Benedictus XIV, *De Synodo Dioecesana* (3 vols., Romae, 1788), Vol. I, lib. 9, c. 1, n. 9.

[32] S. C. Ep. et Reg., *Bilbaonensi,* 25 nov. 1672—Bizzarri, *Collectanea,* p. 728.

[33] *Fontes,* n. 582.

[34] Bizzarri, *Collectanea,* p. 248.

[35] Bizzarri, *Collectanea,* p. 423.

In a dispute which arose over the possession of a church in Cimella in Italy, the local ordinary sought to settle the difficulty by making a contract with the Regulars who claimed the church. The bishop proposed that the sacristy and church furnishings be used in common, and an agreement be drawn up to define the times at which parish functions would take place. The Sacred Congregation of Bishops and Regulars rejected this contract in a reply dated April 8, 1839.[36]

The same Sacred Congregation appended conditions to a decree of erection granted for a Dominican College in Santiago de Chile on March 6, 1846. (1) The foundation was to be known as a college, not a seminary; (2) the rights of the local ordinary, of the pastor, and of the religious were to be scrupulously safeguarded, and (3) a domestic oratory, not a public one, was to be erected in the institution.[37]

The Provincial and Plenary Councils of Baltimore were intent on eradicating the evils of the trustee system. Accordingly the legislation was directed towards this end, rather than to the aim of regulating the contractual relations between bishops and religious congregations. However, the sixth decree of the I Plenary Council of Baltimore (1852), urging that consultors be chosen whose opinions were to be sought in the administration of the diocese, did affect these contracts, since the bishop thus was required to consult this council before entering into such contracts.[38]

More pertinent to the present discussion was the decree of the I Provincial Council of Cincinnati in 1855, which called upon religious congregations to carry out faithfully the contracts they had made with the bishops.[39] The II Plenary Council of Baltimore (1866)

[36] Bizzarri, *Collectanea,* p. 440.

[37] Bizzarri, *Collectanea.* p. 534.

[38] *Acta et Decreta Sacrorum Conciliorum Recentiorum, Collectio Lacensis* (7 vols., Friburgi Brisgoviae, 1870-1890), III, 146. Hereafter cited *Coll. Lac.*

[39] Decretum XVIII: "Cum neminem lateat quanto cum studio fructuque animarum curam egerint Collegiaque regenda susceperint viri religiosi diversorum Ordinum in hac Provincia, et quanto cum scandalo et religionis detrimento Missiones et instituta ipsis commissa, insciis seu invitis Ordinariis locorum, relinquerent et [ad?] alias se transferrent, haud inopportunum esse censuere Patres, quae bona sunt firmare, quae autem mala avertere providentes, in mentem omnibus revocare Decretum Summi Pontificis Bonifatii VIII (c. un., *de*

accepted this resolution of the I Provincial Council of Cincinnati as its own.[40]

ARTICLE 5. CONTRACTS WITH CONGREGATIONS OF SIMPLE VOWS

It was not until the eighteenth century that religious congregations professing simple vows were approved by the Holy See. Inasmuch as they were ecclesiastical bodies, they had to submit to the canonical legislation concerning contracts. Furthermore, they were bound by the particular laws as defined in their constitutions. The papal Constitution *Apostolicae Sedis* of October 12, 1869,[41] made the provisions of the former law applicable to them, since it renewed the former law and made no exception in favor of congregations of simple vows, as can be deduced from a reply of the Sacred Congregation of the Holy Office.[42]

The intention of the Holy See to bind religious congregations of simple vows to the general law concerning contracts is evidenced by replies of the Sacred Congregation of Bishops and Regulars. Observations to this effect were made in numerous cases in which this Sacred Congregation examined the constitutions of religious institutes submitted for approval. The insistence is especially noticeable regarding the establishment of a chapter to guide the Moderator General in formulating contracts. Regarding the constitutions of the Sisters of St. Vincent de Paul, Servants of the Poor, the Sacred Congregation observed that the Moderator General needed the consent of her con-

excessibus praelatorum, V, 6, in VI°) et S. C. de Propaganda Fide (D. 3. Jun. 1822. a S. P. Pio VII d. 21. Jul. ejusd. anni approbatum), ex quibus constat societates religiosas a conventionibus cum Episcopis initis resilire non posse nec pastores et rectores religiosos ab Ecclesiis et locis quibus praepositi sunt a superioribus suis removeri, nisi iis alii societatum sodales, cum consensu Ordinarii, subrogentur. His sapientissimis summorum Pontificum Decretis omnes morem gerere obsequiumque praestare in Domino monemus.—*Coll. Lac.*, III, 198a.

40 *Concilii Plenarii Baltimorensis II Acta et Decreta* (2. ed., Baltimorae, 1894), nn. 406, 407. Cf. Hannan, "The Juridical Status of the Parishes of Religious,"—*The Jurist* (Washington, D. C., 1941—), I (1941), 329-335; Dooley, "The Juridical Status of the Parishes of Religious: Another View,"—*The Jurist,* III (1943), 117-128.

41 *Fontes,* n. 552.

42 S. C. S. Off. (*Ratisbonen.*), 22 dec. 1880, ad V—*Fontes,* n. 1068.

sultors in order to enter into contracts, as well as the *beneplacitum* of the Holy See in the cases specified in Canon Law.[43] That this vote was to be definitive is evident from replies to the Sisters of St. Joseph in the Diocese of Belley in France,[44] and to the Sisters of the Immaculate Heart of Mary in Bayeux, France.[45] Similar replies were made to congregations of men who, when submitting their constitutions for approval, had not insisted on the provision which demanded the definitive vote of the chapter before the superior could enter into contracts.[46]

The Constitution *Conditae a Christo* of Pope Leo XIII (1878-1903), promulgated on December 8, 1900, clarified many issues concerning the status of congregations of simple vows in their relations with bishops. It clearly distinguished between congregations of pontifical approval and congregations of diocesan approval.[47] These laws were supplemented with the *Normae* of the Sacred Congregation of Bishops and Regulars, issued on June 28, 1901,[48] and with the Instruction *Inter ea* of the Sacred Congregation of Religious, issued on July 30, 1909.[49]

A. *Congregations of Pontifical Approval*

The Constitution *Conditae a Christo* gave the councils of congregations of pontifical approval the right to appoint those in charge of the temporal management of the affairs of the institute. In congregations of women, the local ordinary was to preside at such chapter meetings either personally or by delegate.[50] The bishops could

[43] S. C. Ep. et Reg., *Gandaven.*, 30 apr. 1860—Bizzarri, *Collectanea*, p. 779.

[44] S. C. Ep. et Reg., *Bellicen.*, 6 iun. 1860—Bizzarri, *Collectanea*, p. 781.

[45] S. C. Ep. et Reg., *Baiocen.*, 20 febr. 1861—Bizzarri, *Collectanea*, p. 789.

[46] S. C. Ep. et Reg., *Rhedonen.*, 2 mart. 1861—Bizzarri, *Collectanea*, p. 790.

[47] Leo XIII, const. *Conditae a Christo*, 8 dec. 1900—*Fontes*, n. 644.

[48] *Normae secundum quas S. Cong. Episcoporum et Regularium procedere solet in approbandis novis institutis votorum simplicium* (Romae, Typis S. C. de Propaganda Fide, 1901). Hereinafter cited *Normae of 1901*.

[49] S. C. de Rel., instr. *Inter ea*, 30 iul. 1909—*Fontes*, n. 4394.

[50] Cap. II, n. 1—*Fontes*, n. 644.

not modify the provisions of the constitutions regarding contracts after the approval of the Holy See had been obtained.[51]

Though the religious be subject to the local ordinary in spiritual matters, contracts, being a matter of temporal administration, were to be made by the Supreme Moderator and the council guided by the particular constitutions of the institute. Properties and moneys donated to a particular house for the needs of divine worship and local charity were to be administered by the religious superiors under the supervision of the local ordinary. The latter was to receive a report on the administration of these goods which would indicate whether his instructions concerning them had been carried out.[52]

Academies, hospitals and asylums were subject to the supervision of the local ordinary in spiritual matters, e. g., in the teaching of religion, in matters concerning good morals, and in the exercises of piety. In the administration of temporalities they were subject to the same provisions as other houses.[53] This papal constitution did not derogate from the faculties and privileges obtained in the past through immemorial custom, or from the Holy See either directly or by communication or by way of their inclusion in the constitutions already approvel by the Holy See.[54]

The *Normae* of the Sacred Congregation of Bishops and Regulars, issued in 1901, demanded the approval by decisive vote of the council for all contracts made in the name of the institute, and for mortgages or alienations of immovable and precious movable goods.[55]

In the house in which the Moderator General resided a safe secured with three keys was to be kept, so that titles to property and copies of contracts as well as money not used for current expenses might be properly safeguarded. The Moderator General, the First Assistant and the Treasurer General were each to retain possession of one of these keys.[56]

The council of the Moderator General was bound to reside in the

[51] *Ibid.*, n. 2.
[52] *Ibid.*, n. 9.
[53] *Ibid.*, n. 10.
[54] *Ibid.*, n. 11.
[55] *Normae of 1901,* art. 271, nn. 13, 15.
[56] *Ibid.*, arts. 286, 287.

principal house of the congregation with the Moderator General, but if necessity demanded it, two of the councillors could reside elsewhere, provided that they could be present at the council's deliberations when the contracts were being discussed.[57] For contracts concerning mortgages and alienations of immovable or precious movable goods, in addition to the decisive vote of the council, the approbation of the Sacred Congregation of Bishops and Regulars was necessary.[58]

The *Normae* of 1901 were supplemented with the instruction which the Sacred Congregation of Religious issued on July 30, 1909. This Instruction ordered congregations, if they lacked councils for discussing and approving the contracts of the institute, to establish such councils within three months.[59] Should the constitutions of the congregation contain stricter provisions for entering contracts than those contained in the Instruction, the particular constitutions were to be observed. All provisions which in particular constitutions stood opposed to the Instruction were considered abrogated.[60]

B. *Congregations of Diocesan Approval*

Pope Leo XIII devoted the first chapter of his Constitution *Conditae a Christo* to congregations of diocesan approval. In these institutes bishops had much greater supervision than they had in congregations of pontifical approval. These powers were held cumulatively with other bishops as the congregation spread to other dioceses.

Bishops were cautioned against founding or approving new congregations as long as other congregations organized for similar purposes existed in their dioceses. An exception to this rule was made in favor of missionary countries.[61] In order to make a contract for the erection of a foundation in another diocese, diocesan congregations had to obtain the permission of the bishop in whose diocese they had originally been established.[62]

[57] *Ibid.*, art. 276.

[58] *Ibid.*, art. 272.

[59] S. C. de Rel., instr., *Inter ea*, 30 iul. 1909—*Fontes*, n. 4394.

[60] *Ibid.*, n. 10.

[61] Leo XIII, const. *Conditae a Christo*, 8 dec. 1900, cap. II, n. 3—*Fontes*, n. 644.

[62] *Ibid.*, n. 4.

The local ordinary, in addition to the supervision over spiritual matters, had the right to supervise the administration of temporal goods of institutes of diocesan approval. From this it can be concluded that the local ordinary's permission had to be obtained before a diocesan congregation could make a contract concerning these goods. If there was question of the congregation entering into a contract with another bishop, the permission of the local ordinary of the mother house was necessary.[63]

The diocesan congregations had to observe these regulations in addition to those outlined above for congregations of pontifical approval, and also the provisions of their particular constitutions, provided that they were not contrary to the Instruction *Inter ea.*[64] Once they had spread to other dioceses, the local ordinary of the place of their foundation could not change any constitutional provision regarding contractual procedure, unless the approval of all the bishops in whose dioceses the congregation had become established was obtained.[65]

[63] *Ibid.*, n. 10.
[64] S. C. de Rel., instr. *Inter ea,* 30 iul. 1909—*Fontes,* n. 4394.
[65] Leo XIII, const. *Conditae a Christo,* cap. I, n. 5—*Fontes.* n. 664.

PART II

CANONICAL COMMENTARY

CHAPTER VIII

CANONIZATION OF CIVIL LAW REGARDING CONTRACTS

Article 1. GENERAL NOTIONS

Canon 1529.—Quae ius civile in territorio statuit de contractibus tam in genere, quam in specie, sive nominatis sive innominatis, et de solutionibus, eadem iure canonico in materia ecclesiastica iisdem cum effectibus serventur, nisi iuri divino contraria sint aut aliud iure canonico caveatur.

Prior to the Code, the Church generally adopted Roman Law in contractual matters. There was no universal law of the Church on contracts, since Roman Law was the accepted guide in this field. Ecclesiastical law did, however, supply what was lacking in Roman Law, and corrected those laws which were obviously contrary to Catholic teaching.[1]

The codifiers of Canon Law were anxious to reduce the voluminous collection of laws to an orderly and concise collection which would be available to all who needed to consult it. Of necessity, this operation demanded the discarding of much repetitious and obsolete material. Roman Law had lost its position as a body of laws with which the legal world was familiar, just as Latin had lost its pre-eminence of usage in the field of languages. Having discarded Roman Law

[1] "Ecclesiae enim in huiusmodi rebus temporalibus, quae in suo foro sive ratione rei sive ratione personae fuerunt definiendae, generatim adoptaverat ius Romanum. Quare in libro tertio universum ius de rebus ecclesiasticis, contractibus, negotiis legitimis propriam sedem non obtinuit, nisi quid in iure Romano fuit corrigendum vel supplendum".—Wernz, *Ius Decretalium,* III, n. 252.

as the common juridical ground in contractual matters, the codifiers had two alternatives. They could have drawn up an entirely new system of laws governing all phases of contractual legislation. The Church as a perfect society was free to adopt a system of laws concerning contracts which would become part and parcel of her own legal system, as she did in the case of judicial procedure. The other alternatives was to adopt a current system of laws which would serve as a foundation to govern the formation of contracts. In her desire to simplify the legal system and to avoid, wherever possible, conflicts with civil law, the Church incorporated the civil law of each territory concerning contracts in the present Code. By this act she made the civil law on contract her own.

The Church remained fully aware of her right to legislate on individual points of contract, and she was not so rash as to relinquish this right entirely. The prudence of her judgment is apparent in the final clause of canon 1529, "*nisi iuri divino contraria sint aut aliud iure canonico caveatur.*" Coronata ascribes the action of the Church in foregoing her right in this matter to her meekness of spirit.[2] The Church retains her right radically, but foregoes it in this particular instance to avoid conflicts and confusion.

By virtue of canon 1529 all civil legislation regarding contracts is considered as incorporated into the body of Canon Law, except those laws which are contrary to divine law or to some provision of the Code. Both in the statement of the general acceptance of civil law on contracts, and also in the clause which takes exception to two large categories, wide fields in contractual legislation are covered. In practice, each contract must be carefully examined if one is to determine whether the provisions of canon 1529 are fulfilled. Prescriptions contrary to divine law embrace the whole field of moral and dogmatic theology. In an examination of the terms of a contract, contrary provisions would be relatively easy to recognize. Having established the fact that no contrariety exists between the terms of the contract and the divine law or canonical legislation, one may deem the contract to be valid and the effects ordained by the civil statutes would follow.

[2] *Institutiones,* II, n. 1069.

A. *Civil Law Provisions Contrary to Divine Law*

The following provisions would have to be rejected because of their failure to comply with divine law:

(1) Enactments which permit contracts to be made concerning things or actions morally evil.[3]

(2) A provision whereby the status of the Church as a moral person was denied would be contrary to the divine law. Denial of the right of this moral person to enter into contracts would constitute a refusal to recognize the Church's inherent right of ownership.[4]

(3) Recognition of adverse possession based on bad faith is an unacceptable provision of civil law. Property so acquired, even though the acquisition is recognized by civil law, could not be the subject matter of a contract, since such acquisition violates a fundamental concept of justice.[5]

(4) Laws forbidding bequests to pious causes are contrary to the Church's divine right to carry on her mission by using these bequests to further her religious, charitable, and educational aims.[6]

(5) Denial of the natural right of persons to dispose freely of their goods by wills in favor of the Church, or placing such a limitation on this right that such a devise would be illegal if certain formalities decreed by the state were omitted.[7]

(6) Since the Church has the right to acquire and use temporal goods in carrying out her divine mission, the state cannot frustrate

[3] Merkelbach, *Summa Theologia Moralis* (3 vols., Parisiis: Typis Desclée de Brouwer et Soc., 1931-1933), II, n. 464, 8.

[4] Canons 100, § 1; 1499, § 1 and § 2; cf. Brown, *The Canonical Juristic Personality with Reference to its Status in the United States of America*, The Catholic University of America Canon Law Studies, n. 39 (Washington, D. C.: The Catholic University of America, 1927) pp. 108, 109, 190; Coronata, *Institutiones*, I, n. 137; Vermeersch-Creusen, *Epitome*, II, n. 850.

[5] Canon 1512; cf. Cocchi, *Commentarium in Codicem Iuris Canonici ad Usum Scholarum* (5 vols. in 8, Taurinorum Augustae: Officina Libraria Marietti, 1920-1930), VI, 365. Hereinafter cited *Commentarium.*

[6] Canons 1499, § 1; 1513, § 2; cf. Cocchi, *Commentarium*, VI, 344.

[7] Canon 1513, § 1 and § 2; Vromant, *De Bonis Ecclesiae Temporalibus ad Usum Utriusque Cleri, praesertim Missionariorum et Religiosorum* (Louvain: Desbarax, 1927), p. 292. Hereinafter cited *De Bonis Ecclesiae Temporalibus.*

this right by refusing to recognize trusts in wills made to advance pious causes.[8]

(7) Failure to recognize the distinction between clerics and laymen in contractual matters is contrary to the distinction made by divine institution.[9]

(8) Contractual legislation which denies the Church her inherent right of ownership or of jurisdiction over her subjects. Such would be a statute forbidding a contract of sale involving the transfer of land into the Church's possession.[10]

The State of Maryland has adopted the policy of the old English mortmain statutes to the degree that the approval of the legislature is required to enable a religious corporation to acquire real property.[11] The inconvenience brought on by this statute can be forestalled by an antecedent affirmation in the corporation's charter of the right to acquire realty.[12] Limitation of the amount of land which a religious corporation may legally acquire ranges from two acres in the District of Columbia[13] to fifty acres in Kentucky.[14] It is to be noted, however, that what is forbidden by statute may be permitted in virtue of adverse possession. Acquisition of realty or of more land than the charter permits is recognized as valid in the eyes of the civil law.[15]

[8] Canons 1515, 1516; cf. Vermeersch-Creusen, *Epitome*, II, n. 850.

[9] Canon 107; cf. Downs, *The Concept of Clerical Immunity*, The Catholic University of America Canon Law Studies, n. 126 (Washington, D. C.: The Catholic University of America Press, 1941), p. 129; Ottaviani, *Institutiones Iuris Publici Ecclesiastici* (2. ed., 2 vols., Civitate Vaticana: Typis Polyglottis Vaticanis, 1935-1936), I, 406.

[10] Canons 218, 335, 1499, 1530-1543; Coronata, *Institutiones*, I, n. 309; Cocchi, *Commentarium*, VI, 344.

[11] Grove v. Trustees of Congregation of Disciples of Jesus Christ (1870), 33 Md., 451.

[12] Rogers v. Sisters of Charity of St. Joseph (1903), 97 Md. 550, 55 Atl. 318.

[13] Dangerfield v. Williams (1906), 26 App. D. C. 508, 516.

[14] Compton v. Moore (1916) 167 Ky., 657, 181 S. W. 360.

[15] Dangerfield v. Williams (1906) 26 App. D. C. 508, 515.

B. *Civil Law Provisions Contrary to Canon Law*

Besides the civil enactments which would be unacceptable for the reason that they are contrary to divine law, the following provisions of civil law would also have to be repudiated inasmuch as they contravene explicit provisions of Canon Law:

(1) The Church's right to establish moral persons within her own structure to further the charitable or religious ends of the Church is explicitly affirmed in Canon Law.[16] Hence provisions of civil law which deny recognition to dioceses or religious congregations in contractual matters are unacceptable. A provision declaring that a moral collegiate body in the Church could be constituted by less than three members is also contrary to Canon Law.[17]

(2) The right of clerics to an honorable sustenance in the event that creditors have to be satisfied is guaranteed by Canon Law.[18] A statute which deprived a cleric of this honorable sustenance would be unacceptable in the province of Canon Law.

(3) The right of religious congregations to acquire temporal goods by the efforts of their members cannot be withdrawn by civil law provisions.[19]

(4) Whatever temporalities are acquired by religious in solemn vows in any way whatever become the property of the institute if the Order is capable of acquiring property. If the Order is not capable of acquiring temporal goods, acquisitions of the members become the property of the Holy See. Civil statutes declaring that goods acquired through contract by those in solemn vows belong to the person, rather than to the institute, would be contrary to the provisions of Canon Law. Likewise, the refusal to recognize the acquisition of property by the Holy See rather than by the institute itself in contracts of Orders incapable of possessing temporal goods would be an unacceptable provision of civil law.[20]

[16] Canon 100, § 1.

[17] Canon 100, § 2.

[18] Canon 122.

[19] Canon 580, § 2.

[20] Canon 582.

(5) Canon 614 affirms for religious the right given to all clerics by canon 122.[21]

(6) The right to possess cemeteries is affirmed for the Church and for exempt religious institutes. Enactments prohibiting the sale of land to the Church for burial purposes are contrary to the provisions of Canon Law.[22]

(7) The Church has the right to be the beneficiary of bequests and donations. Although the Church urges all her subjects to follow the solemnities prescribed by civil statutes in these matters, she asserts her right to be the beneficiary of wills even though the formalities enjoined by civil law are omitted.[23]

(8) Canon Law declares the competence of the bishop regarding donations and last wills made in favor of pious causes. Clerics and religious who accept such bequests are bound to render an account of such properties to the bishop. So insistent is the Church on the bishop's competence in these matters that she forbids their acceptance when the bishop's competence is excluded. A contract designed to exclude the bishop's supervision over such donations would be inadmissible in Canon Law even though civil authorities recognized its validity.[24]

(9) Canon Law favors the presumption that donations given to rectors of churches are given to the church, and not to the rector personally. A contrary provision of civil law would have no effect on the disposition of such a donation as far as the Church is concerned. So also, civil enactments granting the rector the right to refuse donations to the church, or the right to a donor, because of the ingratitude of a rector or a prelate, to recall donations once made would not be acceptable in Canon Law.[25]

(10) Finally, it is evident from a reply of the Sacred Congregation

[21] Cf. *supra*, p. 56.

[22] Canons 1206, 1208, § 2.

[23] Canon 1513, § 1 and § 2.

[24] Canon 1516.

[25] Canon 1536.

of the Council that civil law is not necessarily to be followed when an inequitable loss to the Church would result.[26]

Although the civil law permitted the payment of obligations in government securities whose nominal value was 100 francs, but whose real value was quoted at 70 francs or less, the Sacred Congregation of the Council declared that the bishop should accept payment only on the basis of the real or current value of such securities.[27]

Article 2. The Province of the Civil Law in Contracts Involving Two Ecclesiastical Moral Persons

That the civil law on contract should bind the members of the Church when they enter into contracts with those who are not of the fold is understandable. Especially is this so in view of the fact that in many places the members of the Church are in the minority and frequently enter into contracts with non-Catholics. Such a situation exists in our own country. To have two separate bodies of rules governing contracts would be to invite confusion and uncertainty in the entire field of contracts. The Church's possession of temporal property acquired through contract would be attacked at every turn

[26] *S. C. C., Resolutio,* 23 ian. 1923, *Acta Apostolicae Sedis* (Romae, 1909 ———), XV (1923), 513. Hereinafter cited *AAS*.

[27] The case in question involved a contract of emphyteusis. The government securities were being used to redeem the rental, a procedure which is permitted according to canon 1542. Emphyteusis is a contract unknown by that name in American law, but it corresponds very closely to 99-year lease, or to a sale with the reservation of ground rent. Redemption of the rental may be compared to purchase under option on the part of the lessee. Upon payment of a lump sum, the legal title of the property is transferred to the lessee, and he is relieved forever of the burden of paying the annual rental. In its reply the Sacred Congregation of the Council pointed out that canon 1542, by using the word *saltem*, did not preclude the possibility of asking for a higher sum than that corresponding to the aggregate rental. Further, the bishop was bound to protect the interests of the minor person (the Church, in this instance, according to canon 100, § 2), since he was designated as guardian. It has been the practice of the Sacred Congregation of the Council to require the lessee who redeems the rental to pay something in advance in compensation of a lower revenue which is substituted for the rental. In the present case, the lessee would be required to pay, in whole or in part, the difference between the nominal and actual value of the securities.

if the Church provided by law for all the details of contract with prescriptions that are at variance with the civil legislation on contracts. Non-Catholics would refuse to recognize the Church's right to formulate a body of contractual legislation differing from that enacted by civil authorities. Civil suits arising from inital misapprehension would be the rule rather than the exception, and the title to property would be continually colored by doubt arising out of the conflict of laws.

The situation is admittedly otherwise when contracts involving two or more moral persons within the Church are contemplated. It may reasonably be objected that these contracts concern so clerical an organism that it is totally improper to invoke the civil law in any detail. Especially is this true when the parties to the contract are the bishop who represents the moral person of the diocese, and religious superiors, who represent the moral person of the religious congregation. By the positions they hold, both profess acceptance of the Church's exclusive power of administration over ecclesiastical goods. There is not in these instances the danger of misunderstanding and of consequent civil suits as there is in the case of contracts involving the diocese or the congregation on the one hand, and non-Catholics on the other. Ecclesiastics, the parties to the agreement, are aware of the *privilegium fori* [28] and, in consequence, of the proper forum for the adjudication of possible disputes.[29] It would seem that all the details of contractual relations between ecclesiastics as parties to a contract could be harmoniously governed without reference to the provisions of the civil law at all.

Nevertheless, the subject matter of contracts between persons within the Church so often concerns temporalities regarding which civil authorities have legislated that conflicts of law would, even in such instances, be inevitable. By neglecting the civil law provisions, even in contracts between ecclesiastical moral persons, a great deal of confusion concerning real property might easily arise. This would hold true despite the fact that the danger of civil court action would in practically all cases be eliminated in view of the persons involved.

[28] Canon 120.

[29] Canon 1557, § 2, 2°.

Although the Church might recognize the transfer of ownership of land in virtue of a contract between two moral persons within her jurisdiction, civil law might declare such a transfer illegal because of the failure of the parties to comply with the provisions of civil law. Positing a series of such transfers of the same property, the chain of title would become more confused with each transfer as far as the civil authorities could ascertain. This is but one of the many problems which would arise if two distinct sets of provisions existed to govern the one contract—one, the general statutes set up by the State to govern its subjects, and the other, those set up by the Church to govern contractual relations of moral persons constituted by her.

Canon 1529 makes no distinction, therefore, between contracts entered into between physical or moral persons within the Church, and contracts between moral persons bound by Canon Law and those outside the Church. The law as stated in canon 1529 embraces all types of parties to contracts and applies the same law to all cases, namely that the civil statutes of the territory are to be followed, provided that they do not legislate contrary to divine or Canon Law. In the face not only of the absence of a particular prescript providing special rules for ecclesiastical moral persons when they contract with each other, but also of an inescapable juridical implication that no such special rules were intended by the legislator, the general rule must be followed. Hence, it must be concluded that moral persons within the Church are also bound to follow the acceptable provisions of civil law when they contract with each other. The rule, *ubi lex non distinguit, nec nos distinguere debemus,* finds application in this case.

Since canon 1529 is a departure from the earlier ecclesiastical law, it cannot be interpreted in the light of laws existing before the present Code. Older authors cannot be sought for commentary upon it. Rather, since it is such a decided innovation, it must be examined on the basis of the wording of the law itself, as the general principles prescribe in such cases.[80] The wording of the law leaves no doubt that it comprehends all contracts, since no exceptions are noted except

[80] Canon 6, 3°.

those provisions which run contrary to divine or Canon Law. The grave consequences of such a wide acceptance of civil law are noted by Vermeersch-Creusen, who offer the opinion that many private responses and authentic interpretations will be given before the full force of the true meaning of canon 1529 becomes evident.[81]

ARTICLE 3. ANGLO-AMERICAN LAW NOTIONS OF CONTRACT

Both Canon Law and civil law commentators have formulated definitions of contract. Canon Law itself formulates no definition, but canonists delineate the elements in the notion of contract when they comment upon the law itself. Modern canonists accept the definition proposed by the commentators on the former law. This acceptance of the definition of contract involves no acceptance of the former law concerning contract. The notion of contract involves a moral concept, which has not changed with the innovation of the adoption of the civil law on contract as stated in canon 1529. Since there is to be a juridical meeting ground in ascertaining the institute for which canon 1529 adopts the civil law, the definitions proposed by canonists and civilists must of necessity be found to be in agreement regarding their essential notes. If there is a disagreement on the very definition of contract, then there is no civil counterpart which could offer rules to be adopted by canon 1529.

From the bare statement of the definitions as given by canonists and civilists, there seems to be some disagreement even on this most basic point. The canonist stresses the notion of consent in contract: *duorum vel plurium in idem placitum consensus.*[82] The civil lawyer stressed the aspects of obligation, consideration, and the protection afforded by the civil law. The definition of a contract as "a promise or set of promises for the breach of which the law gives a remedy,

[81] Valde magni momenti est iste canon, et refertus est gravibus consectariis. Antequam ipso usu et variis declarationibus significatio eius et propria vis magis certo innotescant, plura privati interpretis responsa facile authenticis explicationibus cedere debebunt—*Epitome,* II, n. 850.

[82] Wernz, *Ius Decretalium,* III, n. 230; cf. also, Vermeersch-Creusen, *Epitome,* III, n. 849; Vromant, *De Bonis Ecclesiae Temporalibus,* p. 284.

or the performance of which the law in some way recognizes as a duty," [33] stresses the protection guaranteed by the civil law.

Robinson (1834-1911), following Blackstone (1723-1780), adds the note of consideration as essential to a contract, since he defines contract as "an agreement between two or more persons upon a sufficient consideration." [34] Blackstone's definition, "an agreement upon sufficient consideration to do or not to do a particular thing," [35] although adopted by Kent (1763-1847) and other high authorities, has been criticized for including the notion of consideration as an essential note of the definition. Stephens criticized Blackstone on this score and declared that the existence of a consideration, though essential to the validity of a parol contract, forms properly no part of the essential idea of the institute.[36]

The *Corpus Juris* defines contract as "an agreement which creates an obligation." [37] This latter definition approximates the definition as contained in manuals of Moral Theology.[38]

The differences of terminology adopted in the two systems to formulate the definition of contract are not so great as to be beyond reconciliation. They result chiefly from the approach to the same subject from different points of view. If the modern civilist stresses the protection guaranteed by the law, and the canonist, as well as the older civilists, stresses the notion of assent, it is for the reason that the former is taking a strictly pragmatic view, while the latter seeks to incorporate the ethical element in this juridical notion. In reality,

[33] *Restatement of the Law of Contracts* (2 vols., St. Paul: American Law Institute, 1932), I, n. 1. Hereinafter cited *Restatement.*

[34] Robinson, *Elementary Law* (Boston, 1910), n. 158.

[35] Blackstone, *Commentaries on the Law of England* (12. ed., 4 vols., Dublin, 1775) II, 446.

[36] Stephens, *New Commentaries on the Law of England* (6. ed., 4 vols., London, 1868), II, 108-109.

[37] *Corpus Juris, A Complete Restatement of the Entire American Law as Developed by all Reported Cases* (Mack-Hale-Kiser, 72 vols., Brooklyn: The American Law Book Co., 1914-1935), XIII, n. 1. Hereinafter cited 13 C. J., n. 1.

[38] "Contractus definitur: conventio qua una vel plures personae se obligant erga unam vel plures alias ad aliquid dandum, faciendum vel non faciendum."—Merkelbach, *Summa Theologiae Moralis,* II, n. 451.

although the definitions seem to indicate wide differences of opinion as to what constitutes the essential elements of the definition, even the most modern of Anglo-American civil lawyers are agreed as to what constitutes the necessary elements of the contract itself. These are strikingly in accord with the teaching of canonists. The apparent conflict is seemingly due to the fact that neither the definition given by canonists nor that given by civilists is sufficiently comprehensive to include all the necessary elements of contract as understood by both alike.

A. *Necessary Elements in Contracts According to Civil Law*

Anglo-American law stresses five elements as necessary for the validity of contracts.

(1) Capacity of the parties to enter into a valid contract. There must be at least two competent parties, since one cannot enter into a contract with himself alone.[39] This holds true even to the extent that one person acting in two distinct capacities cannot contract with himself.[40] He can, however, contract with a partnership of which he is a member, or with a corporation in which he holds stock. In this instance he is acting as a physical person contracting with a corporation.[41]

(2) A sufficient legal consideration.[42] That a consideration is necessary for every contract not under seal is evident from an examination of court decisions both State and Federal. Even in that class of contracts (by specialty) in which no consideration is in fact required, one is always presumed by law. The form of the instrument is held to import a consideration.[43] Although some civilists deny

[39] People's Bank of Butler v. Allen, 125 S. W. (2d.) 829, 831.

[40] In re State Exchange Bank of Stryker, 159 N. E. 839, 26 Ohio App. 142.

[41] *Restatement*, I, n. 15.

[42] Consideration has been defined: "a benefit to the party promising or a loss or detriment to the party to whom the promise is made."—13 C. J., n. 144.

[43] Kent, *Commentaries on American Law* (4 vols., New York, 1848), II, 450.

that a consideration is essential to the definition of contract, all agree that it is a constituitive element of every contract not under seal.[44]

The consideration of a contract need not be money, but it should have pecuniary value. Thus time, money, service, chattels, land, incorporeal rights, or even the surrender or suspension of a right having some real or prospective value, are held to furnish a sufficient legal consideration.[45]

(3) There must be present a subject matter which may include anything not forbidden by law.[46]

(4) A mutuality of agreement—a common intention. A valid consent must be manifested by both parties. The parties must indicate to one another by unequivocal words or acts that they consent and bind themselves to the subject matter and consideration in precisely the same way. The parties must give their assent to the same thing in the same sense.[47]

(5) A mutuality of obligation, which consists in the obligation of each party to do or permit something to be done in consideration of the act or promise of the other. This last requisite applies only to bilateral contracts. The term, unilateral contract, has been criticized in civil courts. It has been called a misnomer,[48] a legal solecism,[49] and a contradiction in terms. [50] In a unilateral contract, the contract is merely the promise, not the mutual manifestation of assent or the consideration paid for the promise.[51] A unilateral contract not under seal which never involved mutuality of obligation is unenforceable in American law.[52]

[44] Cf. the opinion of Stephens, *supra*, p. 62.

[45] Williston, *The Law of Contracts* (4 vols., New York, 1920), I, n. 115.

[46] Tobin v. Insurance Agency Co. (C. C. A. Mo.), 80 F (2d.) 241.

[47] American Lumber & Mfg. Co. v. Atlantic Miller and Lumber Co. (C. C. A. Pa.), 290 F. 632.

[48] Railsbach v. Raines, 203 P. 687, 688, 110 Kan. 220.

[49] High Wheat Auto Parts Co. v. Journal Co. of Troy, 98 N. E. 442, 443, 50 Ind. App. 396.

[50] J. J. Williamson & Co. v. Morgan, 106 S. E. 916, 918, 26 Ga. App. 713.

[51] *Restatement*, I, n. 12.

[52] Williston, *The Law of Contracts*, I, n. 13.

B. *Necessary Elements in Contracts According to Canon Law*

(1) Capacity to contract. Vermeersch-Creusen are unwilling to concede that this capacity comes under the jurisdiction of the civil law, and declare that it is excepted from the rule of canon 1529.[53] Other authors see no reason for excluding the capacity to contract from the provisions of civil law since canon 1529 makes no exception in this matter.[54] It seems that objectionable legislation concerning the capacity to contract would be eliminated in virtue of the final clause of canon 1529, which excludes any contractual legislation which contravenes divine or Canon Law.

That at least two parties are necessary for a valid contract is evident from the definition accepted by canonists: *duorum vel plurium in idem placitum consensus*.[55] On the necessity for a plurality of parties to a contract, Canon Law and Anglo-American Law are agreed.[56] Those incapable of giving true consent, such as infants and the insane, are excluded from entering into contracts by both Canon and Anglo-American Law, since this is a precept of the natural law.[57]

Married women were deemed incapable of contracting at common law, but "it may be assumed in most jurisdictions that a married woman has the power to enter into ordinary contracts and dealings with personal property."[58] The capacity of all persons who are not prohibited by natural or ecclesiastical law to make bequests to pious causes is safeguarded by Canon Law.[59]

(2) Valid consent must be given by both parties to the articles of the contract. This consent must be mutually expressed by the contracting parties.[60] The consent demanded by canonists forms a

[53] Vermeersch-Creusen, *Epitome*, II, n. 850.

[54] Vromant, *De Bonis Ecclesiae Temporalibus*, p. 290; Cocchi, *Commentarium*, VI, 406.

[55] Wernz, *Ius Decretalium*, III, n. 230; cf. *supra*, p. 61.

[56] Cf. *supra*, p. 63.

[57] Vromant, *De Bonis Ecclesiae Temporalibus*, p. 286; *Restatement*, I, n. 18.

[58] Williston, *The Law of Contracts*, I, 268: For a detailed statement of American Statutes, cf. Williston, *op. cit.*, I, 269.

[59] Canon 1513.

[60] Cocchi, *Commentarium*, VI, 405.

counterpart of the mutuality of agreement which the civilists consider a necessary element of contract.[61] The consent given must be free from error, fear, or force. The civil law legislates on the influence of duress, violence, and error in the field of contracts.[62] Canon Law likewise legislates concerning the influence of error, fear, and force.[63] Should there be a disagreement as to what constitutes these elements, Canon Law would prevail in accordance with the general principle of canon 1529, which excludes those provisions of civil law which are at variance with Canon Law.

(3) Subject matter of the contract. This must be physically and morally possible; actually existing or existing *in spe;* and it must be proper to one of the parties entering into the contract.[64] Anglo-American Law excludes subject matter which is intrinsically evil, or impossible, or immoral, and thus seems to be in substantial agreement with Canon Law on this point.[65]

(4) Reason for entering into the contract. This was known as the *causa* in Roman Law. It is still maintained as a necessary element of contract by modern canonical authors. The reason for entering into a contract is utility in onerous contracts, and liberality in gratuitous contracts. If one of these elements is not present, consent is not present, and the contract is invalid.[66] This is an element which civil law commentators do not include among the necessary elements of contract. It undoubtedly presumes that some reason exists in the minds of the contracting parties.

From the foregoing analysis, it may be observed that Anglo-American law commentators and canonists differ in only two points, which may be considered substantially one, regarding the necessary elements of a contract. The civilists fail to include a reason for contracting as a necessary element, whereas the canonists omit consideration as a necessary element of the contract. This difference seems to be due

[61] Cf. *supra*, p. 64.

[62] *Restatement*, nn. 500-511.

[63] Canons 103 and 104.

[64] Vromant, *De Bonis Ecclesiae Temporalibus*, p. 287.

[65] Robinson, *Elementary Law*, n. 158.

[66] Cocchi, *Commentarium*, VI, 405; Vromant, *De Bonis Ecclesiae Temporalibus*, p. 288; Wernz, *Ius Decretalium*, III, n. 243.

to the fact that they view the same subject under different aspects. The canonist looks for the cause, and the civilist for the effect. For the *causa* of Canon Law and the consideration of civil law bear the relation of cause and effect toward each other. Consideration is given because there is a reason for entering into the contract. The reason or *causa* according to the canonist is liberality or utility.[67] It is precisely for these reasons that the consideration of civil law is given. Even the gratuitous donor is compensated in the gratification incident to the giving. One of the parties thus contracts for a benefit, and is willing to make the sacrifice which the civil law calls consideration. Consideration may thus be said to import an adequate reason for the contract. However, when there is no mutuality of obligation and the contract is not under seal, Anglo-American law will not enforce the unilateral obligation, which is held to lack a consideration.[68] This seems to be the principle adopted by canon 1529 also, except in the case when an ecclesiastical moral person is the donee.[69] The word "consideration" has actually been declared to be the "cause" of the contract in the statement that a contract involves a mutual promise upon lawful consideration or cause which binds the parties to a performance.[70]

C. *Promise and Agreement*

The element of mutual consent in a contract contains the notion of a promise by one party and its acceptance by the other. As a result of this promise made and accepted, agreement is arrived at. Proposal, in the eyes of the civil law, arises when one party signifies to another his willingness to do or abstain from doing a certain thing with a view to obtaining the assent of the other party.[71] "Promise" has been defined as the declaration by any person of his intention to do or forbear from anything at the request, or for the use, of another. A proposal when accepted becomes a promise.[72] Specific

[67] Cf. *supra*, p. 66.
[68] Cf. *supra*, p. 64.
[69] Cf. canon 1516.
[70] 2 Hill (N. Y.) 551.
[71] Williams v. Rogan, 59 Tex. 438, 440.
[72] Finlay v. Swirsky, 131 A. 420, 423, 103 Conn. 624.

words are not required to constitute the promise. It may even be inferred without the actual use of the word "promise." [73] A promise has been said to be a contract, a pact, or an agreement, and in a loose, incorrect sense to be synonymous with agreement.[74] In the present sense it is best understood as an accepted proposal.

"Agreement" in the law of contract has a well defined legal meaning which implies the expression by two or more persons of a common intention to affect their legal relations.[75] It consists in their being of the same mind and intention concerning the matter agreed upon.[76] "Agreement" has also been defined as the "concurrence of two minds on the object and consideration of the contract." [77] It connotes a mutual obligation [78] and indicates that the bargain is closed.[79]

It is sometimes used as a synonym for contract to indicate a binding result on the mutual relations of the parties. It differs also from the agreement of a bench of judges, which is an agreement of opinion, and does not affect the legal relations of the judges one to another.[80] It has sometimes been used as a synonym for "promise," or "undertaking," [81] or "compact," although the latter is generally used with reference to more formal and solemn engagements, such as the contracts between sovereign nations.[82] It has been said that agreement is one of the necessary essentials of a contract,[83] althongh it is more properly combined with promise to form the notion of mutual consent, which has been declared to constitute a necessary element of contract.[84]

[73] Louisiana Oil Refining Co. v. Scroggins, 74 S. W. (2d) 971, 973, 189 Ark. 707.

[74] Sage v. Wilcox, 6 Conn. 81, 86, 90.

[75] Buffalo Pressed Steel Co. v. Kirwan, 113 A. 628, 630, 138 Md. 60.

[76] Tucker v. Sheeran, 160 S. W. 176, 155 Ky. 670, 672.

[77] Figgins v. Life & Casualty Ins. Co. of Tenn., La. App. 151 So. 129, 130.

[78] Rocha v. Hulen, 44 P. (2d) 478, 482, 6 Cal. App. (2d) 245.

[79] Gonte v. Rosenberg, 191 N. W. 198, 200, 221 Mich. 283.

[80] Tucker v. Sheeran, 160 S. W. 176, 178, 155 Ky. 670.

[81] Sage v. Wilcox, 6 Conn. 81, 90.

[82] Virginia v. Tennessee, 13 S. Ct. 728, 734, 148 U. S. 503, 37 L. Ed. 537.

[83] Stuckert v. Cann, 111 A. 596, 597, 1 W. W. Harr. (Del.) 129.

[84] *Supra*, p. 64.

D. *Express and Implied Contracts*

This classification has been criticized on the grounds that the terms do not denote different types of contracts, but only different kinds of evidence by which the agreement between the parties is shown.[85] An express contract is one in which the intentions of the parties and the terms of the agreement are fully set forth orally or in writing at the time the contract is entered into.[86] It is an express contract even though some of its terms are dependent on the happening of a future event.[87] If the contract is consummated through an agent, it is still held to be an express contract.[88]

Express contracts fall into two classes: contracts under seal or specialties, and contracts by parol.[89]

The distinction between an express and an implied contract is that in an express contract there is an actual promise; when there is no actual promise, the contract is said to be implied.[90] Since the proposal and acceptance are manifested by words in an express contract, the meaning of the words in each must correspond exactly with the meaning in the other. If the meanings differ, there can be no contract. In an implied contract the circumstances as to the parties' intention and interpretation must be certain, so that the conclusion reached by law is inescapable.[91]

The distinction between the two involves no difference as to legal effect, since both are of equal obligation, but it lies in the manner of manifesting consent [92] or in the form and mode of proof.[93] The nature of the understanding is the same in both contracts. Both express contracts and contracts implied in fact are based on the mutuality of agreement, and a meeting of minds is required for both.[94]

[85] Skelly v. Bristol Sav. Bank, 26 A. 474, 475, 63 Conn. 83, 38 Am. S. R. 340, 19 L. R. A. 599.

[86] Stipp v. Doran (C. C. A. Pa.) 18 F. (2d) 83, 84.

[87] Voorheis v. Bovell, 20 Ill. App. 539.

[88] Duie v. Shipmann, 46 N. C. 10.

[89] Whitehill v. Wilson, 3 Penr. & W. 405, 414, 24 Am. D. 326.

[90] Danron v. Stewart & Weir, 69 S. W. (2d) 685, 687, 253 Ky. 394.

[91] Williston, *The Law of Contracts;* I, n. 23.

[92] McArdle v. Williams, 258 N. W. 818, 820, 193 Minn., 423.

[93] Stipp v. Doran (C. C. A. Pa.), 18 F. (2d) 83, 84.

[94] Boyd v. Chase, 166 N. E. 611, 612, 89 Ind. App. 374.

They differ in this that in an express contract words are used, either oral or written, sealed or unsealed, in manifestation of the agreement, while in an implied contract the agreement is arrived at by the consideration of acts and conduct.[95] In other words, to prove an express contract, the actual agreement must be adduced, whereas in an implied contract it will be presumed that the party did make such an agreement as under the circumstances disclosed he ought in fairness to have made.[96]

Implied contracts fall into two classes; those implied in fact and those implied in law. Although this terminology is generally used, it has been declared that it is a misnomer to call a contract implied in law a contract at all, since it is wanting in all the elements of a true contract.[97] A more accurate designation which is frequently employed to signify a contract implied in law is the use of the term quasi-contract or constructive contract.[98] The theory of contract implied in law was originated for the purpose of giving a remedy *ex contractu* for certain wrongs.[99]

A contract implied in fact is one, not expressed by the parties, but deduced from circumstances which indicate a mutual intention to contract.[100] This intention is implied or presumed from the acts of the parties, or when the circumstances are such that, according to the ordinary course of dealing and the common understanding of men, a mutual intention to contract is manifest.[101]

The implication must be a reasonable deduction from all the circumstances and relations of the parties.[102] These deductions must

[95] Anderson v. Beisman and Carrick Co., 4 N. E. (2d) 639, 641, 287 Ill. App. 507.

[96] Marr-Piper Co. v. Bullis (Com. App.), 1 S. W. (2d) 572, 575 reversing Bullis v. Marr-Piper Co. (Civ. App.), 296 S. W., 624.

[97] Willard v. Doran 1 N. Y. S. 345, 588, 48 Hun. 402.

[98] B. & O. Ry. Co. v. U. S. 43 S. Ct. 425, 426, 261 U. S. 592, 67 L. Ed. 816; Stipp v. Doran (C. C. A. Pa.), 18 F. (2d) 83, 84.

[99] Nevada Co. v. Farnsworth (C. C. A. Utah), 89 F. 164.

[100] W. Ross Campbell Co. v. Herbert's of Los Angeles, 293 P. 805, 806, 110 Cal. App. 244.

[101] B. & O. Ry. Co. v. U. S. 43 S. Ct., 425, 426, 261 U. S. 592, 67 L. Ed. 816.

[102] Inman v. Stephenson 40 P. (2d) 1107, 170 Okla. 548.

have been contemplated by the parties when they entered into the contract, or they must have been deemed necessary for carrying their intention into effect.[103] The implication need not be evidenced by any precise words, but may result also from uncertain language.[104]

E. *Written and Oral Contracts*

A written contract is one which, in all its terms, is in writing.[105] It is still a written contract although its operation depends upon some future contingency. The meeting of the minds of the parties as to all the terms of the contract is assumed to take place when the contingency becomes a reality.[106] It is not necessary upon the development of the contingency that the contract be rewritten.[107]

The writing must be in legible characters. When its crucial terms are expressed in symbols or characters so illegible that the tribunal established to judge the facts cannot determine the signification of what is on paper, it is deemed that no contract in writing has been made.[108] A contract which is not entirely in writing is judged to be an oral contract.[109]

A confirmatory letter of a former oral contract does not make the contract a written one, except when both parties mutually adopt the terms of the letter.[110] On the other hand, the necessity of parol evidence to explain some of the terms of a written contract does not render it oral.[111]

[103] Edwards v. Surety Finance Co. of Seattle, 30 P. (2d) 225, 226, 176 Wash. 534.

[104] Tulsa Fuel & Mfg. Co. v. Gillchrist Drilling Co., 190 P. 389, 400, 79 Okla. 82.

[105] Westphal v. Buenger, 154 N. E. 426, 427, 324 Ill. 77.

[106] C. H. Lowenthal Co. v. McCormack Bros. Co., 257 P. 632, 634, 114 Wash. 229.

[107] *Loc. cit.*

[108] Aradalou v. N. Y. etc. R. Co., 114 N. E. 297, 299.

[109] G. M. Shutt Co. v. Andrews, 171 S. E. 219, 47 Ga. App. 530.

[110] Cook, Borden & Co. v. R. Z. L. Realty Corp., 147 A. 891, 50 R. I. 375.

[111] National Bank of Commerce of Houston v. Moody (Civ. App.), 90 S. W. (2d.) 279.

An oral contract usually consists of mere conversation, but it also may be created without a spoken word. Further, the conversation which creates the oral contract may be deficient or redundant.[112]

[112] Finnerty v. Shade, 228 N. W. 889, 890, 210 Iowa 1338.

CHAPTER IX

CONTRACTUAL CAPACITY OF BISHOPS

ARTICLE 1. DERIVATION OF THIS POWER IN THE CODE

IT has been noted above [1] that the incapacity to contract arises from the natural law, Canon Law, or civil law. Inability to perform a human act is the principal impediment contemplated by the natural law. A bishop capable of administering his diocese would not fall under this prohibition. In the event that a bishop should become so impeded, the Code has provided for the appointment of a coadjutor bishop who enjoys all the rights and administers all the offices of the bishop except those withheld from him in his letters of appointment.[2]

When a bishop is wholly incapacitated and a coadjutor bishop having the right of succession under ecclesiastical law has been duly appointed and installed, his status is so recognized by the civil law. Whatever administrative functions regarding church revenue and church property accrue to him because of his ecclesiastical status are recognized and enforced by the civil courts.[3] Since the contracts contemplated in this work are those which affect the relations of the diocese with religious congregations, the contracting bishop would of necessity be the bishop who administers the affairs of the diocese.

Although the determination of the capacity to enter into contracts is generally admitted to be within the province of the civil law in accordance with the general principle stated in canon 1529,[4] the denial of contractual capacity to the bishop in regard to the affairs of his diocese would be an encroachment upon the rights of the Church and a clearly unacceptable provision of civil law.

[1] *Supra*, p. 21.

[2] Canon 351, § 2.

[3] Blanc v. Aglesbury, 63 Tex. 489.

[4] Vromant, *De Bonis Ecclesiae Temporalibus*, p. 290; Cocchi, *Commentarium*, VI, 404.

The power of the bishop is twofold. The power which he receives in virtue of his episcopal consecration is exercised in reference to the administration of the sacraments and sacramentals. This is called the power of orders. By his appointment to a particular see, the bishop receives the power of jurisdiction.[5]

Episcopal jurisdiction gives the bishop power to govern his diocese in both spiritual and temporal matters. It is to be exercised according to the rules of Canon Law, and manifests itself in a fivefold manner. It is legislative, judicial, and coercive,[6] as well as doctrinal [7] and administrative.[8] The capacity to enter into contracts in the name of the diocese derives from the administrative power of the bishop. Since this power is properly and exclusively the power of the residential bishop, it is one which an auxiliary bishop may exercise by delegation only.[9]

The bishop's administrative power comprehends the episcopal benefice and the property of the diocese as such. In addition he has a supervisory and directive power over the administration of other non-exempt ecclesiastical property within his territory. It is important to determine to what extent the bishop is the administrator of any given ecclesiastical property, in order to evaluate his contractual capacity regarding that property. His capacity to enter into contracts

[5] "Episcopi residentiales sunt ordinarii et immediati pastores in dioecesibus sibi commissis"—Canon 334, § 1.

[6] "Ius ipsis et officium est gubernandi dioecesim tum in spiritualibus tum in temporalibus cum potestate legislativa, iudiciaria, coactiva ad normam sacrorum canonum exercenda."—Canon 335, § 1.

[7] "Advigilent ne abusus in ecclesiasticam disciplinam irrepant, praesertim circa administrationem Sacramentorum et Sacramentalium, cultum Dei, sacras indulgentias, implementum piarum voluntatum; curentque ut puritas fidei ac morum in clero et populo conservetur, ut fidelibus, praecipue pueris ac rudibus, pabulum doctrinae christianae praebeatur, ut in scholis puerorum ac iuvenum institutio secundum catholicae religionis principia tradatur."—Canon 336, § 2.

[8] "Loci Ordinarii est sedulo advigilare administrationi omnium bonorum ecclesiasticorum quae in suo territorio sint. . . ."—Canon 1519, § 1; "Habita ratione iurium, legitimarum consuetudinum et circumstantiarum, Ordinarii, opportune editis peculiaribus instructionibus intra fines iuris communis, universum administrationis bonorum ecclesiasticorum negotium ordinandum curent."—Canon 1519, § 2.

[9] Canon 352.

will be defined by the limits of his administrative jurisdiction, since it is obvious that he must possess at least some power of administration over goods in order to contract concerning them. Thus the bishop cannot make the property of an exempt religious institute within his diocese the subject matter of a contract, since it has been withdrawn from his administrative jurisdiction.

The bishop contracts concerning diocesan property as the representative of the moral person of the diocese. He is not the owner of these goods, but acts as guardian of the minor person, since the diocese is considered as such in Canon Law.[10] The majority of the authors opposes the position of Wernz (1842-1914) that the bishop is the supreme administrator of the diocese.[11]

De Meester refers to the discussion as a quarrel about words and uses Wernz's terminology by designating the bishop as the supreme administrator under the guidance of the Holy See. He says that this follows from the hierarchical constitution of the Church. This does not mean that the bishop is the sole administrator of the ecclesiastical goods in his diocese, nor even that he is the immediate administrator, but rather that the bishop must prosecute his right according to the canons, customs and circumstances.[12]

In a reply of the Sacred Congregation for the Propagation of the Faith, it was stated that the bishop has the right of administering

[10] "Personae morales sive collegiales sive non collegiales minoribus aequiparantur."—Canon 100, § 3.

[11] Wernz, *Ius Decretalium,* III, n. 151. Raus (*Institutiones Canonicae,* [Lugduni: Typis Emmanuel Vitte, 1931], p. 200) goes farther and calls the bishop, "bonorum ecclesiae . . . supremus administrator et dispensator." The opposite opinion is held by: Prümmer, *Manuale Iuris Canonici in Usum Scholarum* (3 ed., Friburgi Brisgoviae: B. Herder, 1922), q. 449: Hereinafter cited *Manuale Iuris Canonici;* Vromant, *De Bonis Ecclesiae Temporalibus,* n. 182; Coronata, *Institutiones,* III, n. 1060; Couly, "Les Biens Temporels de l'Eglise"—*Le Canoniste Contemperain* (Paris, 1878-), XLV (1922), 315; Blat, *Commentarium Textus Codicis Iuris Canonici* (5 vols., Romae, 1919-1927), III, Partes II-VI, n. 434: Hereinafter cited *Commentarium;* Vermeersch-Creusen, *Epitome,* II, n. 840. However in treating of the residential bishop, Vermeersch-Creusen state: "Suprema administratio dioecesis ipsi committitur."—*Epitome,* I, n. 406.

[12] De Meester, *Juris Canonici et Juris Canonico-Civilis Compendium,* (3 vols. in 4, Brugis, 1921-1928), III, n. 1473. Hereinafter cited *Compendium.*

the goods acquired by the church, but that he was to be guided by the canons and the intention of the founders.[13] The Rota in the solution of a case in 1919 referred to the bishop as the supreme administrator of the ecclesiastical goods of his diocese.[14]

The Code itself refrains from using the term "supreme administrator" in defining the bishop's administrative powers in canon 1519, although it applies this term to the Roman Pontiff in reference to the universal administration of ecclesiastical goods.[15] The Code in fact states that the local ordinary's duty is to supervise rather than directly administer the ecclesiastical goods in his diocese. He has the immediate supervision only of the goods of the *mensa episcopalis* and of those possessions which are common to the entire diocese. The bishop would act illicitly were he to demand the exclusive right of administration over all the ecclesiastical goods of his diocese. He would act invalidly if he were to administer goods which are not subject to his administration.[16]

The individual ecclesiastical moral persons hold the title to their property, and their responsible officers are the administrators of ecclesiastical goods under their care. Even in the case wherein goods are given to pious causes in general, an administrator is required to be appointed, and the bishop merely inspects and watches over the administration of these goods.[17] There is no doubt that the bishop has much to do indirectly with the temporal administration of all ecclesiastical goods in his diocese, but it remains true that in the organization of the Church each individual moral person enjoys real autonomy in financial matters, and has the administration of its own property subject to proper control and direction on the part of the hierarchy. The ordinary cannot dispose of it except in certain cases, and in this he is very definitely and restrictively guided by the

[13] S. C. Prop. Fide, 1. apr. 1816, ad 2—*Collectanea S. Congregationis de Propaganda Fide*, n. 712.

[14] S. R. R., *S. Angeli de Lombardis Iurium*, 28 febr. 1919, *coram R. P. D. Friderico Cattani-Amadori—AAS*, XII (1920), 90.

[15] "Romanus Pontifex est omnium bonorum ecclesiasticorum supremus administrator et dispensator."—Canon 1518.

[16] Vermeersch-Creusen, *Epitome*, II, n. 840.

[17] Canon 1522; Coronata, *Institutiones*, III, n. 1060.

general law. Further, all administrative acts must in any event be executed in the name of the moral person.[18]

In general, the administrators of ecclesiastical goods are:

(1) The bishop and the cathedral chapter for the cathedral church.

(2) The collegiate chapter for a collegiate church. If the collegiate church is also a parish church, the administration is divided. To the pastor belongs the administration of alms collected for the poor of the parish. In this administration he must follow the will of the donors.[19] The chapter administers the pious legacies of the church edifice as such, and takes care of its repair and maintenance.[20] Surely, canon 415, § 3, 3°, contemplates only the church, and not the schools, the lyceums, or similar institutes. These latter are properly eleemosynary, supported by the alms of the parishioners, and therefore are subject to the administration of the vicar, since they are not connected with the benefice as such.

(3) If the church is attached to a religious house, the religious appointed to the care of souls has the same administrative rights as the pastor of the collegiate parish church, while the religious superior has the administration of the buildings, grounds, stable capital, and pious legacies.[21] By way of comparison with the collegiate chapter, it should be said that all buildings not properly church buildings, as well as all pious legacies not properly destined for the benefit of the church buildings, are subject to the administration of the religious vicar, since they are eleemosynary and not connected with the benefice as such.

(4) For other churches, secular parish churches or public oratories, the administrator is the rector of the church or of the oratory.[22]

Besides the direct administration over the goods of the *mensa episcopalis,* and over the goods of the diocese as such, the Code gives the local ordinary wide powers of supervision and direction. He has the duty of diligently supervising the administration of all non-exempt

[18] Ayrinhac, *Administrative Legislation,* p. 426.

[19] Canon 415, § 2, 5°.

[20] "Ecclesiae curam habere eiusque bona administrare cum piis legatis"—Canon 415, § 3, 3°.

[21] Canon 609, § 1; cf. *infra,* p. 147 et seq.

[22] Vromant, *De Bonis Ecclesiae Temporalibus,* pp. 204-205.

ecclesiastical goods in his territory. He may acquire greater rights by prescription.[23] The bishop's duty of supervision imports the necessity of taking the proper precautions to assure the faithful performance of their duties by all administrators of the individual moral persons. His supervision extends to all ecclesiastical goods in his territory which have not been withdrawn from his jurisdiction, and pertains to all important administrative acts. Special stipulations in the charters of foundations may augment this supervisory power to the extent that the bishop himself shares directly in the administration.

Local ordinaries are empowered to regulate matters pertaining to the administration of ecclesiastical goods by enacting statutes or issuing special instructions when circumstances demand such action. In regulating the administration of ecclesiastical goods, the local ordinary must not go beyond the limits indicated in the common law. He cannot modify any of its provisions, or trespass upon the acquired rights of others, or abstract from legitimate customs, or ignore the circumstances of place or time as established in the foundations.[24] He must not, then, proceed arbitrarily in formulating the regulations within his competence, but must show a proper regard for the limitations imposed by the law as indicated above.[25] Obviously, he cannot interfere in the ordinary administration of ecclesiastical moral persons as long as the accredited administrators perform their duties according to the law.[26]

Article 2. Bishops' Contractual Capacity According to Civil Law

In the United States proper the Universal Church and the Holy See are not recognized as juristic personalities in the sense of canons 100 and 1499. However, in the insular possessions ceded to the United States by Spain, this status is recognized by virtue of Article

[23] Canon 1519, § 1.

[24] Ayrinhac, *Administrative Legislation*, p. 425.

[25] Vermeersch-Creusen, *Epitome*, II, n. 840.

[26] Woywod, *A Practical Commentary on the Code of Canon Law* (7. ed., 2 vols., revised by Callistus Smith, New York, Joseph F. Wagner, Inc., 1943) II, n. 1511. Hereinafter cited *Commentary*.

8 of the Treaty of Paris.[27] This article, preserved the status of the Church as it existed in the Philippines, in Puerto Rico, and in Cuba when they were Spanish possessions. It stated specifically that the treaty which brought to an end the Spanish American War did not impair property rights which by pre-existing law were enjoyed by civil and ecclesiastical bodies. Among these rights was the acknowledged juristic personality of the Church, and the legal capacity of the Church to acquire and possess property.[28]

Individual dioceses are not recognized in the continental United States as juristic personalities despite their canonical establishment as moral persons. In order to exercise the right of ownership and to realize the consequent power to enter into contracts as a corporate body, they must obtain from the state their establishment as corporations.[29] In order that they may stand before the law with the rights of corporations, three ways are open to them. A special decree issued for the United States by the Sacred Congregation of the Council in 1911 declared that the holding of ecclesiastical property by a physical person in *fee simple* was to be abolished entirely, and advocated that the method popularly known as the parish corporation was to be established wherever possible.[30]

The form of corporation approved by the Sacred Congregation of the Council is constituted of five members—three of whom are the bishop, the vicar general, and the pastor. As constituted in New York, the parish corporation is within the definition of a corporation

[27] U. S. Statutes at Large, XXX, 55th Congress 1897-1899 (Washington, 1899), 1758.

[28] Treaty of Paris, Art. 8, cited in Ponce v. Roman Catholic Apostolic Church in Porto Rico (1908) 210 U. S. 296, 310, 28 S. Ct., 737, 52 L. ed 1068; cf. Zollmann, *American Church Law* (St. Paul: West Publishing Co., 1933), n. 202; Brown, *The Canonical Juristic Personality with Reference to its Status in the United States of America*, p. 115; Dignan, *A History of the Legal Incorporation of Catholic Church Property in the United States* (1784-1932) (Washington, D. C.: *The Catholic University of America*, 1933), pp. 237-238; Hannan, *The Canon Law of Wills*, The Catholic University of America Canon Law Studies, n. 86 (Washington, D. C.: The Catholic University of America, 1934), n. 526.

[29] Brown, *op. cit.*, pp. 133, 135; Hannan, *op. cit.*, n. 525.

[30] 21 iul. 1911—*The American Ecclesiastical Review* (Philadelphia, 1889-1943, Baltimore, 1944-), XLV (1911) 585-586. Hereinafter cited *AER*.

aggregate. It has distinct advantages over the usual form of religious corporations aggregate, since the three *ex officio* members appoint the remaining two lay members.[31] Where it is impossible under the civil law to set up a corporation of this type, preference is given by the Sacred Congregation, in the declaration cited, to the corporation sole whereby the bishop is incorporated and his successors in office succeed him without dissolution of the corporation.

It has not been found possible to abolish the holding of property in *fee simple* in certain places in view of the failure of civil enactments to make provision for the hierarchical organization of the Church. Thus in the States of Missouri and Indiana where the old trustee system still prevails, *fee simple* tenure by the local ordinary has been retained.[32]

The incorporation of the bishop as a corporation sole is permitted in Alabama,[33] Arizona,[34] California,[35] Idaho,[36] Maine,[37] Montana,[38] Nevada,[39] Oklahoma,[40] Utah,[41] Washington,[42] and Wyoming.[43] There is a possibility that the bishop could be incorporated as a corporation sole in New Hampshire. This conclusion is based on the statute giv-

[31] *Cahill's Consolidated Laws of New York* (2. ed. by Basil Jones, Chicago, 1930) nn. 2071, 2072.

[32] *The Revised Statutes of the State of Missouri, 1939* (Jefferson City, Mo.: Millard Printing Co., 1940), Const. art. 2, § 8; *Indiana Annotated Statutes* (Indianapolis: Bobbs-Merrill Co., 1934), § 25-1511.

[33] *Code of Alabama* (St. Paul: West Publishing Co., 1941), tit. 10, § 115.

[34] *Arizona Code* (Indianapolis: Bobbs-Merrill Co., 1940), § 53. 402.

[35] *California Civil Code*, § 6059.

[36] *Annotated Code of Idaho, 1932* (Indianapolis: Bobbs-Merrill Co., 1932), § 29-1201.

[37] *The Revised Statutes of the State of Maine* (Augusta, Kennebec: Journal Press, 1945), c. 53, § 11.

[38] *The Revised Code of Montana, 1935* (Great Falls, Mont: Tribune Printing & Supply Co., 1935), § 6453.

[39] *Nevada Compiled Laws, 1929* (San Francisco, 1930), §§ 3223, 3224.

[40] *Oklahoma Statutes, 1941* (St. Paul: West Publishing Co., 1942) tit. 8, § 541.

[41] *The Utah Code Annotated, 1943* (Chicago: Callaghan & Co., 1943), tit. 18, § 6.1.

[42] *Pierce's Code of the State of Washington* (Seattle: Frank Pierce, 1944), § 456-1.

[43] *Wyoming Revised Statutes, 1931* (Cheyenne, 1931), § 28.610.

ing a minister and his successors the power to hold property.[44] However, the Bishop of Manchester and his successors were established as a corporation sole by a special act of the legislature.[45] Other dioceses so incorporated by special acts are Baltimore, Boston, Charleston and Providence.[46] Provisions similar to those enabling a bishop to become a corporation sole are found in the statutes of Michigan.[47]

The trustee system still prevails in the states of Arkansas,[48] Colorado,[49] Mississippi,[50] North Dakota,[51] North Carolina,[52] Ohio,[53] South Carolina,[54] South Dakota,[55] Tennessee,[56] and Texas,[57] as well as in the District of Columbia.[58]

Besides New York, the following states permit the establishment of the favored type of corporation aggregate with various modifica-

[44] *The Revised Laws of the State of New Hampshire* (Concord, N. H.: H. H. Rumford Press, 1942), c. 281, § 4.

[45] *Laws of the State of New Hampshire, 1901* (Concord, 1901), c. 232, p. 723.

[46] Dignan, *op. cit.*, pp. 259-263; Hannan, *op. cit.*, n. 533.

[47] *The Compiled Laws of the State of Michigan, 1929* (Lansing, 1930), § 10090.

[48] *A Digest of the Statutes of Arkansas* (Holms Printing Co., 1937), § 11368.

[49] *Colorado Statutes Annotated, 1935* (Denver: Bradford, Robinson Printing Co., 1936), c. 41.180.

[50] *Mississippi Annotated Code, 1942* (Atlanta, Ga.: Harrison Co., 1943), §§ 5350, 5351.

[51] *North Dakota Revised Code of 1943* (Fargo: Knight Printing Co., 1944), § 10-0802.

[52] *The North Carolina Code of 1931* (Charlottesville, 1931), §§ 3568, 3569.

[53] *Throckmorton's Ohio Code, 1940* (Cleveland: Banks-Baldwin Co., 1940), § 100011.

[54] *South Carolina Code of Laws, 1942* (Clinton, S. C.: Jacobs Press, 1942), § 8158.

[55] *South Dakota Code of 1939* (Pierre, So. Dak.: State Publishing Co., 1939), §11.1801.

[56] *The Tennessee Code of 1932* (Kingsport, Tenn., 1932), § 4408.

[57] *Complete Texas Statutes, 1928* (Kansas City, 1928), § 1396.

[58] *The Code of the District of Columbia* (Washington, D. C., 1930), tit. 5, § 312.

tions: Connecticut,[59] Delaware,[60] Maryland,[61] Massachusetts,[62] Minnesota,[63] New Jersey,[64] Nebraska,[65] Oregon,[66] and Wisconsin.[67] Although the provisions of the Iowa code are not very specific, there seems to be possible the establishment there also of this type of corporation aggregate. In the diocese of Des Moines, church property is held by parish corporations composed of five members—the bishop, the vicar general, the pastor, and two laymen elected by them. The bishop's signature is necessary to bind the corporation legally in financial matters.[68] Ohio seems to provide for a diocesan corporation holding all diocesan property by permitting the incorporation of the cathedral church.[69]

By special act, the Bishop of Natchez, his Vicar-general and four diocesan consultors were created a corporation for a period of fifty years, and given the power to hold in trust the title to the property of several parishes and missions.[70] By special charter secured from the legislature of Vermont, the diocese of Burlington was constituted a corporation in 1896. The Board of Trustees is composed of five members chosen for life. The Bishop is *ex officio* President of the

[59] *The General Statutes of Connecticut, Revision of 1930* (Published by authority of the State Secretary, 1930), §§ 3574, 3576.

[60] *Delaware Revised Code of 1935* (Wilmington, Del.: Star Publishing Co., 1936), § 2471.

[61] *The Annotated Code of the Public General Laws of Maryland* (Baltimore, 1939), art. 23, § 287.

[62] *Tercentenary Edition of the General Laws of the Commonwealth of Massachusetts* (Boston, 1932), c. 67, § 44.

[63] *Mason's Minnesota Statutes, 1927* (St. Paul, 1927), §§ 7975, 7976.

[64] *Revised Statutes of New Jersey, 1937* (4 vols., ed. by the State Commission, 1938), I, 16:15-1.

[65] *Revised Statutes of Nebraska, 1943* (ed. by Statute Commission, 1943), 21-801 to 21-804.

[66] *Oregon Compiled Laws Annotated* (San Francisco: Bancroft, Whitney Co., 1940), 77-419.

[67] *Wisconsin Statutes, 1943* (Racine, Wisc.: Former Co., 1944), § 187.12.

[68] Synod of the Diocese of Des Moines (1923), 94-96—as cited by Dignan, *op. cit.*, p. 264; *Iowa Code of 1939* (Des Moines, 1939), § 10183.

[69] *Throckmorton's Ohio Code, 1940*, §§ 10011, 10022-1; cf. Hannan, *op. cit.*, n. 535.

[70] Constitutiones Dioceseos Natchetensis (1922), 63—as cited by Dignan, *op. cit.*, p. 254.

Board.[71] In 1869, Rhode Island authorized an act of incorporation of the Bishop and Vicar-general of the Diocese of Hartford together with two laymen of any Roman Catholic Church or Congregation in Rhode Island. In 1900, the Bishop of Providence was empowered to become a corporation sole.[72]

In Florida,[73] Georgia,[74] Kansas,[75] Kentucky,[76] and New Mexico,[77] a diocesan corporation may probably be formed to hold diocesan property for the promotion of education, charity, and religion.

The Illinois law as amended July 17, 1943 permits the holding of property by religious corporations composed of "two or more members or trustees according to its usages or custom or such other officers whose powers are similar to trustees." [78]

Until 1935, Pennsylvania did not recognize a corporation if the majority of the incorporators were clergymen, but this did not prohibit the forming of a corporation by Brothers or Sisters. However, in 1935 the law was revised so as to permit the holding of ecclesiastical property in a way which seems to justify the agents of a canonical corporation to act in corporate capacity with effects which the secular law recognizes even as to property rights.[79]

West Virginia and Virginia retained a constitutional provision originally directed against the Protestant Episcopal Church in Virginia, which forbade corporate rights to any religious society. In 1942 Virginia passed a provision similar to the Pennsylvania Act of

[71] Dignan, *op. cit.*, p. 261.

[72] Dignan, *op. cit.*, p. 259.

[73] *Florida Statutes, 1941,* § 617.01.

[74] *Code of Georgia Annotated, 1943* (Atlanta: Harrison Publishing Co., 1943) § 22-415.

[75] *General Statutes of Kansas, 1935* (Topeka: W. C. Austin, 1936), §§ 17.701, 17.702.

[76] *Kentucky Revised Statutes, 1944* (Kentucky Statute Revision Commission, 1944), § 273.020.

[77] *New Mexico Statutes of 1941* (Indianapolis: Bobbs Merrill Co., 1942), § 54-306.

[78] *Illinois Revised Statutes, 1945* (Chicago: Burdette Smith Co., 1945), c. 32, § 164.

[79] *Purdon's Pennsylvania Statutes of 1936* (St. Paul: West Publishing Co., 1936), tit. 10, § 81: cf. "Decrees and Decisions"—*The Jurist*, I (1941), 163.

1935, permitting the holding of ecclesiastical property by the ecclesiastical officers authorized by their own rules to do so.[80] West Virginia, however, has still retained the former prohibitory law.

While the aims of religious corporations differ from those of other corporations, their rights and liabilites regarding the property they manage are substantially the same under Anglo-American law as those of private corporations.[81]

Article 3. Limitation of the Bishop's Contractual Capacity

Although the Code of Canon Law gives the bishop wide administrative powers in his diocese, it prudently places various limitations on this power. These limitations are not placed upon the bishop to hinder him in the performance of his duties but rather to assure him of efficacious help in his many and complex assignments.

A. *The Diocesan Consultors*

The institution of the body of diocesan consultors had its foundation in a decree of the II Plenary Council of Baltimore (1866), which recommended that such a board be set up. The III Plenary Council (1884) made their institution obligatory.[82] The Fathers of the Council realized the necessity for advisers to the bishop in his work. They were also aware that it was impossible to establish cathedral chapters in view of the double lack of funds and of priests. To overcome these obstacles a board of diocesan consultors was proposed. This institution was embodied in the Code of Canon Law to take the place of the cathedral chapter as the senate of the bishop in those places where cathedral chapters could not be established.

The requisite qualities of the consultors as outlined in canon 423 are substantially the same as those demanded by the II and III

[80] *The Virginia Code of 1942* (Charlottesville: Michie Co., 1942), § 38a, c. 261.

[81] Zollmann, *American Church Law*, n. 126.

[82] *Concilii Plenarii Baltimorensis II Acta et Decreta* (2. ed., Baltimorae, 1894)), n. 71; *Acta et Decreta Concilii Plenarii Baltimorensis III* (Baltimorae, 1886), n. 18.

Plenary Councils of Baltimore.[83] The Code prescribes that they be chosen by the bishop, and that they be at least six in number, or in dioceses where the number of priests is small, at least four.[84] These rules are a departure from the III Plenary Council of Baltimore, which permitted two as a minimum number, and also provided that one half of the number should be chosen upon nomination of the clergy.[85]

The diocesan consultors are chosen for a term of three years, and are to reside in the episcopal city or in nearby territory.[86] Canon 427 describes their duties in a general way. Since they are to take the place of the cathedral chapter, their functions relative to the government of the diocese are determined by the part played by the cathedral chapter in administrative matters. Although the Code does not prescribe any regular meetings for the diocesan consultors, the rule of the III Plenary Council, which provides for four annual convocations at stated intervals, is to be followed. When this is impossible, it is within the province of the bishop to limit the meetings to two each year.[87]

The consent of the body of diocesan consultors is to be sought in the specific instances stated in the Code:

(1) For the alienation of church property whose value is between one thousand and thirty thousand lire.[88]

(2) For a contract of lease for not over nine years when the value exceeds thirty thousand lire.[89]

(3) For a contract of lease for more than nine years when the value is between one thousand and thirty thousand lire.[90] Since the

[83] *Concilii Plenarii Baltimorensis II Acta et Decreta,* n. 71; *Acta et Decreta Concilii Plenarii Baltimorensis III,* n. 18.

[84] Canons 424, 425, § 1.

[85] *Acta et Decreta Concilii Plenarii Baltimorensis III,* nn. 18, 19.

[86] Canons 426, § 1, 425, § 1.

[87] *Acta et Decreta Concilii Plenarii Baltimorensis III,* n. 21.

[88] Canon 1532, § 3.

[89] Canon 1541, § 2, 1°.

[90] Canon 1541, § 2, 2°. For the computation of the equivalent of thirty thousand lire or francs in the currency of various countries, the reader is referred to Ellis, "Triginta Millia Libellarum seu Francorum"—*Periodica de Re Morali, Canonica, Liturgica* (Brugis, 1928-1936; Romae, 1937—) XXVII

Code demands the consent of the diocesan consultors in these cases, acts placed without the obtaining of their consent are invalid.[91]

The advice only of the body of diocesan consultors is to be sought in the following cases:

(1) Appointments to fill vacancies in the offices of synodal examiners and parish priest consultors.[92]

(2) The removal of synodal examiners and of parish priest consultors.[93]

(3) The changing of parochial status which implies irremovability for the previously removable pastor.[94]

(4) The establishment of a new parish which in its future status involves removability for its pastor.[95]

(5) The reservation of cases outside of those proposed in the diocesan synod.[96]

(6) The appointment of the two seminary boards.[97]

(7) The union, division, transfer or dismemberment of benefices.[98]

(8) The appointment of the board of administrators for diocesan church property.[99]

That the bishop need not follow the advice of the diocesan consultors for the validity of his action is apparent from canon 105, 1°. However, it is a much controverted question whether the bishop can

(1938), 348-349; Doheny, "Church Finance and Problems of Alienation"—*The Jurist*, I (1941), 101; and Heston, *The Alienation of Church Property in the United States*, The Catholic University of America Canon Law Studies, n. 132 (Washington, D. C.: The Catholic University of America Press, 1941), p. 110. The sum fixed for the United States and Canada is ten thousand dollars which has been declared to be a safe norm to follow in practice.

[91] Canon 105, 1°.

[92] Canon 386, § 1.

[93] Canon 388.

[94] Canon 454, § 3.

[95] Canon 454, § 3.

[96] Canon 895.

[97] Canon 1358, § 2.

[98] Canon 1428, § 1.

[99] Canon 1520, § 1.

act validly without first seeking the consultors' advice.[100] It is not sufficient to inquire the opinion of each consultor individually; the group of consultors is to be heard in its capacity of an advisory body.[101]

B. *The Diocesan Board of Administrators*

To aid the bishop in the administration of the temporal goods of the diocese, canon 1520 provides for the establishment of a board of administrators. It is to be set up in the episcopal city, and consists of the bishop, who is the president of the board, and two or more members who should be familiar with the civil law. In the constitution of this board the advice of the diocesan consultors is to be sought, unless some other provision has been made by special law or custom. Persons related to the bishop by ties of blood relationship or affinity in the first or second degree are excluded from the board unless an apostolic indult dispenses from this impediment. The men who constitute this board are to be consulted on the more important administrative matters. Their vote is only consultative, unless the common law explicitly states otherwise, or unless the charter of a foundation demands that their consent be obtained.

[100] Maroto, *Institutiones Iuris Canonici* (2 vols., Madrid, 1918-1919), I, n. 471; Leitner, *Handbuch des katolischen Kirchenrechts* (5 vols.. Vol. I, 2. ed., Regensburg: Kösel & Pustet, 1921), I, n. 77; Ojetti, *Commentarium in Codicem Iuris Canonici* (4 vols., Romae, 1927-1931) II, 186, et seq.—Hereinafter cited *Commentarium;* Ojetti, "In Canonem 105 Codicis J. C."—*Jus Pontificium* (Romae, 1921—) VII (1927), 13; Augustine, *The Rights and Duties of Ordinaries* (St. Louis: B. Herder Book Co., 1924), p. 149. All the foregoing maintain that it is *ad validitatem* that the bishop hear the diocesan consultors. The contrary opinion is maintained by Vermeersch-Creusen (*Epitome,* I, n. 197 bis), Boudinhon ("An nullus semper sit actus superioris non petito consilio"—*Jus Pontificium,* VIII [1928], 29) and Vromant (*De Bonis Ecclesiae Temporalibus,* p. 53). Since the force of the words, *"satis est ad valide agendum"* in canon 105, 1° does not seem to contain the express or equivalently invalidating clause demanded for all invalidating laws by Canon 11, the arguments of the latter authors adhere more closely to the concept of invalidating laws. The writer, therefore, holds with the opinion which declares that it is not necessary for the validity of an act that the bishop give a hearing to the consultors when their advice only is required.

[101] Canon 105, 2°; cf. Coronata, *Institutiones,* I, n. 154.

The consent of the Board of Administrators must be obtained in the following cases:

(1) Alienation of goods whose value is between one thousand and thirty thousand lire.[102]

(2) Contracts of lease for less than nine years when the value is beyond thirty thousand lire.[103]

(3) Contracts of lease beyond nine years when the value is between one thousand and thirty thousand lire.[104]

The advice only of the Board of Administrators is to be sought in the following cases:

(1) The erection of a benefice when the endowment consists of a set sum of money which is to be invested as soon as possible in safe and fruitful real estate or bonds.[105]

(2) The alienation of goods whose value does not exceed the sum of one thousand lire.[106]

(3) Contracts of lease for less than nine years when the value is between one thousand and thirty thousand lire.[107]

(4) Contracts of lease beyond nine years when the value does not exceed one thousand lire.[108]

When the consent of the board is necessary, the bishop acts invalidly if he does not first obtain this consent. When advice only is demanded, it is sufficient that he summon the board and request their opinion without obliging himself to follow their advice.[109]

C. *Other Limitations*

In entering into a bilateral contract, the contractors each seek to gain something, while at the same time they realize they must forfeit something they now possess. In order to gain they have to sacrifice. Both parties feel that there is an equation between the thing gained

[102] Canon 1532, § 3.
[103] Canon 1541, § 2, 1°.
[104] Canon 1541, § 2, 2°.
[105] Canon 1415, § 2.
[106] Canon 1532, § 2.
[107] Canon 1541, § 2, 2°.
[108] Canon 1541, § 2, 3°.
[109] Canon 105, 1°; cf. *supra*, p. 86, for various opinions on this question.

and the sacrifice made. Otherwise they would be reluctant to enter into a contract at all. There are limits, however, placed upon the rights of administrators to forfeit goods or rights, or to accept obligations, since they act not as individuals but as the representatives of a moral person.

Some privilege or right may be a desirable object of sacrifice in the matter of contract, since its forfeiture may have a great bargaining power in the eyes of one of the parties to a contract. Paramount among the rights which a bishop exercises over religious bodies is the right of visitation. It may be inquired here whether the bishop may forfeit this right to gain the help of a religious congregation in carrying out his work. In the eyes of the religious congregation exemption is desirable for the free exercise of its works. It is a desirable asset also for the bishop to have the power of visitation in the administration of his diocese.

Exemption from the visitation of bishops is considered a privilege by the religious congregation, and it is in fact a papal privilege, as canon 344, § 1, indicates by demanding proof of its concession by the Holy See.[110] Bishops themselves are given the power of exempting from the authority of a pastor a religious community or a pious institution located within the territory of the parish, even though they are not exempted by the common law.[111] May the bishop relinquish his right of visitation over a religious congregation by including this renunciation as a consideration for services to be rendered?

The Code, in treating of religious, has a rubric *De privilegiis,* but it has only the single rubric, *De Episcopis,* when legislating concerning bishops. In order to formulate an exhaustive list of the bishop's privileges one would have to investigate the entire Code. Some of the privileges of bishops are mentioned in canon 349, but this list is not exhaustive, as the words, *praeter alia privelegia suis in titulis recensentur,* indicate.

[110] "Ordinariae episcopali visitationi obnoxiae sunt personae, res ac loca pia, quamvis exempta, quae intra dioecesis ambitum continentur, nisi probari possit specialem a visitatione exemptionem fuisse ipsis ab Apostolica Sede concessam."—Canon 344, § 1.

[111] Canon 464, § 2.

Although some authors refer to the "right of visitation" when they speak of the bishop's office, the Code treats it as an obligation.[112] Even if the word "obligation" were not used, the reason given in the canon would indicate its obligatory nature.[113] Further, the obligation is of such necessity that it devolves upon the vicar general if the bishop is impeded and upon the metropolitan if the bishop neglects it.[114]

Since it is an obligation, the bishop is not competent to renounce it in formulating a contract. He cannot dispense himself from this obligation of the quinquennial visitation.[115] As a matter of fact, the local ordinary may because of special circumstances be obliged to perform an extraordinary visitation in order to remedy disorders in his diocese.[116]

While the aims of religious corporations are higher than those of other corporations, the status conceded them by the civil law gives them equality only with other societies. They are subject to the same restrictions as other private corporations. Civil law views religious corporations as having been created for the managing of church property. Hence it endows them with substantially the same rights and subjects them to the same liabilities as private corporations.[117] Their contractual rights are "subject to the ordinary rules of law and equity applicable to other contracting parties."[118] "Religious corporations come before the courts in the same attitude

[112] ". . . tenentur Episcopi obligatione visitandae dioecesis. . . ." Canon 343, § 1.

[113] "Ad sanam et orthodoxam doctrinam conservandam, bonos mores tuendos, pravos corrigendos, pacem, innocentiam, pietatem et disciplinam in populo et clero promovendam ceteraque pro ratione adiunctorum ad bonum religionis constituenda. . . ." Canon 343, § 1.

[114] Canon 343, § 1, 3°.

[115] Larraona, "Commentarium Codicis," *Commentarium pro Religiosis* (Romae, 1920-1934; ab anno 1935: *Commentarium pro Religiosis et Missionariis*), VIII (1927), 441. Hereinafter cited *CpR* and *CpRM* respectively.

[116] Reilly, *The Visitation of Religious,* The Catholic University of America Canon Law Studies, n. 120 (Washington, D. C.: Catholic University of America, 1938), p. 87.

[117] Zollmann, *American Church Law,* n. 126.

[118] Bowen v. Trustees of Irish Presbyterian Congregation, 19 N. Y. Super. 245.

as other voluntary associations [when unincorporated] for benevolent or charitable purposes, and their rights of property, or of contract, are equally under the protection of the law and the actions of their members subject to its restraint." [119]

The power of the bishop as a representative of a corporation may be thus *de facto* restricted by the civil law in regard to the transfer of property by the conditions under which this property is held. Disposal in breach of such conditions will result in the *de facto,* though not *de iure canonico* forfeiture of title to the original owner.[120] As long as the true purpose of the church property is preserved, the civil law interposes no objection to its transfer.[121] In the absence of restrictive conditions, the religious corporation has the inherent right without any express authority to dispose of its property, and the courts will uphold this right.[122]

A corporation and an individual do not stand before the civil courts in the same light regarding contractual rights. While an individual may enter into any agreement which does not contravene the interests of society, a corporation may exercise only those rights which are granted it in its charter. The charter of the corporation bears a relation to that corporation analogous to that which the Constitution of the United States bears to the Federal Government. To its charter all the corporation's contractual rights under civil law are traceable either directly or by implication.[123]

Since the idea of the incorporation of any Catholic moral person is intended only to give the corporation's acts valid effects before the civil law, the bishop is not from a canonical point of view restricted to those rights which are given him in the charter of incorporation. His rights of administration derive from his administrative jurisdiction as stated in the Code.[124]

Often civil law forbids the rights which are canonically his. Since the Code declares that the Church may acquire temporal goods in any

[119] Watson v. Jones, 80 U. S. (Wall.) 679, 714, 20 L. Ed. 666.

[120] Patrick v. Y. M. C. A. of Kalamazoo, 120 Mich. 185, 79 N. W. 208.

[121] Zollmann, *American Church Law,* n. 176.

[122] Zollmann, *op. cit.,* n. 177.

[123] Zollmann, *op. cit.,* n. 148.

[124] Canon 335, § 1, 1519, § 2; cf. *supra,* p. 74 et seq.

manner sanctioned by the natural and positive law,[125] civil law restrictions which impede the bishop in any way from the free exercise of this right would have to be considered as unacceptable provisions in the matter of contract.[126]

[125] Canon 1499, § 1.
[126] Canon 1529.

CHAPTER X

CONTRACTUAL CAPACITY OF RELIGIOUS CONGREGATIONS

ARTICLE 1. DERIVATION OF THIS POWER IN THE CODE

As the bishop representing the moral person of the diocese derives his contractual capacity from his power of administrative jurisdiction, so in religious congregations this capacity has its basis in the fact that the congregation as such can perform acts of ownership through the mediation of the legitimately appointed superiors of the congregation. Canon 1495 asserts the right of a moral ecclesiastical person properly constituted to exercise the right of acquisition, retention and administration of temporal goods according to the norms of the sacred canons. Besides the ownership of temporal goods concerning which the congregation has the right to contract, the II Plenary Council of Baltimore (1866) adverted to the fact that religious congregations were accustomed to enter into contracts concerning the service of their members.[1] It was concerning the latter type of contracts that the legislation of the II Plenary Council of Baltimore provided that contracts be drawn up between bishops and religious congregations.

A. *The Right of the Congregation to Acquire and Administer Temporal Goods*

Canon 531 asserts the right of religious institutes to acquire temporal goods unless this capacity is denied them or restricted by their rules and constitutions. The Council of Trent excluded the Friars Minor and the Capuchins from the right to possess property in common.[2] The constitutions of some orders, for example, the Discalced Carmelites and the Jesuits, restrict the right. In the Society of Jesus, colleges in which the religious or externs are edu-

[1] *Concilii Plenarii Baltimorensis II Acta et Decreta*, nn. 406, 407.

[2] Conc. Trident., sess. XXV, *de regularibus*, c. 3.

cated can possess stable incomes; houses in which the professed live can hold in ownership only the house, church, and garden. They can possess movable goods in common, but no stable revenues.[3]

The right of the administration of the temporal goods of the congregation, province or individual house belongs to those designated by the constitutions.[4] Canon 1495 refers to the right of acquiring, retaining and administering temporal goods as the right of the moral person so constituted by the Church. Religious congregations, provinces, and individual houses are considered as moral persons by virtue of their proper canonical erection, and are so referred to in the Code.[5] For the constitution of the individual house as a moral person, at least three members are required.[6]

Temporal goods may be acquired by a religious congregation in any of the various ways sanctioned by the natural and positive law,[7] subject only to the limitations which the Code has seen fit to place upon such acquisition, as it does for example in regard to the collection of alms.[8] Any provision of civil law by which the right of acquisition on the part of the congregation is further limited would be contrary to Canon Law, and would have to be repudiated according to the general principle stated in canon 1529, by which civil law provisions contrary to Canon Law are declared unacceptable.

The administrators of temporal goods in religious congregations are designated by the constitutions of each institute.[9] These, in turn,

[3] Wernz-Vidal, *Ius Canonicum ad Codicis Normam Exactum* (7 vols. in 8, Romae: Apud Aedes Universitatis Gregorianae, 1923-1938), III, n. 342. Hereinafter cited *Ius Canonicum;* Larraona, "Commentarium Codicis," *CpR,* XII (1931), 251.

[4] Canon 532, § 1.

[5] Canons 536, § 1; 1557, § 2, 2°; cf. Coronata, *Institutiones,* I, n. 524.

[6] Canon 100, § 2. Three persons are also required for the constitution of a province or a congregation as a moral person—Vromant, *De Bonis Ecclesiae Temporalibus,* p. 26.

[7] Canons 1498, 1499, § 1.

[8] Canon 622; O'Brien, *The Exemption of Religious in Church Law* (Milwaukee: Bruce, 1942), p. 242.

[9] Canon 532, § 1.

generally follow the principles enacted in the *Normae* of the Sacred Congregation of Bishops and Regulars as issued in 1901,[10] since regarding the administration of temporal goods these principles have not been changed by the *Normae* of 1921.[11]

The exercise of administrative rights in religious congregations is subject primarily to the supreme authority of the Roman Pontiff, who enjoys the right of eminent domain over all ecclesiastical goods,[12] and is the supreme administrator of them.[13] His is the inherent sovereign authority in the protection and administration of ecclesiastical goods according to the ends for which the Church was instituted.[14]

The moral person juridically constituted by the Church in religious congregations is, however, the proprietor of the goods, and their disposition cannot be made arbitrarily even by the Roman Pontiff.[15] Hence, no religious superior, not even the Superior General, may licitly or validly dispose of the goods of any house unless he first obtains the free consent of the legitimate administrators given in accordance with the limitations imposed upon them by the general law or the constitutions.[16]

Not only do the constitutions of the institute designate the various administrators, but they also determine the limits of the administrators' capacity. All acts mentioned by the common law are permitted, then, for the proper conservation of the congregation's temporal goods, but the prescription of canon 142, which forbids habitual

[10] *Normae of 1901,* nn. 283-296.

[11] *Normae secundum quas S. Congregatio de Religiosis in novis congregationibus approbandis procedere solet* (Romae: Typis Polyglottis Vaticanis, 1921), n. 1. Hereinafter cited *Normae of 1921.*

[12] Canon 1499, § 2.

[13] Canon 1518.

[14] Vromant, *De Bonis Ecclesiae Temporalibus,* p. 66; Wernz-Vidal, *Ius Canonicum,* IV, Pars. II, n. 741; Coronata, *Institutiones,* II, n. 1039; De Meester, *Compendium,* III, n. 1499.

[15] Wernz-Vidal, *Ius Canonicum,* IV, Pars. II, n. 741; Prümmer, *Manuale Iuris Canonici,* q. 443; Cocchi, *Commentarium,* IV, 346.

[16] Vermeersch-Creusen, *Epitome,* II, n. 818; Prümmer, *Manuale Iuris Canonici,* q. 443.

trading, must be observed.[17] Since the ultimate norm is that contained in the constitutions of the individual institutes, whenever they set limitations more stringent than the common law, these are to be followed. The constitutions determine the formalities necessary when the more important administrative acts are to be performed, such as the intervention of the chapter or of the council. Implicitly imposed on all administrators in the performance of all acts of administration is the furtherance of the purpose for which the institute was founded.

In modern congregations, wherein a hierarchical organization has been adopted, the right of supervision over the administration of the temporal goods is universally reserved in the constitutions to the Superior General. The Treasurer General, sometimes called the Procurator General,[18] administers the goods belonging to the congregation as a whole under the direction of the Superior General. The provincial and local treasurers administer the goods of the province and of the local house respectively under the direction of the provincial and local superior in the respective case.[19]

Great care is apparent in the precise formulation of canon 516, § 2. It makes it clear that all administrators are subject to the superiors. This power of direction of the superior extends to all acts of ordinary administration. In the first formulation or draft of this canon the words *"sub directione Superioris"* were not included.[20] In the preparatory editions the words *"ad normam constitutionum"* were added along with the words *"sub directione Superioris,"* but they were later omitted since it was feared that anxiety and confusion would result from the fact that often particular constitutions do not

[17] Fanfani, *De Iure Religiosorum ad Normam Codicis Iuris Canonici,* (2. ed., Taurini-Romae: Ex Officina Libraria Marietti, 1925), p. 155. Hereinafter cited *De Iure Religiosorum.*

[18] This latter usage is confusing, since canon 517 describes the Procurator General as the agent of the congregation in conducting its affairs with the Holy See.

[19] "Sint etiam pro administratione bonorum temporalium oeconomi: generalis qui religionis universae bona administret, provincialis qui provinciae, localis qui singularum domorum; qui omnes officio suo fungantur sub directione Superioris."—Canon 516, § 2.

[20] Vermeersch-Creusen, *Epitome,* I, n. 585.

specify the duties of extraordinary administrators. Such extraordinary administrators are those who are appointed to collect alms for the missions; administrators of building funds for the erection of shrines; administrators of funds to be expended in the celebration of congresses. These administrators are appointed according to the nature and end of their work by one or the other superior, who also gives them special directions for their particular work.[21]

Neither the constitutions nor custom can exempt the various treasurers from the supervision of and dependence on their superiors. It is true that they are permitted a reasonable degree of initiative and liberty, but they must always keep the superiors informed concerning their transactions.[22] In Benedictine communities the local bursar is chosen from among the members of the community by the abbot without whose command he can do nothing.[23]

In using the word *direction*, the Code gives superiors more than a supervisory power over their treasurers. The bishop, for example, is accorded the power of vigilance over the ecclesiastical goods in his territory,[24] but the power of superiors in religious congregations over inferior administrators is more extensive than vigilance. This fact is evident from canon 532, § 2, where superiors are conceded power to perform administrative acts. It was precisely to show that superiors have power to perform administrative acts that the word *superiors* was inserted in this canon according to Larraona.[25] He continues:

> "Logically and practically the right to perform acts of administration is necessary to them. Administration is a part of government. Though generally entrusted to officials, radically it cannot be denied to those having the right to govern. Moreover, the faculty must be reserved to them of placing economic acts directly, at least in certain cases, as for example to remedy

[21] Larraona, "Commentarium Codicis," *CpR*, X (1929) 34, 35.

[22] Creusen-Ellis-Garesché, *Religious Men and Women in the Code* (4. English ed., Milwaukee: The Bruce Publishing Co., 1940), n. 99. Hereinafter cited Creusen, *Religious Men and Women in the Code*.

[23] Augustine, *Commentary*, III, 150.

[24] Canon 1519, § 1; cf. *supra*, p. 76.

[25] Larraona, "Commentarium Codicis," *CpR*, XII (1931), 358.

the negligence of an administrator or to repair an injury done by him." [26]

From canon 516, § 2, it is apparent that the normal exercise of administration is in the hands of the treasurer. Canon 532, § 2, vindicates this right for the superior also, but it is not to be exercised habitually by him. Otherwise the prescription of canon 516, § 3, which forbids the Superior General and the provincial to assume simultaneously the office of treasurer would be frustrated entirely. It may be concluded, then, that the superior has administrative power, as has also the treasurer. The treasurer is completely under the direction of the superior in administrative matters, but he usually performs the administrative acts. The superior's province is principally to watch over the spiritual welfare of his subjects. By dissociating himself as much as possible from the administration of temporalities, he will not neglect the higher good of those placed under his care.[27]

It seems unlawful for a congregation or a province to have a standing rule of not appointing treasurers in individual houses, since the Code permits the fusion of this office with that of the local superior, even in a local house, only when necessity demands it. By combining this office with that of the assistant superior the spirit of the law is more nearly satisfied.[28]

The various administrators are to be chosen in the manner prescribed by the constitutions of the religious organization. In the absence of explicit legislation as to their election, they are chosen by the major superior with the consent of his council. Hence, the Treasurer General is chosen by the Superior General and his council, while the provincial and his council select both the provincial and local treasurers.[29]

It must be kept in mind that the canonical provision instituting the office of treasurer does not duplicate the office of superior in the congregation, in the province, or in the local house. There is

[26] *Loc. cit.* The translation is the writer's.

[27] Vromant, *De Bonis Ecclesiae Temporalibus*, p. 243.

[28] Coronata, *Institutiones*, I, n. 524.

[29] Canon 516, § 4.

but one superior who is the supervisor of the administration of the temporal goods. The treasurer is bound to render an account to the superior as required by the constitutions or whenever the superior demands it. The treasurer cannot dispose of the goods under his care without the superior's permission; obviously the superior cannot grant him unlimited power in this regard.[80]

The former legislation ruled that the administrators of temporal goods in religious institutes should be removable at the will of the superior.[81] Today the constitutions of each institute determine the length of their term of office, and it seems that the superior would have to have weighty reasons in order to remove them. If, in the absence of a particular statute, the administrator is chosen, as stated above, by the major superior and his council, it seems that for his removal the same intervention would be requisite, and that the consent of the council would have to be obtained before he could be removed from his office.[82]

B. *The Right of the Congregation to the Service of Its Members*

The temporal goods of any institute play an important part in the usual contracts whereby property is acquired and the life of the members is sustained. However, the consideration for a contract between bishops and religious congregations usually revolves around the right of the congregation to the service of its members. This is the type of contract which the Fathers of the II Plenary Council of Baltimore (1866) contemplated when they decreed that religious superiors should not remove members from services which they had agreed to render without supplying adequate substitutes.[83]

The right of the religious congregation to the service of its members arises from religious profession, which is a contract by which a qualified Catholic freely gives himself to the religious institute by pronouncing the three vows and is in turn accepted by the institute

[80] Wernz-Vidal, *Ius Canonicum,* III, n. 156.

[81] Conc. Trident., sess. XXV, *de regularibus,* c. 2.

[82] Augustine, *Commentary,* III, 150.

[83] *Concilii Plenarii Baltimorensis II Acta et Decreta,* n. 406.

as a member.[34] By virtue of this free contract the superiors and chapters possess dominative power over their subjects.[35] This power is also possessed by superiors of societies in which promises only are taken.[36]

Dominative power is described as the faculty which, as possessed by the head of any society, authorizes him to give precepts, to direct and to correct the members of the society in order to obtain the ends for which it was instituted.[37] Most authors hold to the twofold distinction of power in religious organizations as stated in canon 501, § 1, namely, dominative power and jurisdiction.[38] Besides jurisdiction, other authors distinguish dominative power and domestic power,[39] also called social power,[40] and a third power referred to as power arising from the vow.[41] Larraona distinguishes these as species of dominative power rather than as powers separate from it. His division falls into the threefold species: social dominative power; governing dominative power; and dominative power arising from the vow.[42] Wernz- (1842-1914) Vidal (1867-1938) also maintain

[34] Leo XIII, const. *Conditae a Christo,* 8 dec. 1900,—*Fontes,* n. 644; Wernz-Vidal, *Ius Canonicum,* III, n. 300; Battandier, *Guide Canonique pour les Constitutions des Instituts a Voeux Simples* (6. ed., Paris, 1923), p. 87. Hereinafter cited *Guide Canonique.*

[35] Canon 501, § 1.

[36] Coronata, *Institutiones,* I, n. 527.

[37] Wernz-Vidal, *Ius Canonicum,* III, n. 93.

[38] Cf. Coronata, *Institutiones,* I, n. 527; Wernz-Vidal, *Ius Canonicum,* III, n. 93; Augustine, *Commentary,* III, 103; Chelodi, *Ius de Personis iuxta Codicem Iuris Canonici* (Tridenti, 1927), p. 205. Hereinafter cited *Ius de Personis;* Schaefer, *Compendium de Religiosis ad Normam Codicis Iuris Canonici* (Muenster i. W.: Ex Officina Libraria Aschendorff, 1931), n. 105. Hereinafter cited *De Religiosis;* Balmes, *Les Religieux a Voeux Simples d'apres le Code* (Paray-le-Monial, 1921), p. 57. Hereinafter cited *Les Religieux a Voeux Simples.*

[39] Vermeersch-Creusen, *Epitome,* I, n. 573.

[40] Biederlack-Führich, *De Religiosis* (Oeniponte, 1919), n. 36.

[41] Raus, *De Sacrae Obedientiae Virtute et Voto* (Lugduni: Typis Emmanuel Vitte, 1923), n. 39.

[42] "Quatenus est societas iuridica . . . potest soletque appellari *socialis* . . . Quatenus est societas iuridica *non mere privata* sed quae continet *statum publicum* totaque ad ipsum ordinatur . . . *gubernativa* appellatur . . . Denique Religio est sua specifica natura theologica et iuridica, votum obedientiae secum

that the various powers spoken of by the authors are species or parts of the one power, the dominative.[43]

Authors are agreed on the basic point that all superiors possess at least dominative power by virtue of which they can give precepts according to the constitutions and the common law. This power is the foundation upon which rests the obligation of service which the religious owes to his congregation. The constitutions determine the degree to which each superior can exercise this power. The extent of the individual superior's dominative power is coterminous with the ends of the congregation and the sphere over which the superior exercises his influence. The constitutions should clearly indicate the extent of each superior's dominative power, since the Code is content to leave this matter to particular law, provided that it does not contravene the common law.[44]

Regarding the phrase *ad normam constitutionum,* one may well inquire whether it applies also to those congregations whose constitutions are not as yet approved by the Holy See. Larraona maintains that it applies to these congregations also.[45] This opinion is founded on a sound basis, since to hold otherwise would be to encourage possible disregard for superiors' orders, and could lead to eventual confusion and instability of disciplinary restraint in those congregations whose constitutions are not as yet approved by the Holy See.

Certainly the exercise of dominative power permits the designated superior to command his subjects to undertake work which is within the scope of the institute's ends. Generally, the Provincial and his council have the power to assign members of the province to various

fert ex quo potestas omnis qua regitur habitu confirmatur et actu confirmari potest, religionis vinculo. Facultas quae ex voto Superiori obvenit quandoque *potestas ex voto* simpliciter dicitur."—"Commentarium Codicis," *CpR,* VII (1926), 32, 33.

[43] *Ius Canonicum,* III, n. 93.

[44] "Superiores et Capitula, ad normam constitutionum et iuris communis, potestatem habent dominativam in subditos."—Canon 501, § 1.

[45] "Nihil refert an hae constitutiones seu regulae seu statuta vel ordinationes sint approbatae a Sede Apostolica. Tam illae quae approbatae sunt, etiam approbatione expressa et specifica, quam illae quae hac approbatione carent, veniunt sub nomine constitutionum."—"Commentarium Codicis."—*CpR,* VII (1926), 30; IV (1923), 139, footnote 389.

houses of the congregation within the province. It is not within the power of the local superior to effect these changes, since his power is restricted to his own house. He may, however, contract for the services of his subjects by permitting them to assist temporarily in a neighboring parish, provided that this work is not forbidden them by the nature of their organization. Such a prohibition would exist in a strictly contemplative Order such as the Trappists. Local superiors may also contract for the services of their subjects in the discharge of their offices for short periods on individual occasions or even habitually.

Article 2. Service Beyond Six Months

There is a general prohibition enacted in canon 606, § 2, which limits the period of time during which a religious may live outside the house to which he has been assigned. Except for purposes of collecting alms,[46] a grave cause is necessary in order that the superior may permit even a short absence. The duration of this brief absence is to be determined according to the constitutions of each institute. An exception is made in favor of those who are assigned to pursue courses of study outside the religious house, but for all other cases the permission of the Holy See is required if absences beyond six months are to become allowable.[47]

Authors are inclined to give a strict interpretation to this canon, and unanimously insist that even for the cause of sickness, permission of the Holy See must be obtained for absences which exceed six months. This is held to be true even though the religious is confined to a hospital or to a convalescent center conducted by religious of another congregation. This position is maintained because the Code commands residence in a house of the religious' own congregation.[48]

[46] Canons 621-624.

[47] "Superioribus fas non est, salvis praescriptis in can. 621-624, permittere ut subditi extra domum propriae religionis degant, nisi gravi et iusta de causa atque ad tempus quo fieri potest brevius secundum constitutiones; pro absentia vero, quae sex menses excedat, nisi causa studiorum intercedat, semper Apostolicae Sedis venia requiritur."—Canon 606, § 2.

[48] Vermeersch-Creusen, *Epitome*, I, n. 706; Cocchi, *Commentarium*, II, 208; Fanfani, *De Iure Religiosorum*, n. 318; Schaefer, *De Religiosis*, n. 364; Creusen, *Religious Men and Women in the Code*, n. 292.

The present law relaxes to a great degree the former legislation on residence of religious in that it permits absences for periods beyond six months for purposes of study. Formerly, ordinaries were empowered to remand religious to their own houses if they found them unlawfully residing in their dioceses outside the cloister.[49] Pope Alexander III (1159-1181) prohibited religious from leaving their monasteries to attend lectures on civil law and the sciences.[50] The present law makes the concession general, and does not restrict the type of studies to the ecclesiastical branches. There is a prohibition, however, which forbids attendance at secular universities without the permission of the ordinary.[51] As a safeguard to religious discipline, the prescription of canon 587, § 4, must be fulfilled.[52]

The question arises as to the possibility of religious remaining outside their proper house for periods longer than six months in order to aid in the works of the sacerdotal ministry. Authors who discuss this question incline towards the opinion that in such cases the permission of the Holy See is not required. The general permission given to those who pursue studies outside their own religious houses was given, they say, because such studies were deemed necessary for the advancement of the aims of the institute. By comparison, it seems that the exercise of the sacred ministry affords even greater reason for absences beyond six months without implying any need for recurring to the Holy See for permission in each case. It is argued that the exercise of such works as the giving of missions, which demands prolonged absences, is a part of the ministry and, like the pursuit of studies, furthers the ends of religion.[53] But this position is not without its opponents.[54]

[49] C. 7, X, *de officio iudicis ordinarii,* I, 31.

[50] C. 3, X, *ne clerici vel monachi saecularibus negotiis se immisceant,* III, 50.

[51] S. C. Consist., 30 apr. 1918—*AAS,* X (1918), 237.

[52] "Religiosis, qui studiorum causa longe a propria domo mittuntur, non in privatis domibus habitare, sed opus est in aliquam suae religionis domum se recipiant, vel, si id fieri non possit, apud religiosum aliquod institutum virorum, vel Seminarium aliamve piam domum, cui sacri ordinis viri praesint, quaeque ab ecclesiastica auctoritate approbata sit."

[53] Wernz-Vidal, *Ius Canonicum,* III, n. 382; Schaefer, *De Religiosis,* n. 364.

[54] "Religiosi, qui vocationis aut muneris sui uti praedicatoris, missionarii, directoris exercitiorum ultra sex menses extra conventum commorantur indigent

It is maintained that the necessity of obtaining the permission of the Holy See for absences beyond six months applies to those cases only in which the absence is necessitated by the performance of works foreign to the religious state.[55] Vermeersch (1858-1936) adduces the following arguments in favor of this opinion:

(1) The *Fontes* of canon 606 indicate that the law was prescribed for the sake of preventing religious from leaving the cloister without their superior's permission even when pious works were involved.

(2) The force of this prohibition is to be restricted to residence outside the religious house for reasons alien to the religious vocation, for example, for the sake of recuperating from sickness.

(3) This interpretation conforms to the practice of the Sacred Congregation of Religious in giving such permission. In such cases this Sacred Congregation applies the same rules as it does in the case of exclaustration, which bars the wearing of the religious habit. This prohibition clearly could not be applied to those who are absent to perform the customary works of the ministry.

(4) The words, "outside of a house of his own institute," are understood to mean "outside of a house where by reason of his vocation a religious can or should dwell." One who, by reason of his vocation, is appointed to be spiritual director or superior of a seminary dwells there as though he were in a house of his own institute.[56]

A literal interpretation of this restriction would introduce a new and rigorous discipline, which could not be complied with if the works of many institutes are to be continued.[57] Hence, it is inferred by Vermeersch, and also by the authors who are in accord with him, that if a religious is performing the works compatible with the sacred ministry or the religious state, he cannot be regarded as being absent from his religious house. Religious superiors may, according to this view, assign their subjects to the care of souls in hospitals

licentia Sanctae Sedis."—Oesterle, *Praelectiones Iuris Canonici* (Romae, 1931), p. 340; Augustine, *Commentary,* III, 507.

[55] Coronata, *Institutiones,* I, n. 612; Vermeersch, "De commoratione extra propriam religionis domum."—*Periodica,* X (1922), 36.

[56] Vermeersch, *ibid.,* pp. 36, 37.

[57] Cocchi, *Commentarium,* II, 208.

or in parishes or in any branch of religious work which conforms to the aims of their institute.[58]

If this opinion may be held for clerical religious in general inasmuch as the nature of the sacerdotal ministry at times necessitates absences for periods beyond six months, an even more cogent argument is to be found in the examination of particular works specified in the constitutions of certain religious institutes. Congregations whose constitutions mention specifically the fact that they are to aid the diocesan clergy when this help is needed seem to be excused from the requirement of obtaining permission from the Holy See each time a member is assigned to assist in a diocesan parish for longer than six months. The approval of their constitutions by the Holy See seems implicitly to contain the permission necessary.[59] The permission is understood to be given in order to carry out the aims of the institute as specified in its constitutions.[60]

In the case of such congregations at least, the superior could contract with a bishop for the services of the religious to assist in a parish even for periods beyond six months without recurring to the Holy See for permission to authorize them to remain outside the religious house. Such an opinion seems sufficiently safe to follow in view of the preponderant number of authors who maintain that the permission of the Holy See is implied in such cases.[61] The opinion of Creusen is typical of these authors: "If the constitutions approve the exercise of the sacred ministry outside the houses of the institute, if, in par-

[58] Coronata, *Institutiones*, I, n. 612; Biederlack-Führich, *De Religiosis*, p. 242; Schaefer, *De Religiosis*, n. 364: Vermeersch, *loc. cit.*

[59] Vermeersch, *loc. cit.*; Schaefer, *De Religiosis*, n. 364; Cocchi, *Commentarium*, II, 208, Creusen, *Religious Men and Women in the Code*, n. 292.

[60] Goyeneche, *Iuris Canonici Summa Principia*, Pars II, *De Religiosis* (Romae: Tip. Pol. "Cuore di Maria," 1938), p. 157. Hereinafter cited *De Religiosis*.

[61] Vermeersch, *Theologia Moralis, Principia, Responsa, Consilia* (4 vols., Romae: Università Gregoriana, 1922-1924), III, 121; Vermeersch, "De commoratione extra propriam religionis domum"—*Periodica*, X (1922), 36, 37; Coronata, *Institutiones*, I, n. 612; Wernz-Vidal, *Ius Canonicum*, III, n. 382; Schaefer, *De Religiosis*, n. 364; Cocchi, *Commentarium*, II, 208; Biederlack-Führich, *De Religiosis*, n. 242; Goyeneche, *De Religiosis*, p. 157; Creusen, *Religious Men and Women in the Code*, n. 292.

ticular, they approve the accepting of the post of parish vicar or of parish priest, the religious thus employed outside the house may remain more than six months outside their convents." [62]

In some institutes an attempt has been made to mitigate the dangers which might result from prolonged absences from the rest of the community. Sometimes, in mission countries, a central house is established as a *domus formata,* and the individual missionaries reside in that house, although they are entrusted with different missions in the area. Such a system commends itself because it preserves the advantages of the cloister and fosters religious discipline and the common life. However, the presence of the priest among his flock to direct and edify them is sacrificed by this plan. The accessibility to a priest in time of emergency is a consolation which the faithful are forced to forego. The system of utilizing a central house is not practical in places where individual priests must of necessity cover large areas which are sparsely populated. To assign several priests to an area, although large, which contains a handful of Catholics, while other sections suffer for want of priests, is not utilizing missionaries to produce the best results.

Where the practice of assigning a religious as assistant in a non-religious parish because of the scarcity of diocesan priests obtains, the custom is sometimes followed of attaching the religious to a local house of his congregation, to which house he returns one day a month. He is theoretically missioned to the religious house while still performing the duties of a parish assistant. By periodic returns to his religious house, the letter of canon 606, § 2, is satisfied. Although this would not be necessary if the opinion espoused above is followed, the practice is commendable from the point of view that it fosters in the religious a deeper devotion to community life.

The power to assign a religious to a particular work for six months or longer seems to be within the competence of only the higher superiors, since such an assignment analogously takes on the character of a transfer from one house to another. In this hypothesis it is the provincial who is empowered to enter into contracts for the service of his subjects for these longer periods. A proportionate power could

[62] Creusen, *loc. cit.*

then be conceded by the provincial or by the constitutions to lower superiors.

The establishment of such a proportion is at least consonant with the Code's legislation on other matters in which a gradation of power from the highest to the lowest superiors is recognized. Such a gradation is evidenced in the legislation on alienation, in which the competent superior for permitting an alienation which involves the maximum amount of property is the Holy See, while lower superiors are empowered to alienate property of graduated values according to their precedence in the hierarchy of authority.[63] Since specific provisions are not found in the common law concerning the authority necessary for the making of contracts for services, the constitutions of each institute must be investigated on this point for a determination of the powers conceded to the various types of superiors.

Article 3. Service for Shorter Periods

Superiors themselves are restricted in contracting for their own services in assisting in the works of the sacred ministry, since canon 508 binds them to residence in the house which is under their care. This obligation, as it is expressed in the common law, is not as strict as a pastor's or a bishop's obligation of residence, for the Code relinquishes the right of its determination to the constitutions of the religious institute. The constitutions, of course, may demand a relatively grave reason for a superior's absence from his house.[64]

Legitimate absence in the case of superiors is to be determined not according to time but according to the reason and manner of absence permitted by the constitutions.[65] Superiors would not be restricted to the extent that they could never absent themselves in order to offer their services for parochial work, such as "week-end work" or preaching. In assuming such obligations they must follow the norm stated in their particular constitutions. It must above all be established that no detriment will come to the religious discipline

[63] Canons 534, 1532, 1541.

[64] Coronata, *Institutiones,* I, n. 540.

[65] Vermeersch-Creusen, *Epitome,* I, n. 580.

of their house because of such absences, no matter how brief they may be.

The Code seems to propose that, rather than to perform these services themselves, superiors should designate their subjects to undertake the work of helping out in parishes. Assistance in parochial work is directed by the Code primarily toward the benefit of parishes in the diocese where the religious house is located, but assistance in other dioceses is not precluded.[66] The Code, in expressing this preference, contemplates the usual situation in which there is a balanced proportion of religious houses in each diocese. In the case wherein one diocese has many religious congregations in view of peculiar circumstances, assistance in an adjacent diocese where priests are needed would not be precluded, but would rather be encouraged in order to enable the faithful of the latter diocese to attend religious services.

It seems, then, to be within the competence of the local superior, unless the constitutions contain a limitation in this respect, to contract for the services of his subjects for assistance at parochial functions for short periods such as a funeral Mass, "week-end work," preaching a sermon on a special occasion, or a retreat. The Code does not specify in canon 608, § 1, which superiors are empowered to make contracts for such services to be rendered by religious, nor do authors restrict this right to the higher superiors.[67]

Habitual assistance at these functions on the part of the same religious would not be prohibited as the subject matter of contracts within the competence of the local superior, provided that proper safeguards are maintained to protect religious discipline.[68] It does not seem to be compatible with the office of the Master of Clerics in a religious house of studies to be separated from his charge in order to give retreats habitually. Consequently, even provincial superiors seem to be prohibited by the general law from making such services the subject matter of a contract.

The assignment of priests for the purpose of giving missions in

[66] ". . . praesertim in dioecesi in qua degunt."—Canon 608, § 1.

[67] Vermeersch-Creusen, *Epitome,* I, n. 710; Coronata, *Institutiones,* I, n. 615; Augustine, *Commentary,* III, 322.

[68] Canon 608, § 1.

parishes seems to be reserved to the provincial rather than to the local superior, since this duty assumes the aspect of a continuous charge. Contracts for missions, therefore, seem to be reserved to the provincial if the constitutions do not grant this authority to the local superiors. In practice, a religious is usually assigned to a Mission Band for this purpose. His charge, therefore, appears to partake of the nature of a full time duty separate from any office in the religious house. It is comparable to a full time duty such as that of an assistant superior or a treasurer, rather than one which could be combined with either of these two offices. Hence, this assignment falls within the competence of the provincial and his council, since it is a selection of a member of a province for a particular work.

The Code is silent as to the amount and type of reimbursement to be offered to religious in consideration for their services. This factor must be determined by custom, local legislation and, in particular, by the circumstances attendant upon each case. Attention should be directed towards the labor and inconvenience involved, and with a view to reimbursement for expenses incurred in travel. The celebration of the two late Masses in parishes on Sundays or the preaching at Masses celebrated by some other priest, involves a certain amount of inconvenience for the religious. A just recompense for this added inconvenience is generally deemed to be due him. The determination of this recompense is left to the local ordinary, and may well be the matter of particular legislation in diocesan synods.[60] In the absence of positive synodol legislation local custom and equity must determine the norm to be followed.

Article 4. Rights and Privileges of Religious in Contracts

The Code grants religious certain rights in virtue of the erection of a house of their congregation in a diocese. The house becomes a

[60] The Diocesan Statutes of the Diocese of Toledo have specific legislation on this point. "No. 397. Priests who assist in parochial work on Saturday and Sunday and who receive no regular salary from another diocesan assignment shall receive fifteen ($15) dollars. If they assist Sunday only, they shall be remunerated with ten ($10) dollars; however, their traveling expenses shall be added thereto."—*Acta et Decreta Synodi Diocesanae Toletanae, Excellentissimo ac Reverendissimo Carolo Josepho Alter, Episcopo Toletano, Convocante ac*

juridical personality.[70] In clerical religious congregations the faculty to erect a church or a public oratory and to perform the sacred functions therein is included in the authorization to erect a religious house.[71]

In every contract the notion of consideration demands that certain sacrifices be made with a view to gaining the advantage of the contract. In the contract of sale, the purchaser is willing to sacrifice a specified amount of money in order to acquire a desirable property. By permitting a religious congregation to enter his diocese, the bishop suffers a diminution of authority in the sense that the religious are in varying degrees withdrawn from his jurisdiction. He makes this sacrifice in order to secure help in the carrying out of his apostolic mission, since he rightfully expects that the religious congregation will further the aims of the Catholic faith by its pious works. There may well be proposed here the question to what extent the religious congregation may sacrifice its rights in contracting for the erection of a house in a particular diocese.

A. *The Privilege of Exemption*

The most powerful of the privileges accorded to religious institutes is the privilege of exemption, by which certain religious organizations are withdrawn from the jurisdiction of the local ordinary. Regulars enjoy this privilege by law,[72] while some congregations have acquired it by concession from the Holy See.[73] Congregations of pontifical approval enjoy exemption in a restricted sense, namely, inasfar as the administration of the institute and of its religious discipline is with-

Praeside, A. D. 1941—as cited by Piontek, "A Gentleman's Agreement."—*The Jurist,* III (1943), 304.

[70] Coronata, *Institutiones,* I, n. 524.

[71] Canon 497, § 2.

[72] Canon 615. "Regulares, novitiis non exclusis, sive viri sive mulieres, cum eorum domibus et ecclesiis, exceptis iis monialibus quae Superioribus regularibus non subsunt, ab Ordinarii loci iurisdictione exempti sunt, praeterquam in casibus a iure expressis."

[73] Canon 500, § 1. "Subduntur quoque religiosi Ordinario loci, iis exceptis qui a Sede Apostolica exemptionis privilegium consecuti sunt, salva semper potestate quam ius etiam in eos locorum Ordinariis concedit."

drawn from the jurisdiction of the local ordinary.[74] The exemption of Regulars has been held by many authors to be a privilege contained in the Code.[75]

Exemption, being an institute of a papal law, produces its effect independently of the will of Regulars, since it is a status accorded to them by the Code. This status depends entirely upon the will of the Sovereign Pontiff, and like other laws it became obligatory when promulgated.[76] Since this status has been determined by the Holy See, it is not within the power of Regulars to renounce this privilege, and in consequence they are obliged to use it. The privilege of exemption is given not only for the common good of the particular institute, but also for the good of religion in general. Renunciation of the privilege by Regulars would be the equivalent of withdrawing themselves from the immediate jurisdiction of the Holy See in favor of submission to the immediate jurisdiction of the local ordinary.[77]

Exemption is granted not so much in favor of the exempt as in favor of the Apostolic See, for the sake of furthering the supernatural end of the Universal Church and of each particular diocese.[78] Hence its renunciation would be prejudicial not only to those who possess it but also to the Church as a whole. It is not a private privilege to be renounced by an individual superior,[79] even though certain benefits would accrue to the exempt community through its renunciation. Not even the community as a whole may renounce it, since it would then be detrimental to the interests of others who might be expected to relinquish their privilege in order to gain other benefits.[80]

[74] Schaefer, *De Religiosis*, n. 419; Prümmer, *Manuale Iuris Canonici*, q. 239.

[75] Ojetti, *Commentarium*, II, 302; Maroto, *Institutiones*, II, 291; Melo, *De Exemptione Regularium*, The Catholic University of America Canon Law Studies, n. 12 (Washington, D. C.: The Catholic University of America, 1921), p. 32; O'Brien, *The Exemption of Religious in Church Law*, p. 10.

[76] O'Brien, *op. cit.*, p. 12.

[77] Michiels, *Normae Generales Iuris Canonici* (2 vols., Lublin: Universitas Catholica, 1929), II, 401.

[78] Schmalzgrueber, Lib. III, tit. 13, n. 112.

[79] Canon 72, § 2.

[80] "Nec ipsi communitati seu coetui integrum est renuntiare privilegio sibi dato per modum legis, vel si renuntiatio cedat in Ecclesiae aliorumve praeiudicium." Canon 72, § 4.

The Holy See has constituted itself as the exclusive authority over exempt religious institutes, and it is obviously, as just established, not within their competence to withdraw themselves from the immediate subjection to that supreme authority in favor of immediate subjection to a lesser one.[81] In every case and by the general provision of the law, the cessation of privileges is an accomplished fact only when the renunciation is accepted by the competent superior.[82] Since the Holy See is the grantor of the privilege of exemption, any contract in which a renunciation of this privilege were contemplated would have to be submitted to the Holy See for final approval.

Issuance of orders contravening the rights of exempt religious would be an illicit and invalid use of authority on the part of the local ordinary, and the religious would not be bound to submit to such orders.[83] Superiors of exempt religious institutes have an obligation to resist any illegal interference with their office, and hence they cannot tolerate any violation of their right of exemption. Since acts which violate this right are illicit and invalid, even the avoidance of greater harm or of serious inconvenience would not offer a sufficient excuse to justify their submission.[84]

The fact that the exemption granted to certain religious congregations, such as the Redemptorists and the Passionists, is given by way of privilege rather than in consequence of law does not lessen their obligation to use it in behalf of the congregation and of religion as a whole. It cannot be regarded as a privilege granted in favor of the congregation only, nor can it, as a consequence, be considered merely as a convenience to be used or forsaken as circumstances vary. The congregation cannot relinquish it in order to gain a present good or make it the consideration of a contract. Although the Code grants the bishop the right to append certain conditions upon the concession of the permission to erect a religious house in his diocese, he cannot place conditions contrary to the privilege of exemption, and the exempt religious institute cannot acquiesce in such conditions. In

[81] O'Brien, *op. cit.*, p. 12.

[82] "Privilegia cessant per renunciationem a competente Superiore acceptam." —Canon 72, § 1.

[83] Melo, *op. cit.*, p. 34.

[84] O'Brien, *op. cit.*, p. 13.

order that such a condition may be placed in a contract, the permission of the Holy See will have to be obtained.[85]

B. *Renunciation of the Right to a Church or Public Oratory*

In contracting for the erection of a school or other religious house in his diocese, the local ordinary is aware that certain privileges accrue to the religious house by virtue of the permission given to begin this new work. While desiring that the religious house be erected in order that salutary results for the fostering of religion may follow, the local ordinary may also have misgivings as to the possible clashes which may arise between the new establishment and ecclesiastical works already functioning in his diocese. According to canon 497, § 2,[86] permission having been obtained to erect a house of a clerical congregation, the religious automatically acquire permission to erect a church or public oratory. Since a church is destined for the use of the faithful,[87] and a public oratory for their use at least during the time of religious services,[88] conflicts may arise between the local parish and the church or public oratory of the religious congregation. The faithful may be drawn to the services of the religious congregation to the detriment of their own parish church.

The local ordinary is at liberty to grant the minimum which the law requires by conceding permission for a public oratory only. This follows from the disjunctive construction of the canon, in which either a church or a public oratory is permitted.[89] Since no exceptions are

[85] Prümmer, *Manuale Iuris Canonici,* q. 181; Schaefer, *De Religiosis,* n. 84.

[86] "Constituendae novae domus permissio facultatem secumfert pro religionibus clericalibus habendi ecclesiam vel publicum oratorium domui adnexum, salvo praescripto can. 1162, § 4, et sacra ministeria peragendi, servatis de iure servandis; pro omnibus religionibus, pia opera exercendi religionis propria, salvis conditionibus in ipsa permissione appositis."

[87] Canon 1161.

[88] Canon 1188, § 2, 1°.

[89] Larraona, "Commentarium Codicis"—*CpR,* V (1924), 427; cf. Flanagan, *The Canonical Erection of Religious Houses,* The Catholic University of America Canon Law Studies, n. 179 (Washington, D. C.: The Catholic University of America Press, 1943), p. 83. Oesterle (*Praelectiones Iuris Canonici,* I, 246) contends that the religious congregation decides this status.

permitted in the law itself, it appears that no condition derogating this privilege is permitted.[90]

The omission, in the canon which guarantees this right, of any clause permitting the local ordinary to derogate this privilege is apparently intentional, for other limiting clauses and conditions do appear in the same canon. For instance, the approval of the local ordinary is necessary for the erection of the religious church or oratory in a particular location.[91] Moreover, a limitation upon the exercise of the pious works of the religious congregation is proposed as a possibility in the final clause of canon 497, § 2. Consequently such a limitation could enter into a contract, imposed by the local ordinary, and accepted by the religious congregation.[92]

The condition prescribing that the congregation of clerical religious seek permission for the approbation of the proposed site of the church or public oratory in no way diminishes their right to possess a place of worship itself. This provision is rather an indication that the legislator foresaw the possibility of conflicts arising between the rights of the parish and the religious church. It is an effort to make in anticipation an equitable adjustment of adverse claims, so that the rights of both parties may be safeguarded. The reason for the investigation prior to the granting of permission for the erection of a new church is clearly stated in canon 1162, § 3, i. e., the protection for churches already existing in the vicinity.[93]

In order to obviate the possibility of difficulties arising from any conflict of rights as possessed by the religious church on the one hand and the parish church on the other, it has been suggested that the religious may spontaneously renounce the use of their right to a

[90] Wernz-Vidal, *Ius Canonicum,* III, n. 77; Coronata, *Institutiones,* I, n. 524; Chelodi, *Ius de Personis,* n. 249; Schaefer, *De Religiosis,* n. 84; Augustine, *Commentary,* III, 89; Melo, *De Exemptione Regularium,* p. 125; Fanfani, *De Iure Religiosorum,* n. 21; Flanagan, *The Canonical Erection of Religious Houses,* p. 82.

[91] Canons 1162, § 4; 497, § 2.

[92] ". . . pro omnibus religionibus, pia opera exercendi religionis propria, salvis conditionibus in ipsa permissione appositis"—Canon 497, § 2.

[93] "Ne nova ecclesia ceteris iam existentibus detrimentum afferat"; cf. Melo, *De Exemptione Regularium,* p. 125.

church or public oratory before erecting the religious house.[94] It may consequently be inquired as pertinent to this dissertation, whether the religious community may renounce the use of this right in order to secure the local ordinary's permission to erect a religious house. It seems that this alternative does not offer a juridical solution, since the religious superior is not competent to renounce this privilege or its use for the reason that it is granted by the law of the Code itself. The Code states that the permission to erect a religious house brings with it the additional right to have a church or a public oratory.

From the wording of canon 497, § 2, these two factors seem to be inseparable as cause and effect. The privilege is acquired automatically as something independent of the will of the one acquiring it, and the religious congregation is not at liberty to relinquish the use of the privilege, since it is not conceded for its private good alone. The acquisition of the privilege is the corollary of the permission received. It seems, then, to take on the aspect of a privilege given *per modum legis*, and as such the religious congregation becomes powerless to renounce it or its use.[95] Furthermore, this renunciation could very easily prejudice the rights of others by establishing a precedent whereby all religious congregations seeking authorization to erect a house would be expected to make a spontaneous renunciation of the use of their right.

The objection against the use of this right, namely, the fear that people might be drawn to the services of the religious church and that a loss of alms would be sustained by the parish church, is not confined to any particular territory. Wherever parish churches and religious houses exist in the same neighborhood, the identical contingencies are present. If the use of the right could be renounced by one congregation, it might become the habitual practice to expect all congregations to renounce the use of the right before the permission to erect a religious house is conceded. In this way a right which the Code grants would be rendered absolutely useless.

The legislator gave the privilege of having a church or a public oratory to clerical religious only. The same privilege is not conceded

[94] Flanagan, *The Canonical Erection of Religious Houses*, p. 83.

[95] Canon 72, § 4.

to lay religious, even though they possess the privilege of exemption. The reason for the granting of this privilege exclusively to clerical religious congregations can be explained in the legislator's realization that the possession of a church or of a public oratory is necessary for the full attainment of the clerical organization's ends. At least a public oratory is necessary for the fulfillment of the choir obligation in some religious institutes such as the Franciscans.[96] Augustine (1872-1943) found it difficult to imagine a Benedictine community without a public oratory.[97]

As to clerical congregations of simple vows, the privilege of a church or of a public oratory as connected with their houses is new with the Code. In the former law, although the erection of a house had been authorized, religious in simple vows, whether clerical or lay, had to seek an additional permission in order to establish a chapel.[98] Canon 6 offers the reasons for the various departures from the former discipline, in that such changes are considered opportune. The legislator's reasons for the amplification of the privilege in favor of clerical religious organizations must have been weighty to make such a far-reaching change in Canon Law. Since the right of having a church or a public oratory is conceded to religious institutes of clerics only, the granting of this right must have been induced by the consideration that it is necessary for the complete exercise of the clerical religious vocation.

It was declared in the former law that the objection against the erection of a religious house on the ground that people might be drawn away from the parish church, and that a consequent reduction in alms contributed to that church might thus be sustained, did not constitute a sufficient reason for refusing to the religious the permission that authorizes them to erect a religious house.[99] The loss of parishioners and the loss of funds are the principal objections alleged today.

[96] The assumption that this obligation could be fulfilled in a semi-private oratory is, at best, doubtful. Cf. Bastnagel, "Status of Religious Oratory after Waiver of Right to Public Oratory,"—*The Jurist,* IV (1944), 155-156.

[97] *Commentary,* III, 89.

[98] Battandier, *Guide Canonique,* n. 512.

[99] S. C. Consist., 19 dec. 1772, as cited by Prümmer, *Manuale Iuris Canonici,* q. 357.

In view of the fact that the Code has extended the right of clerical religious to have a church or a public oratory, it seems that these objections should have even less validity now than formerly.

To grant a privilege unconditionally in the Code, and at the same time to relinquish its renunciation to a subordinate authority, or to permit a subordinate authority to urge that it be nullified by non-use, would jeopardize the position of all persons or institutes given privileges by the common law. According to the contrary line of reasoning, the local ordinary could suggest that priests spontaneously renounce their rights to officiate as prospective pastors at various parochial functions as allowed them by canon 462, as a condition for their appointment as pastors. It is obvious that this would be an unjustified restriction upon the rights and liberties granted to pastors by the Code.

This illustration is used in indication of a similar situation in places of contact between religious and local ordinaries. The history of the problems growing out of the privilege of exemption contains many sad stories of disputes in matters concerning jurisdiction. The Code has clearly tried—and not without success—to settle these questions in a juridically acceptable manner. The best basis for a peaceful settlement of the possible conflicts seems to be a ready acceptance by all parties of all the matters at issue as they have been regulated by the Code.

Both sides to the controversy, left to themselves, may err by making demands and claims that are not, by wise anticipation, sustained in the law. Both sides, therefore, would be most prudent in accepting the Code's provisions as a happy solution of problems that affect the good of souls so intimately. If the safeguards provided by the Code are not sufficient for the protection of parish rights, it seems that there are present admissibly weighty reasons to justify a petition for a papal dispensation, in order that the religious may cede their right or its use in a particular case.

C. *Acceptable Limitations*

Even apart from a papal dispensation, the prevention of conflict between the respective claims of the parish and the religious church seems to admit of a more equitable disposition than the wholesale renunciation of rights, or their use, on the part of the religious congregation. The prescription of canon 1162, § 4, gives the local ordinary the opportunity to forestall the danger of loss of revenue by the parish church. A contract could specify the location of the entrance to the church or the public oratory of the religious. In this way access to the place of worship could be determined in such manner that the faithful would find it inconvenient to foresake their parish church in favor of attendance at the services of the religious church.

The local ordinary is at liberty to impose restrictions upon the exercise of the pious works of the religious congregation.[100] Under this prerogative he could impose a condition in his agreement whereby the services at the religious church would be conducted at times when they would not conflict with the parish devotions. The time of Sunday Masses, for instance, could be so designated that they would be said at hours in which there was little likelihood that the people would be drawn away from their parish church.

Where great loss of revenue were feared, the following arrangement could be agreed upon to protect the parish church. The parish church could employ the envelope system for collections. Those attending the religious church or oratory could then be advised, by the agreement on the part of the religious, of their obligation to support their parish church, and urged to drop their envelopes which are designated for parish use into the collection basket of the religious church or oratory. The religious would thereupon assume the obligation of forwarding the parish contributions to the pastor of the parish church.

The legislator has evidently foreseen the possibilty of conflicts arising over the respective rights of various persons, and has afforded the means for an equitable solution in the law itself. The religious are permitted to exercise the sacred ministry, provided that it does not conflict with the rights of others, especially those of pastors.[101]

The local ordinary may also, if he deems it necessary in his contract with the religious, restrict the institute to one of its various works while excluding others mentioned in the constitutions of the

[100] Canon 497, § 2.

[101] Augustine, *Commentary,* III, 90.

congregation. He could limit a teaching congregation to accepting only pupils who intend to become members of that congregation.[102]

In dioceses where it is impossible for the local ordinary to establish his own seminary, he may admit a religious congregation for the purpose of establishing its own seminary, with a proviso in the contract that they agree also to instruct all the seminarians destined for the service of the diocese. In places where a Catholic university is located, the bishop could permit the establishment of a house of studies with a proviso in the contract that the religious were not to organize a curriculum of studies, but were to send all the students of that house to the Catholic university for their lectures.

In the case of an institute of Sisters who have the double aim of teaching and doing hospital work, it is within the power of the local ordinary to restrict them, in his contract with them, to one of these works. He could also similarly limit the number of boarders to be received in a school conducted by them, or require that the establishment be restricted to the service of persons of specified nationalities.[103] These and many other points in which specific contractual undertakings do not contravene the common law should be clearly incorporated in the contract before the bishop authorizes a particular foundation, or the religious agree to undertake a special work.

It is to be noted that the bishop should not proceed arbitrarily in imposing limitations but should be impelled by a grave and reasonable cause for his actions. Institutes which have obtained pontifical approval have an acquired right by virtue of that approval of founding houses universally, provided that they comply with the prescripts of the common law. Their mode of life and operation has been defined by the Holy See in its approval of their constitutions, and it would be imprudent for a bishop, without adequate reasons, to seek to impose conditions in his contracts with them, if such conditions would in any degree contravene the aims for which these institutes were established.[104]

[102] Coronata, *Institutiones*, I, n. 524.

[103] Creusen, *Religious Men and Women in the Code*, n. 39.

[104] Wernz-Vidal, *Ius Canonicum*, III, n. 76.

CHAPTER XI

APPLICATION OF THE NORMS TO CONTRACTS BETWEEN BISHOPS AND RELIGIOUS CONGREGATIONS

Article 1. Formal Requisites

In the absence of canonical provisions to demand any specific formalities in the making of a contract, the meeting of the minds on a particular matter, the proposal and acceptance, and the exchange of consent seem in themselves to be sufficient to make a contract binding upon both parties. In American Law, however, particular statutes determine the nature and the extent of the formalities required to be observed in the making of contracts. It has been declared that, in cases in which no such requisites are decreed by statute or arbitrary rule of law, a contract is valid independent of any formalities.[1]

No particular form of words is demanded for the validity of a contract in the absence of particular statutes legislating otherwise.[2] The promise may be determined from words, conduct or a combination of both.[3] Under the American system of law, the only formal contract in which the form is of the essence, is the contract under seal,[4] which is also called a covenant or specialty in which the seal raises the presumption of a consideration for the promise given.[5] All other contracts are considered parol, and their validity is based upon the consideration involved, whether the contract itself be oral or written.[6]

A contract is construed according to the intention of the contractors, whose agreement may be expressed in words, acts or relations from which the terms of contract may be implied.[7]

[1] McArdle v. Williams, 258 N. W., 818, 193 Minn. 433.

[2] Muse v. E. A. Whitney & Son, 56 S. W. (2d) 848, 227 Mo. App. 640.

[3] Greiner v. Greiner, 293 P. 759, 131 Kan. 760.

[4] Stabler v. Cowman, 7 Gill & J. 284.

[5] Williston, *The Law of Contracts*, I, n. 5.

[6] Stabler v. Cowman, 7 Gill & J. 284.

[7] Williston, *The Law of Contracts*, II, n. 602.

Civil law also presupposes that the agents of a corporation are acting with due authority and within the scope of that authority, and that they are acting in accordance with their by-laws. If the contract is made otherwise, it is invalid. The officers of the corporation are the joint possessors of the church property and are charged with the duty of executing contracts. In order to avoid personal liability, they must act as agents of a society which has a legal personality, and whatever contracts are entered into must be approved by the agents as a board by majority vote. The by-laws may demand certain consultations and approval analogous to those demanded by Canon Law.[8]

In Canon Law, the subject matter involved will usually demand that certain formalities be undergone. This is especially true when the contractants are representatives of moral persons of such rank as a diocese and a religious congregation. The Code has decreed that the bishop seek the advice or obtain the consent of his diocesan consultors in many affairs in the administration of his diocese.[9] The bishop is also bound to consult or obtain the consent of his board of administrators in many matters concerning the administration of the temporal goods of his diocese.[10]

The religious superior likewise has similar limitations placed upon his contractual capacity. Sometimes the common law states specifically that the consent of the superior's council is necessary for the validity of certain acts. This is true in administrative matters when there is question of the alienation of temporal goods whose value does not exceed thirty thousand lire or francs.[11]

More frequently, however, the determination of those cases in which the consent or advice of the council is necessary is left to the constitutions of individual institutes. The constitutions should state specifically those occasions in which the deliberative vote of the council is needed, and in these matters the superior is bound to follow the will of the majority in order to act validly. When the Code

[8] Zollmann, *American Church Law*, pp. 480, 483, 494.

[9] Canons 386, § 1; 388; 454, § 3; 895; 1358, § 2; 1428, § 1; 1520, § 1; 1532, § 3; 1541, § 2, 1° and 2°. Cf. *supra*, p. 84 et seq.

[10] Canons 1415, § 2; 1532, §§ 2, 3; 1541, § 2, 1°, 2°, and 3°. Cf. *supra*, p. 87 et seq.

[11] Canon 534, § 1.

or the constitutions do not state whether the vote of the council is deliberative or merely consultative, it suffices for the validity of the act to have consultation only.[12] Even in these cases, however, the rules of canon 162 concerning the convocation of the entire council must be followed.[13] So necessary is this convocation that many authors hold that its omission renders the act invalid, even though the Superior had obtained consent in other ways.[14]

If the Code or the constitutions demand that the entire council be heard, it seems that by analogy with canon 655, § 1, members may be substituted for those councillors who are unable to attend the session.[15] However, this substitution is not mandatory unless the constitutions specifically demand that the entire council be in session in a given case.[16]

When the Code or the constitutions prescribe that the council be consulted or heard only, there is no obligation on the part of the superior to follow the advice given. If their opinion is unanimous, although prudence demands that due consideration be given this unanimity, the superior cannot be held to have acted invalidly if he should have acted contrary to the advice given.[17] The Code is itself quite explicit in demanding that the superior have weighty reasons in acting contrary to the advice of his councillors, especially when there are several who express the same opinion.[18]

The common law does not determine the number of councillors, their mode of election, their necessary qualifications, or the duration of their term of office. These details are left to the constitutions of

[12] Coronata, *Institutiones*, I, n. 541; Fanfani, *De Iure Religiosorum* n. 467; Schaefer, *De Religiosis*, n. 155.

[13] Wernz-Vidal, *Ius Canonicum*, II, n. 33; Vermeersch-Creusen, *Epitome*, I, n. 197 bis; Fanfani, *De Iure Religiosorum*, n. 66; Creusen, *Religious Men and Women in the Code*, n. 98.

[14] Chelodi, *Ius de Personis*, n. 252; Goyeneche, "Consultationes," *CpR*, III (1922), 215; Coronata, *Institutiones*, I, n. 541; Ojetti, *Commentarium*, II, 183.

[15] Coronata (*Institutiones*, I, n. 541) so declares, arguing from the *Normae of 1901*, n. 273.

[16] Goyeneche, "Consultationes," *CpR*, III (1922), 333-335; Schaefer, *De Religiosis*, n. 155.

[17] Canon, 105, 1°; cf. Coronata, *Institutiones*, I, n. 153.

[18] Canon 105, 1°; cf. Augustine, *Commentary*, II, 35.

each institute. The Code does prescribe, however, that councils be established for the Supreme Moderator, for the Provincial and for the local superior in a religious house set up in its full juridical organization (*domus formata*).[19]

According to the mind of the Code, even local houses which are not *domus formatae* should establish councils also.[20] This is a licit deduction, first, from the nature of the office of a councillor, which is to provide advice in affairs of government and, secondly, from the fact that the word *saltem* is used in canon 516, § 1. The local superior of a small house is no less in need of advisers than are the superiors of *domus formatae*. However, in the absence of explicit provisions in the Code or in particular law, the strict necessity for their institution cannot be urged.

Concerning the number, the method of election, the qualifications, and the place of residence of the various types of councils, the *Normae* of 1901 and the Instruction of the Sacred Congregation of Religious as issued in 1909 indicate specific rules. The General Council should have at least four members in congregations with twelve capitulars or more, but two members are permitted in those congregations which have a smaller number of capitulars. The councillors' term of office in the General Council is three years.[21] They should be elected by the General Chapter.[22] They should be at least thirty five years old and in perpetual vows.[23] The place of residence designated for the General Council is identified with that of the Supreme Moderator in the principal house of the congregation. Two may live elsewhere, provided that they are easily accessible when their advice is needed.[24]

Since these norms do not contravene the present law, they may still be followed, even though they do not now constitute strict law.[25] The constitutions are now the ultimate norm in regard to members of all types of councils, even the General Council, in reference to

[19] Canon 516, § 1.

[20] Coronata, *Institutiones*, I, n. 541.

[21] S. C. de Rel., instr. *Inter ea*, 30 iul. 1909—*Fontes*, n. 4394.

[22] *Normae of 1901*, n. 242.

[23] *Normae of 1901*, n. 240.

[24] *Normae of 1901*, n. 276.

[25] Coronata, *Institutiones*, I, n. 541.

their number and qualifications, the method of their election and, with the exception of certain specific provisions of the Code, the determination of the cases in which the Council's consent or advice must be obtained. The Code, as just intimated, has determined certain matters of administration in which the consent of the various types of councils is necessary,[26] but particular constitutions may prescribe other matters for the administration of which it is also required.

Regarding the method of the election of Provincial and General Councillors, the nature of their office seems to require that they be chosen by the Chapter, and not by the superior alone. Since they are the official advisers of the superior, if he had a free hand in their appointment, the objectivity of their advice would conceivably be suspect. By choosing those who would accede to his views each time that consent or advice was required by law, the superior could frustrate the law which calls for their institution. Such is neither the intention of the legislator nor the purpose for which they were instituted.[27] It is a practice which is certainly alien to the reason for which the law was prescribed, and this is the more evident from a comparison with the former law, which permitted that the superior alone should choose his councillors.

The methods of election are diverse in the various older institutes, but in congregations of more recent institution the local Councillors are usually designated by the Provincial and his Council.[28] The General Council is usually elected in the same chapter in which the Supreme Moderator is chosen, and the Provincial Council is elected in the same chapter in which the Provincial is chosen,[29] although the Provincial Council, under some constitutions, is appointed by the Supreme Moderator.[30]

The affairs in which the advice or consent of the council is necessary should be minutely determined by the constitutions of each

[26] Canons 516, § 4; 534, § 1; 575, § 2; 650, § 1.

[27] Augustine, *Commentary,* III, 149.

[28] Larraona, "Consultationes," *CpR,* V (1924), 225.

[29] Vermeersch-Creusen, *Epitome,* I, n. 584.

[30] Wernz-Vidal, *Ius Canonicum,* III, n. 155.

institute. The *Normae* of 1901 [81] stated that the councillors had a vote in the matters of greater importance. Among these affairs, the following may be appropriately enumerated as involving the intervention of Provincial or General Councils: (1) The erection of new houses with the consent of the local ordinary and, when there is question of mission territory, of the Sacred Congregation for the Propagation of the Faith.[82] (2) The suppression of existing houses with the permission of the local ordinary and of the Sacred Congregation of Religious. Now only the permission of the local ordinary is needed for the suppression of houses of non-exempt congregations unless there is question of the only house of the institute, or unless the house exists in territory subject to the Sacred Congregation for the Propagation of the Faith. For the suppression of a house in an exempt institute, permission of the Holy See is required.[83] (3) The erection of a new house of novitiate. In congregations of pontifical approval the permission of the Holy See is required for this action also.[84] (4) The transfer of the novitiate to another place. (5) The erection of a new province. The permission of the Holy See is necessary for the erection of new provinces, or for the division of old ones in congregations of pontifical approval.[85] (6) The transfer of the residence of the Supreme Moderator and his Council. (7) Alienation.

To this list may be added the undertaking of any project for which the permission of the Holy See is necessary. In this category would fall those contracts between a bishop and a religious congregation by virtue of which the religious congregation assumes the care of a parish either perpetually or for a time. The relationships between a parish and a religious institute fall into two general classes: (1) *Pleno iure* effected unions, in which the parish is united to the moral person of the religious institute with regard to both its temporalities and its spiritualities; and (2) *Semipleno iure* effected unions, in which the parish is united to the moral person of the

[81] N. 271.

[82] Cf. canon 497, § 1.

[83] Canon 498.

[84] Canon 554, § 1.

[85] Canon 494, § 1.

religious institute either regarding its temporalities or its spiritual matters, but not as to both, or at least not perpetually.[86]

Since these relationships between a parish and a religious congregation constitute the principal matter of contracts between bishops and religious congregations, a detailed examination of the manner in which they are effected, and of the juridical effects of each, will be discussed in the succeeding articles.

Article 2. Contracts Concerning *Pleno Iure* Effected Unions

Of themselves parochial benefices are secular benefices. Therefore, in a secular parish only rarely and by special dispensation of the Holy See are religious permitted to be pastors. An exception is made in favor of mission territories. The ordinaries of mission territories have special authority to appoint religious to parishes in order to supply the needs of the faithful when there are not enough priests available among the secular clergy to meet all the territorial demands.[87]

Canon 297 declares that prefects and vicars apostolic have the right to constrain religious, even those of exempt congregations who live within their territory, to undertake the care of souls in case there are not sufficient members of the secular clergy to cope with the situation. In this case the prefect or vicar apostolic has only the obligation of consulting the religious superior without being bound to accede to his objections.

The Council of Trent made the distinction between secular and religious benefices, and declared that to the former only secular priests could be appointed, and to the latter only religious, whenever there existed a *pleno iure* effected union.[88]

In order to have a true religious parish, the parish must be incorporated or united with the religious house. Since this changes the nature of the parochial benefice in that it is transformed from a sec-

[86] Canon 1425, §§ 1, 2; Coronata, *Institutiones,* I, n. 469. Augustine (*Commentary,* II, 515) mentions a *plenissimo iure* effected union. But this kind of union is simply the one that obtains in connection with an *abbatia nullius.*

[87] S. C. Prop. Fide, decr. 9 dec. 1920—*AAS,* XIII (1921), 17.

[88] Conc. Trident., sess. XIV, *de ref.,* c. 11.

ular to a religious parish, only the Holy See is empowered to perform this juridical act.[39]

To effect this transformation, the following procedure is outlined. First, the boundaries of the parish are agreed upon by the local ordinary with the consent of his diocesan consultors[40] and the religious congregation. According to the *Normae* of 1901, the competent superior is the Supreme Moderator with the consent of his council.[41] Next, conditions binding both contracting parties are to be clearly specified. The bishop must state the reason for requesting this union, and explain the reasons proposed. The document of transfer must be signed by both contracting parties, and the seal of each party impressed thereon. A copy of the contract is to be kept by both contractants.

The local ordinary then submits to the Sacred Congregation of the Council a copy of the contract, outlining the reasons for the transfer, and stating also that the consent of the diocesan consultors has been given and that the other interested parties have been heard on the matter. The religious superior submits to the Sacred Congregation of Religious a copy of the contract, in which he states his reasons for accepting the parish, and indicates also the fact that he has acted with the consent (if the constitutions so demand; otherwise, the advice) of the chapter or councillors. Both documents may be sent to the Sacred Congregation of Religious, which in turn sends the document of the local ordinary to the Sacred Congregation of the Council. In the latter case the instruments are sent in separate envelopes. Both requests are directed to the Roman Pontiff with the salutation, *Beatissime Pater.* If an affirmative reply is received from the Holy See, the full union is effected, and the religious house acquires the vested title of pastor in relation to the parish.

The Sacred Congregation of the Council makes this declaration, and then a copy of the indult is to be given to the religious congregation to be preserved along with the contract in the archives of the congregation. The local ordinary sends this copy to the religious

[39] Canons 1422; 1423, § 2.

[40] *Acta et Decreta Concilii Plenarii Baltimorensis III*, n. 20.

[41] *Normae of 1901*, n. 271.

superior with the annotation, *Concordat cum originali,* followed by his signature and seal. The original instrument granting the indult is kept in the diocesan archives.[42]

The transformation from a secular to a religious benefice obtains only in the case of a *pleno iure* effected union. The parish itself is then a religious parish, although the church need not be a religious church. This determination should be made at the time of entering into the contract. The local ordinary could specify that in the *pleno iure* effected union he is turning over to the religious congregation the parish only, and that the church itself is not ceded to them. In this case the church cannot properly be called a religious church.[43]

When the union has taken place, the parochial office becomes shorn of its own erstwhile juridical personality, and is thereupon incorporated with the juridical personality of the religious house to which it is united.[44] This union does not necessarily imply that all the missions which are attached to the religious house, or which are served by the members of the religious community, are also incorporated in the same manner. The document drawn up by the local ordinary and the religious superior may specify that these missions also form a part of the union with the religious house. If they are attached to the religious parish, then those who attend to the care of souls must give an account of their administration to the actual pastor of the religious church. If they are given over to the charge of the religious community, but not through a full union of the parish with the religious house, the priests attending to the care of souls are not bound to give an account to the actual pastor of the religious church. In this event their canonical status is vague. A possible remedy is to make accessory benefices, subsidiary vicarages or chaplaincies of them, and to attach them to a canonically established parish. The pastor of the parish would then be responsible for the administration of the accessory benefices, and

[42] Cf. Coronata, *Institutiones,* I, n. 469.

[43] *Schaefer, De Religiosis,* n. 499; Coronata, *Institutiones,* I, n. 469; Nebreda, "Studia Canonica," *CpR,* VII (1926), 263; Reilly, *Visitation of Religious,* p. 130.

[44] Wernz-Vidal, *Ius Canonicum,* III, n. 414.

those who have the care of souls in them would be bound to make a report to him.[45]

When a union is effected *pleno iure,* both the office and the benefice attach to the religious house, and this moral person is constituted as bearing the title of pastor.[46] The parochial benefice and the office of pastor can never be considered vacant, inasmuch as its incumbent, the religious house, lives on with permanency of duration.[47] The moral person, the religious house, acquires the vested title of pastor of the parish along with the obligation of constituting a priest of the congregation as the vicar who will exercise the actual care of souls.[48]

The superior authorized to present the candidate as the congregation's vicar in the actual exercise of the care of souls is determined by the constitutions of each institute. It would seem that this power would be one of those reserved to the provincial superior, since it is an assignment of prolonged duration. If the constitutions provide otherwise by restricting or extending the superior's powers, they are, of course, to be followed.[49] The priest presented must belong to the congregation to which the parish is united, since only members of the religious institute to which a benefice is united are eligible for that benefice.[50]

In virtue solely of his nomination by the superior the candidate does not obtain possession of the parish. He must first be approved by the local ordinary, who may submit him to an examination in order to determine whether he possesses the necessary qualifications of learning and piety. However, the bishop is not obliged to subject the candidate to an examination, if he is morally certain that the latter possesses the requisite qualities for the office. On the other hand, if the candidate is found to be fit for the office, the bishop

[45] Augustine, *The Canonical and Civil Status of Catholic Parishes in the United States* (St. Louis: B. Herder Book Co., 1926), pp. 141-143.

[46] Canon 452, § 2.

[47] Schaefer, *De Religiosis,* n. 500; Fanfani; *De Iure Religiosorum,* n. 447. Wernz-Vidal, *Ius Canonicum,* III, n. 414.

[48] Canons 452, § 2; 471, § 1.

[49] Canon 456; cf. Augustine, *Commentary,* II, 526.

[50] Canons 456, 1422; cf. Fanfani, *De Iure Religiosorum,* n. 447.

is obliged to give his approval. He may not demand that the religious presented by his superior be subjected to a *concursus,* since this is not prescribed by the Code, nor was it favored by the old law.[51] Having been approved by the bishop, the religious candidate must pronounce the Profession of Faith before the bishop or his delegate.[52] To this Profession of Faith must be added also the Oath against Modernism.[53]

It is disputed whether a formal act of taking possession of the parochial office is required in the case of the religious vicar. Some authors contend, that since the true pastor is the religious house itself, this procedure is not necessary. It is maintained by them that the institution by the local ordinary is sufficient and that from the moment when it is given the religious obtains the care of souls.[54] Others maintain that the common law of taking possession of the parochial benefice must be followed.[55]

Institutio is described in canon 148, § 1 as a process of approval by the bishop subsequent to presentation by one having the right of patronage. The appointment of the religious vicar is not comprehended by the word *institutio* as used in canon 148, § 1 since there is not a question of the right of patronage in the presentation of the religious vicar.[56] A similar process is mentioned in canon 456 in reference to the canonical institution of the religious vicar.

Canon 461 provides that the pastor obtains the care of souls from the moment he takes possession of the benefice according to the norms outlined in canons 1443-1445.[57] Canon 1443 forbids

[51] Augustine, *Commentary,* II, 526.

[52] Canon 1406, § 1, 7°.

[53] S. C. S. Off., decr. 22 mart. 1918—*AAS,* X (1918), 136.

[54] Fanfani, *De Iure Religiosorum,* n. 447; Schaefer, *De Religiosis,* n. 500; Vermeersch-Creusen, *Epitome,* I, n. 502.

[55] Coronata, *Institutiones,* I, n. 635; Goyeneche, "Consultationes"—*CpR,* VI (1925), 484-486.

[56] The right of patronage is described in canon 1448: "Ius patronatus est summa privilegiorum, cum quibusdam oneribus, quae ex Ecclesiae concessione competunt fundatoribus catholicis ecclesiae, cappellae aut beneficii, vel etiam eis qui ab illis causam habent."

[57] "Curam animarum parochus obtinet a momento captae possessionis ad normam can. 1443-1445. . . ."

anyone from taking possession of a non-consistorial benefice unless he is placed in possession of the benefice by the local ordinary or his delegate. This act on the part of the local ordinary is called the *institutio corporalis,* and is sometimes referred to as "installation." [58]

While it is true that the parochial benefice does not become vacant inasmuch as the religious house is the incumbent of the benefice, canon 461 clearly has reference to that pastor who has the care of souls. Hence, in the case of the religious parish, the religious vicar is referred to and not the religious house in which the title of pastor vests. In so far as reference is had to the pastor having the care of souls, religious parishes become vacant in the same way as other parishes. This is evident from the wording of canon 472, 1°, which makes explicit reference to a religious parish.[59] The ecclesiastical office to which the care of souls is attached may be said, therefore, to become vacant by the death, removal or resignation of the religious vicar.

Further, canon 451, § 2, 2°, declares that parochial vicars are held to be equal to pastors in the eyes of the law with regard to their rights and duties. Canon 471, § 4 provides that the religious vicar has all the rights and duties of other pastors. There seems, therefore, to be no valid reason to excuse the religious vicar from the obligation of the *institutio corporalis* by the local ordinary or his delegate as provided for by canon 1444, § 1. In the United States there is no form of taking possession of the parish prescribed by the Plenary Councils of Baltimore. The determination of the procedure to be followed is left to the statutes of each diocese or to the customary usage followed in each.[60]

The bishop obtains the right of visitation, jurisdiction, and correction over the religious vicar in all those matters which pertain to the care of souls. The religious vicar is subject to the bishop in all things in which a secular pastor is responsible to him in his parochial office. On the other hand, the question of his religious ob-

[58] Woywod, *Commentary,* II, n. 1451; Vermeersch-Creusen, *Epitome,* I, n. 502.

[59] "Vacante paroecia: Ordinarius loci in ea quamprimum constituat idoneum vicarium oeconomum, de consensu Superioris, si de religioso agatur. . . ."

[60] Woywod, *Commentary,* I, n. 337.

servance is under the supervision and correction of his religious superior.[61]

The bishop has the right of personal visitation over the religious vicar and his assistants, and he may inquire of them whether they perform their parochial duties properly, and whether they have fulfilled the other obligations of parish priests, such as attendance at the conferences of the deanery. He may also inquire into their way of life to discern whether there is anything in their mode of life contrary to their moral obligations. Regarding their sacred ministry, the bishop may inquire whether they have taken proper care of the sick and the dying, whether the *Missa pro populo* has been said on the appointed days, and whether they have observed the law of residence.[62]

The bishop may also visit the parish church, even though the church itself belongs to an exempt congregation, and may inquire concerning those matters which have reference to the care of souls. Hence, he has the right and duty to make the following the subject of his visitation: the altar at which the Blessed Sacrament is reserved, the tabernacle, the sacred vestments and vessels destined for parish use, the parish cemetery, and the bell tower.[63]

A. *Juridical Status of the Religious Vicar*

By his assignment as the vicar in actual charge of souls, the religious takes on, as it were, a dual personality. He must fulfill certain offices in his person as a religious, and others as vicar in the care of souls. As a religious he is subject to his superior; as pastor he is subject to the bishop of the diocese.

As a religious the parochial vicar is still bound by his vows and by the requirements of the constitutions of his institute, in so far as their observance is compatible with his parochial office.[64] Should

[61] Canon 631, § 1.

[62] Fanfani, *De Iure Religiosorum,* n. 449; Coronata, *Institutiones,* I, n. 624.

[63] Melo, *De Exemptione Regularium,* p. 154; Coronata, *Institutiones,* I, n. 624; Goyeneche, "Consultationes"—*CpR,* VI (1925), 359-360.

[64] "Religiosus, qui paroeciam regit sive titulo parochi sive titulo vicarii, manet adstrictus ad observationem votorum et constitutionum, quatenus haec observatio potest cum muneris sui officiis consistere."—Canon 630, § 1.

a conflict arise between the diverse offices, between his attendance, for example, at a religious exercise and a parochial duty, the parochial duty takes precedence.[65]

In matters of religious observance, he is entirely under the supervision of the religious superior. Concerning these matters the religious superior is free to inquire, to the exclusion of any interference by the local ordinary. In cases wherein correction or punishment are necessary for the violation of any religious observance, the superior determines the manner and extent of the disciplinary measures to be taken.[66] The religious vicar may, on the other hand, freely dispatch and receive correspondence concerning parochial affairs. These letters are free from the inspection of the superior. All other correspondence is subject to the superior's supervision, since this inspection is not an infringement on the parochial office.[67] It cannot be deduced from the wording of canon 630 itself whether the parochial vicar has the right to a separate safe for the safekeeping of his correspondence, or whether he has a right to a separate key to the common safe.[68]

Without prejudice to the exercise of his parochial ministry, the vicar is bound to obtain the permission of his religious superior before leaving the house if the constitutions of the congregation have determined that this procedure is to be followed by its members.[69] Should the constitutions of his institute demand that before leaving the religious house the religious request the blessing of his superior, the religious vicar would obviously be bound to the performance of this act of submission as often as it did not interfere with his parochial office. Common sense demands that the vicar be given by legitimate dispensation a certain amount of liberty in these matters, in order that he may the better perform his parish duties. He should be conceded habitually wider faculties in this regard than the rest of his confrères, who have no parochial obligations. This concession of wider faculties should be given him even though they

[65] Schaefer, *De Religiosis*, n. 501.
[66] Coronata, *Institutiones*, I, n. 625.
[67] Fanfani, *De Iure Religiosorum*, n. 451.
[68] Larraona, "Annotationes," *CpR*, II (1921), 183-185.
[69] Schaefer, *De Religiosis*, n. 501.

may not seem absolutely necessary for the exercise of his duties as pastor.[70]

Regarding his subjection to the local ordinary, the Code states that the religious as vicar is subject immediately and entirely to the bishop, and that the latter has the right of visitation, jurisdiction and correction over him. This holds true even though the vicar has his parochial charge in the house where the major superior has his ordinary residence.[71] Some authors have understood this to mean that the right of exemption is thereby abrogated for such religious parishes.[72] But most of the authors have maintained that the privilege of exemption in such parishes still holds. The bishop has, however, the right of personal visitation over the religious who is actually in charge of the parish.[73]

Coronata states that this determination of personal subjection of the religious vicar in the residential houses of major superiors was necessary, since it constitutes a departure from the old law according to which such pastors were not subject to the local ordinary.[74] The deduction that the right of the local ordinary is a personal one which affects only the vicar is consonant with the wording of the canon which mentions the pastor alone, and says nothing regarding the religious parish.[75]

The matters in which the religious vicar is subject to the local ordinary have already been partially indicated.[76] With regard to

[70] Fanfani, *De Iure Religiosorum,* n. 451.

[71] Canon 631, § 1.

[72] Wernz-Vidal, *Ius Canonicum,* III, n. 415; Biederlack-Führich, *De Religiosis,* n. 160.

[73] Schaefer, *De Religiosis,* n. 506; Vermeersch-Creusen, *Epitome,* I, n. 730; Coronata, *Institutiones,* I, nn. 624, 635.

[74] Conc. Trident., sess. XXV. *de regularibus,* c. 11; Coronata, *Institutiones,* I, n. 635.

[75] "Idem parochus vel vicarius religiosus . . . subest . . . iurisdictioni, visitationi, et correctioni Ordinarii loci. . . ."—Canon 631, § 1. The local ordinary has limited rights in regard to his visitation of the parish church itself, and such as he enjoys concern simply those matters which are connected with the care of souls. All these rights were conceded to the local ordinary under the former discipline by the papal constitution *Firmandis,* issued by Pope Benedict XIV on November 6, 1744.—*Fontes,* n. 349.

[76] *Supra,* pp. 131, 132.

them the Code states in canon 631, § 1, that in this subjection the religious vicar does not differ from other pastors. Hence he is bound to all the obligations imposed upon secular pastors in canons 460-470, 471, § 1, and § 4. He is bound upon the occasion of the visitation by the local ordinary to prove his legitimate title to the parish, and to undergo an examination on that occasion should the bishop so desire. He is also bound to the following:

The law of residence; attendance at the diocesan synod when summoned; attendance at diocesan conferences and at meetings held for the solution of *casus conscientiae;* the application of *Missa pro populo;* the exercise of the function of preaching on the appointed days, and the giving of instruction to children in the rudiments of faith and Christian doctrine; the hearing of the confessions of the faithful; attendance upon the sick and the dying; diligence in the administration of the last Sacraments in due time; the giving of instruction to those who are to receive First Holy Communion and Confirmation; care in making the necessary investigations prior to his assistance at the marriage of his subjects; and orderly preservation of the books in which the baptisms, the marriages, and the deaths of his parishioners are recorded, as well as of the *liber status animarum.*[77]

When the religious vicar has been delinquent in the exercise of his office, he is subject to the correction and punishment of the local ordinary. This punitive power of the local ordinary is exercised cumulatively with the power accorded to the religious superior. Should a difference of opinion arise as to the punishment to be imposed, the decree of the local ordinary prevails.[78] The coercive power of the local ordinary over the religious vicar in those matters which pertain to the care of souls is, as just observed, cumulative with that of the religious superior. The cumulative right is not to be understood in the sense that the local ordinary must proceed in con-

[77] Benedictus XIV, const. *Firmandis,* 6 nov. 1744—*Fontes,* n. 349, §§ 7-9. Cf. canons 804, § 3; 831, § 3; 874; 964, nn. 2-4; 965; 966; 967; 1001, § 4; 1155; 1162, § 4; 1261, § 2; 1265, § 1; 1267; 1274, § 1; 1279; 1291; 1292; 1293; 1303, § 2; 1338, § 2; 1349, § 2; 1355, § 1; 1356, § 1; 1382; 1385; 1386; 1505; 2269.

[78] Canon 631, § 2.

junction with the religious superior, as Augustine states.[79] It seems that the bishop may proceed in the case alone, with the obligation merely of notifying the religious superior in case he desires to remove the vicar.[80]

However, the religious superior has exclusive coercive power regarding the matters of religious discipline. The religious superior could go so far as to remove the offending vicar from office for his breaches of religious discipline, subject only to the obligation of making this fact known to the local ordinary.[81]

The cumulative right of the local ordinary and the religious superior is to be understood in such a manner that either could proceed against the religious vicar, so that the first to proceed to correction excludes the intervention of the other. The cumulative right could be made exclusive by mutual agreement.[82] The two could not simultaneously proceed against the vicar in such a way that there would be promoted two processes against him at the same time for the same offense. This would constitute a grave injustice to the victim. If, however, the penalty inflicted by the initial prosecutor should seem too light, an additional penalty could be imposed by the other.[83]

It has been established that the local ordinary does not have the power, without recourse to the Holy See, to submit a religious vicar to the yearly examination demanded for secular priests in canon 130, § 1, and for religious in canon 590, in case the religious superior neglects to conduct this examination. The Code requires that all priests undergo this examination yearly for at least three years after their ordination. The III Plenary Council of Baltimore requires such examinations for a period of five years.[84] Religious priests are obliged by the Code to undergo this examination each year for five

[79] *Commentary*, III, 363.

[80] Coronata, *Institutiones*, I, n. 635.

[81] Canon 454, § 5; cf. Coronata, *Institutiones*, I, n. 635.

[82] Cf. canon 1568 for an analogical case of cumulative jurisdiction.

[83] Coronata, *Institutiones*, I, n. 635; Fanfani, *De Iure Religiosorum*, n. 449.

[84] Canon 130, § 1; *Acta et Decreta Concilii Plenarii Baltimorensis III*, n. 187.

years after the completion of their studies.[85] The question was submitted to the Pontifical Commission for the Interpretation of the Code. The response received was that recourse should be had to the Sacred Congregation of Religious in such cases.[86]

The religious vicar holds his post subject to removal *ad nutum* by either the local ordinary or his religious superior.[87] Despite the fact that the religious vicar is removable *ad nutum*, the office itself must be considered a stable one even in his case. Stability in office is the desire of the legislator as manifested in canon 454, § 1.[88] Even the religious vicar cannot be appointed for a determined length of time, for example, for three years, if it is thereby meant that when the three years have expired he ceases to be pastor.[89] If the office of local superior of the religious house is joined to that of the parochial vicar, it would seem that the vicar in this case holds his office for a predetermined duration of time. However, it is to be noted that in order to permit such a condition to exist, an indult is required since the two offices are deemed to be incompatible. It is possible that an immemorial custom or a privilege might be adduced as permitting this cumulation of offices.[90]

The notion of pastor in the canonical sense demands permanency or subjective perpetuity in office. To religious vicars is attributed a kind of perpetuity modified by a greater degree of removability than is verified in the case of a pastor of the diocesan clergy.[91] The religious vicar is, as has been asserted above, personally removable

[85] Canon 590.

[86] The question submitted was the following: "Utrum in casu negligentiae Superiorum religiosorum circa examen post absolutum studiorum curriculum quotannis, saltem per quinquennium peragendum (can. 590) Ordinarius loci cogere possit Religiosos (parochos vel vicarios curatos) ut examen, ad normam can. 130, § 1, coram se suisve delegatis subeant. Resp.: Recurrendum esse in casu ad S. Congregationem de Religiosis.—*AAS*, XIV (1922), 526.

[87] Canon 454, § 5.

[88] Melo, *De Exemptione Regularium*, p. 87.

[89] Coronata, *Institutiones*, I, n. 470.

[90] Clancy, *The Local Religious Superior*, The Catholic University of America Canon Law Studies, n. 175 (Washington, D. C.: The Catholic University of America Press, 1943), pp. 108, 109.

[91] Augustine, *Commentary*, II, 519.

ad nutum, but the pastor in title, the moral person of the congregation to which the parochial benefice is annexed, is irremovable as is evidenced by the fact that the religious benefice cannot be extinguished, transferred or divided without the intervention of the Holy See.[92]

The religious vicar is removable at the will of either the local ordinary or the religious superior without the institution of the process determined in Book IV, Title 28, of the Code. The prudent judgment of the bishop or of the religious superior is sufficient for effecting his removal. However, the canons of the title concerning the method to be followed in the removal of removable pastors may well serve as a norm in determining the causes justifying the removal of the religious vicar.[93] Since the stability in office of all pastors is directed, not towards the pastor's own good, but towards the common good of the faithful, the reason for the removal of the religious vicar should generally be equally directed towards and in its causes be measured by the good of the faithful involved.[94]

The fact remains, however, that despite the equities involved, the religious vicar is subject to removal *ad nutum* by either the local ordinary or the religious superior. Both have equal rights in the matter, with the sole obligation of advising each other of their action. Hence, if the local ordinary removes the vicar, he makes this fact known to the religious superior, and if the religious superior removes him, he makes this fact known to the local ordinary. Neither is further obliged to explain the reasons for his action. It seems, however, that the local ordinary may withdraw the vicar's jurisdiction only for reasons which have reference to the care of souls.[95]

There is open to both the local ordinary and the religious superior the option of invoking a recourse *in devolutivo* with the Holy See. Some authors hold that the religious who is removed from his parochial post may have recourse to the Holy See only when the removal is made by the local ordinary. If the religious superior removes him, they maintain, he is bound to obey by reason of his vow, whereas he

[92] Fanfani, *De Iure Religiosorum,* n. 448; Schaefer, *De Religiosis,* n. 509.

[93] Schaefer, *De Religiosis,* n. 501.

[94] Coronata, *Institutiones,* I, n. 470.

[95] Wernz-Vidal, *Ius Canonicum,* III, n. 416; Biederlack-Führich, *De Religiosis,* n. 160.

is not so bound to the local ordinary.[96] The opposite opinion [97] seems juridically to be the better founded one, for despite the fact that the vicar is bound to his religious superior by the vow of obedience, the way of recourse is always open to every religious if he feels that an injustice has been done him even by his superior. Canon 454, § 5, discusses only the point in which the religious superior or the bishop objects to the decision of the other, but it does not exclude the right of the religious vicar to have recourse against the decree of his superior as well as against that of the bishop. It remains true, however, that the right of removal by the bishop is a right which he may exercise only in the interests of the faithful, whereas the religious superior is free to change his subjects to another post for reasons merely pertinent to the internal government of the institute. Hence, it seems that recourse by the religious vicar would have little effect against the decree of his superior that he is to undertake another charge. By virtue of his vow of obedience, he is subject to removal from any post, and the religious superior is under no obligation to offer reasons justifying his action in removing his subjects.

The contention that he is also under a vow of obedience to the local ordinary in cases wherein the religious has been appointed as a parochial vicar [98] does not seem to be a valid one. The Code states that subjection by reason of the vow is due the Roman Pontiff,[99] but it concedes no similar power to the local ordinary over the religious in view of the latter's status as a parochial vicar. In case recourse is sought, the religious (whether the superior or the parochial vicar) applies to the Sacred Congregation of Religious, and the local Ordinary to the Sacred Congregation of the Council.

B. *The Administration of Temporal Goods*

In the acquisition and administration of temporal goods in a religious parish, three parties must be considered, namely, the parish,

[96] Wernz-Vidal, *Ius Canonicum*, III, n. 415; Biederlack-Führich, *De Religiosis*, n. 160.

[97] Coronata, *Institutiones*, I, n. 470; Schaefer, *De Religiosis*, n. 509.

[98] Vermeersch-Creusen, *Epitome*, I, n. 496.

[99] Canon 499, § 1.

the religious house, and the religious vicar. Those goods which accrue to the religious in consideration of the parish, the parish acquires; those which accrue to him in other ways are acquired in the manner in which other religious acquire goods.[100] There must also be a distinction made between the goods given to the church and the goods given to the parish. Goods given to the parish are always subject to the jurisdiction of the local ordinary. Goods given to the parish church are subject to the local ordinary in those cases only when the parish church does not belong to the religious, even though the parish is united to the religious house *pleno iure.*[101]

Regarding revenues which come to the religious vicar in consideration of the parish over which he presides, the parish acquires them. Such goods are those which a secular pastor would have to reserve for the secular parish. Goods which are given by the faithful for the propagation of religion, for the furthering of religious ritual, for the support of the clergy, for the relief of the poor and for other similar pious uses are presumed to be given to the parish. Therefore it is imperative that the intention of the donor or testator of such goods be properly discerned, in order that they may be applied to the use for which they were intended. If the church edifice has been erected as a parish church by means of funds collected from the faithful, even though the parish is entrusted to a religious congregation, then the alms collected are presumed to be given, not to the religious house, but for the promotion of divine worship and the relief of the poor of the parish. This holds true also if the church edifice was provided by a single benefactor, unless it was specifically erected, not for the convenience of the faithful, but as a gift to the religious community. Whatever goods, by their nature destined for ecclesiastical uses, are given to the pastor are presumed to be given to the church. Those destined for personal use are presumed to be given to the pastor. Even sacred things, chalices, for example, if clearly and definitely given as expressions of personal esteem by the congregation, accrue in this case to the pastor.[102]

[100] Canon 630, § 3.

[101] Cf. *supra*, p. 128; canons 630, § 4; 1550.

[102] Leo XIII, const. *Romanos Pontifices*, 8 maii 1881—*Fontes*, n. 582.

To the pastor accrue the revenues mentioned in canon 463, § 1, under the general term *praestationes*, which are to be determined by custom or legitimate taxation. This term includes the entire range of income, salary, and stole fees.[103] It does not in the sense of canon 463, § 1, include manual Mass stipends, since these are of too uncertain a nature to constitute a source of regular income.[104]

The word "salary" is not used in the Code, and consequently no sum is fixed by the Code in canon 1410, since varying financial conditions in different countries make this determination impractical. The III Plenary Council of Baltimore (1884) decreed that the individual bishops were to fix the amount of the salary of pastors and assistants in each diocese. The same Council ruled that pastors, if they neglected to draw their salaries within a year from the time it was due, lost the right to it unless a written demand for it was seasonably submitted to and approved by the local ordinary or his chancellor.[105]

Generally, besides the salary, the following items accrue to the pastor: Mass stipends for Masses celebrated by him, and stole fees or offerings given on the occasion of the administration of the sacraments; of the churching of women; and of funerals. Custom reserves the other offerings to the parish. Ends specified by the donors must always control the disposition of their contributions.[106] All the revenues which are added to the patrimony of the secular pastor are acquired by the religious vicar in the manner in which he is permitted to acquire goods.[107] They are, therefore, in so far as they are acquired by the religious as an incumbent of the benefice, acquired by the congregation, or the province, or the religious house, or by

[103] Goyeneche, "Consultationes"—*CpR*, X (1929), 42, 178.

[104] Coronata, *Institutiones*, I, n. 482; Augustine, *Commentary*, II, 541.

[105] *Acta et Decreta Concilii Plenarii Baltimorensis III*, nn. 273, 281.

[106] Nebreda, "De Loci Ordinariorum Iuribus circa Pia Legata Donationesve tum Religiosis tum Eorum Ecclesiis etiam Paroecialibus facta"—*CpR*, VII (1926), 264.

[107] ". . . cetera [bona] acquirit ad instar aliorum religiosorum"—Canon 630, § 3.

the Holy See, and their administration belongs to the institute and not to the religious vicar.[108]

The Code states in canon 630, § 2, that those goods which are not given to the vicar in consideration of the parish are acquired *ad instar aliorum religiosorum.* Canon 580, § 2, explains that even religious who retain the capacity to acquire goods in ownership do not have a right to all the goods given them, since what they acquire by their own industry or in consideration of their status as religious accrues to the religious congregation.[109] The words *industria sua* refer to any personally produced work of art, to any performed labor, or to any executed ministry, and the words *intuitu religionis* comprehend those things which are given to the religious either especially for the congregation, or in view of the fact that he is a religious.[110]

Accordingly, it is possible for the religious vicar to receive goods of three different kinds, inasmuch as they may have been contributed out of as many diverse considerations:

(1) Those given him in consideration of the parish. These remain in the parish for parish uses.

(2) Those given him because he is a religious, or because of some work which he has performed. These belong to the religious congregation.

(3) Those given him not because of his religious state, nor for services performed, nor for parish uses, but precisely as gifts to him personally. The disposition of these goods depends upon the constitutions by which the religious vicar is bound. If he has given up the right to acquire new possessions, either in view of his solemn vows or inasmuch as the constitutions specifically state that he has ceded his capacity for acquiring new possessions, then these goods are acquired by the institute.[111]

[108] Melo, *De Exemptione Regularium,* p. 84-85; Coronata, *Institutiones,* I, n. 625.

[109] "Quidquid autem industria sua vel intuitu religionis acquirit, religioni acquirit"—Canon 580, § 2.

[110] Fanfani, *De Iure Religiosorum,* n. 256; Vermeersch-Creusen, *Epitome,* I, n. 683.

[111] "Quilibet professus a votis simplicibus, sive perpetuis sive temporariis, nisi aliud in constitutionibus cautum sit, conservat proprietatem bonorum suorum et capacitatem alia bona acquirendi. . . ." Canon 580, § 1.

If the constitutions of a congregation in which the members take simple vows do not state that the members cede their capacity for acquiring new possessions in virtue of their religious profession, these gifts accrue to the religious personally, and are added to his patrimony.[112] This opinion is more in keeping with the words of canons 580, § 1, and 630, § 3, than the opinion which simply states that all goods acquired by the religious vicar, except those destined for the use of the parish, accrue to the religious institute or house.[113]

It is true, however, that stole fees, Mass stipends, salaries and other offerings received by the religious in the ministry [114] accrue to him by reason of his own industry, and hence are not added to his patrimony. However, it is quite possible that, while engaged in parish work, he could acquire goods which belong neither to the parish nor to the congregation, but are added to his patrimony. Such would be gifts tendered him as a private person, or legacies specifying that they are made to him personally.[115] The constitutions of most of the congregations are careful to stipulate that the professed religious is prohibited from acquiring new possessions unless the title to such acquisition existed before his profession.[116]

The points outlined above may be summarized as follows:

(1) Whatever the religious vicar receives for the purpose of divine worship becomes the property of the parish.

(2) Mass stipends, stole fees, and salaries become the property of the religious house.

(3) Gifts which are purely personal accrue to the patrimony of

"Post solemmnem professionem, salvis pariter peculiaribus Apostolicae Sedis indultis, omnia bona quae quovis modo obveniunt regulari:

1°. In Ordine capaci possidendi, cedunt Ordini vel provinciae vel domui secundum constitutiones;

2°. In Ordine incapaci, acquiruntur Sanctae Sedi in proprietatem."—Canon 583.

[112] Wernz-Vidal, *Ius Canonicum*, III, n. 416, fn. 18; Vermeersch-Creusen, *Epitome*, I, n. 730.

[113] Fanfani, *De Iure Religiosorum*, n. 451; Schaefer, *De Religiosis*, n. 501.

[114] Cf. *supra*, p. 141.

[115] Cf. Vermeersch-Creusen, *Epitome*, I, n. 683.

[116] Pejska, *Ius Canonicum Religiosorum* (3. ed., Friburgi Brisgoviae: Herder, 1927), p. 126.

the religious if the constitutions do not deny him the capacity of acquiring new possessions; otherwise they become the property of the institute.[117]

In a *pleno iure* effected union of a parish with a religious house, the subject of ownership of the goods contributed for parochial purposes is the religious house itself, which possesses these goods in a fiduciary capacity, with the obligation of expending them for the benefit of the parish, and not for the utility of the religious community.[118] Moreover, goods which are given in consideration of the parish are subject to the supervision of the local ordinary. It is incumbent upon the religious vicar to render an account of them to the bishop.[119]

The following question was submitted to the Pontifical Commission for the Interpretation of the Code:

> "Whether in virtue of canons 631, § 3; 535, § 3, 2°; 533, § 1, 3° and 4°, the local ordinary has the right to demand an account of the administration of foundations and legacies to a religious parish such as is mentioned in canon 1425, § 2 [i.e., a parish united *pleno iure* to a religious organization]."
> The reply received was: "In the affirmative, without prejudice to the prescriptions of canon 630, § 4 and 1550."[120]

Concerning this reply the following remarks may be made. Canon 631, § 3, states that the prescripts of canon 533, § 1, 4°, and canon 535, § 3, 2°, are to be followed regarding the administration of temporal goods in parishes thus united to religious houses. Canon 533, § 3, 2°, asserts the right of the local ordinary to receive a report concerning the administration of funds and legacies, as mentioned in canon 533, § 1, 3° and 4°, which refers to those funds and legacies

[117] Cf. Creusen, *Religious Men and Women in the Code,* n. 324.

[118] Wernz-Vidal, *Ius Canonicum,* III, n. 415; Schaefer, *De Religiosis,* n. 501; Goyeneche, "Consultationes"—*CpR,* X (1929), 39-41. Woywod (1880-1941) said merely "the religious community becomes entitled to the entire revenue of the parish," but he did not state the necessity of using the revenue for parish purposes.—*Commentary,* II, n. 1437.

[119] Coronata, *Institutiones,* I, n. 561; Wernz-Vidal, *Ius Canonicum,* III, n. 415.

[120] Pont. Comm. Intr., 25 iul. 1926—*AAS,* XVIII (1926), 393.

which were given to a superior of a religious congregation to be employed for the purpose of divine worship or for charity in that locality, and to money given to a parish or a mission in consideration of that parish or mission.

If the religious parish is established in a diocesan church, the parish and the church remain under the jurisdiction of the local ordinary, and he has the same right of supervision over the goods of that parish as he does over the goods of other parishes in his diocese. This is true even if the religious congregation is exempt.[121]

If the religious parish is established in a religious church, then canon 630, § 4, governs the case, and the local ordinary has no right to demand an account, since this pertains to the religious superior, whether the congregation be exempt or non-exempt.[122] Pious foundations established for the benefit of the parish or of the church are subject to the local ordinary if the religious parish is established in a secular church, even though the congregation is exempt.[123]

If both the parish and the church are religious, but the congregation is not exempt, the pious foundations are also subject to the local ordinary's jurisdiction. If the religious are exempt, and both the church and the parish are religious, the local ordinary cannot demand an account of the pious foundations. This holds true also for pious foundations which are established for the benefit of the parish.[124] Regarding the investment of funds donated to a non-exempt congregation for projects of divine worship or for works of charity in the parish, the local ordinary's permission must first be obtained, and he has the right to demand an account of the administration of such funds.[125]

If, however, the religious parish is established in the church of an Order, the superiors are exempt from the jurisdiction of the local ordinary in this case. If the religious parish is erected in a church

[121] Cf. canon 1519; Maroto, "Annotationes"—*CpR*, VII (1926), 440.

[122] Maroto, *loc. cit.;* Schaefer, *De Religiosis*, n. 504.

[123] Canons 1545-1549.

[124] Nebreda, "De Loci Ordinariorum Iuribus circa Pia Legata Donationesve tum Religiosis tum Eorum Ecclesiis etiam Paroecialibus facta"—*CpR*, VII (1926), 329-332; Schaefer, *De Religiosis*, n. 504.

[125] Canons 533, § 1, 3°; 535, § 3, 2°.

of an exempt congregation, it is disputed whether the superior must render an account to the local ordinary.[126] Other revenues, whether they are designated as moneys, as in canon 533, § 1, 4°, or as offerings, as in canon 1182, § 2, 3°, are not added to the revenues of the religious church in which a religious parish may be erected. These revenues accrue entirely to the parish, and an account of their administration is due the local ordinary, even though the parish is established in a church of an exempt institute.[127]

Goods given to the church must always be distinguished from those given to the parish. Goods given to the parish or for the good of the parish are always under the jurisdiction of the local ordinary. Goods given to the parish church are under the jurisdiction of the local ordinary only when the parish church is secular.[128]

Notwithstanding his vow of poverty, the religious vicar may collect alms for the benefit of his parishioners, for the parochial schools and for other pious institutions connected with the parish. These alms he may distribute according to his own judgment, but always under the supervision of his religious superior. The collection, retention, and administration of alms intended for the ornamentation or the conservation or the building of the parish church pertain to the religious superior, if the church belongs to the religious; otherwise to the local ordinary.[129]

The wide faculty conceded to the religious vicar by canon 630, § 4, also subjects him to the supervision of his religious superior. In the case of alms collected for charitable uses and for other pious works, the religious superior has a right to know to what uses the alms are being directed. The superior must ascertain whether the will of the donors is being observed, and the religious vicar must render an

[126] Chelodi (*Ius de Personis,* n. 260), Prümmer (*Manuale Iuris Canonici,* q. 194), Fanfani (*De Iure Religiosorum,* n. 155) and Blat (*Commentarium,* II, nn. 597, 599) hold that only regulars are exempt in this case. Vermeersch-Creusen (*Epitome,* I, n. 606), De Meester (*Compendium,* II, n. 980), Biederlack-Führich (*De Religiosis,* n. 54) and Nebreda (*art. cit.,* p. 321) argue that by virtue of canon 1550 all exempt institutes are excused from rendering an account to the local ordinary in this case.

[127] Maroto, "Annotationes"—*CpR,* VII (1926), 442.

[128] Schaefer, *De Religiosis,* n. 504.

[129] Canon 630, § 4.

account of his administration to the religious superior as well as to the local ordinary upon demand.[130]

The religious vicar, on the other hand, is bound to the observance of his vow of poverty in so far as it is compatible with his office.[131] He has no right, therefore, to retain alms collected, but must follow the law as it applies to other religious, and accordingly must deposit the money with the treasurer of the house with which he is affiliated. When he needs money for the distribution of alms, he must ask for what in his prudent estimation is necessary. The treasurer must faithfully keep an account of the funds thus received, and he may not refuse the religious vicar the money requested, since it is destined for parochial and not community uses. There is no incompatibility between the faculty which the religious vicar has, namely, to distribute money, and the obligation which he has as a religious, namely, to deposit such funds with the treasurer.[132]

The right of vigilance accorded to the religious superior concerning alms collected for the pious works of the parish imports the necessity of inquiring himself or through his delegate, as frequently as he judges opportune, how the money is being expended. The religious superior has a right to demand an account of the receipts and expenditures of such funds, in order to determine whether they are being administered in a prudent manner. He has no right, however, to determine the method in which they are to be expended, nor may he reserve to himself the faculty of distributing them partially or entirely. These duties are reserved to the religious vicar. If, however, he disapproves of the manner in which these alms are being administered, and the religious vicar refuses to accept his counsel in the matter, he may remove the vicar from office, with the obligation of notifying the local ordinary, as prescribed by canon 454, § 5.[133] However, the fact remains that the religious vicar is independent in administering these funds. Accordingly the superior's right and duty is one of vigilance only.

130 Coronata, *Institutiones,* I, n. 635.

131 Canon 630, § 1.

132 Wernz-Vidal, *Ius Canonicum,* III, n. 415; Schaefer, *De Religiosis,* n. 501.

133 Fanfani, *De Iure Religiosorum,* n. 450.

Alms given for the building, conservation, repair, and decoration of the parish church are to be collected and retained by the religious superior, if the church belongs to the religious community. Among the superiors in this case the local superior is included. The administration seems to pertain to the office of the treasurer under the direction of the superior.[184] If the church is not owned by the religious community, the right of administration pertains to the local ordinary who may delegate this power to the religious vicar.[185] For the safe investment of money given to the parish the consent of the local ordinary is required, and an account of the administration of the funds of the parish church must be rendered to him. This does not, however, apply to money or to pious foundations given to the church as such, if both the church and the parish belong to Regulars.[186]

Because of the many difficulties and conflicts which may arise concerning the religious vicar's right of administration and the superior's right of vigilance over alms collected for parish uses, and the further right of the administration of certain funds by the superior, authors suggest that in practice the superior delegate wider powers to the religious vicar than those bespoken for him in the common law.[187]

American authors question the practicability of this division of administration. Augustine[188] feared that it could throw an unbearable burden on religious superiors whose communities hold many parochial churches; that it might cause trouble with regard to parish-

[184] Schaefer, *De Religiosis,* n. 501.

[185] Vermeersch-Creusen, *Epitome,* I, n. 730; Schaefer, *De Religiosis,* n. 501.

[186] Melo, *De Exemptione Regularium,* p. 90; Coronata, *Institutiones,* I, n. 635.

[187] Vermeersch-Creusen, *Epitome,* I, n. 730; Wernz-Vidal, *Ius Canonicum,* III, n. 416; Schaefer, *De Religiosis,* n. 501. Vermeersch-Creusen are of the opinion that this expediency is within the scope of the superior or bishop—"canon [630, § 4] ius definit, non prohibens quin, quantum expediat, delegatio seu commissio a Superiore vel ab Ordinario tribuatur."

[188] *Commentary,* III, 361.

ioners and trustees, who are entitled to know how the money is spent; and that the regulation of canon 533, § 1, 4°, in requiring a separate account of the parish money and of the money of the institute, might call for a host of officials in the religious house itself.

Woywod [139] adverted to the manner in which parochial revenues are collected in the United States. The Code prescribes that certain revenues are to be in the hands of the religious vicar, and that others are under the supervision of the religious superior. He declared that in our country all offerings from whatever source constituted the sole revenue which the parish receives. From this revenue all parish expenses have to be paid. The suggestion that wider delegation be given to the parochial vicar is not, in Woywod's opinion, a solution of the problem which is peculiar to our country.

Concerning these opinions, the following remarks may be offered:

(1) A religious superior cannot have many churches united to his house, but only one. Augustine may have had reference to the union which is effected *plenissimo iure* and which exists solely in an *abbatia nullius*.[140]

(2) The parishioners have the same opportunity of knowing how money donated for parish enterprises is being expended whether the religious vicar or the superior has control of these funds. As to money and foundations for the benefit of a parish church that belongs to the religious, there is nothing in the law which would prohibit the religious superior from permitting the vicar to make a report to the parishioners.

(3) The treasurer can handle all the accounts, although the distribution of the funds is made by the vicar.

(4) Woywod implied that no funds are received over which the superior would have supervision. Surely, the superior has supervision, as well as the local ordinary, over all contributions to which Woywod referred.

139 *Commentary*, I, 543.

140 *Commentary*, II, 515.

ARTICLE 3. THE *Semipleno Iure* EFFECTED UNION OF A PARISH WITH A RELIGIOUS HOUSE

Besides the method of the full incorporation of a parish with a religious house, canon 1425, § 1 refers to another type of union.[141] This union is described by authors as being effected *non pleno iure,* or *semipleno iure.*[142] Canon 1425, § 1 mentions specifically this method of the union of a parish with a religious house as a union *ad temporalia tantum quod attinet.* This type of union can be effected by the Holy See only. By this kind of union the temporal goods only of the benefice are transferred to the ownership of the religious house to which the parish is united. The religious house, in turn, has the obligation of providing an appropriate sustenance for the secular priest who is appointed for the care of souls. The office of pastor is independent of the religious house, and the benefice remains a secular benefice.[143]

The phrase, *domus religiosa particeps fit solummodo fructuum paroeciae,* causes some difficulty in maintaining the position that the temporal goods of the benefice are transferred to the ownership of the religious house to which the parish is united. The following arguments are adduced to solve this difficulty:

(1) The word *solummodo* in canon 1425, § 1 is used in contrast to the words *fit religiosa* in canon 1425, § 2 where the *pleno iure* union is described. The contrast of these words brings out the distinction between these two types of union. In the *pleno iure* union not only the temporal goods of the benefice but the parochial office itself is possessed by the religious house, whereas in the union *ad temporalia tantum quod attinet* the religious house receives merely the dominion of the temporal goods of the parish.

(2) The word *fructuum* is not to be interpreted in the restrictive sense of the revenues only of the temporal goods of the benefice. It

141 "Si a Sede Apostolica paroecia domui religiosae uniatur *ad temporalia tantum* quod attinet, domus religiosa particeps fit solummodo fructuum paroeciae, et Superior religiosus sacerdotem e clero saeculari in eadem instituendum, assignata congrua portione, Ordinario loci praesentare debet."

142 Coronata, *Institutiones,* I, n. 469; Cocchi, *Commentarium,* VI, 214; Vermeersch-Creusen, *Epitome,* II, n. 752; Augustine, *Commentary,* II, 515.

143 Cocchi, *Commentarium,* VI, 214.

refers rather to the temporal goods of the benefice itself. This usage of the word *fructus* is found elsewhere in the Code.[144]

(3) If the word *particeps* is taken in its proper signification as meaning that only a part of the temporal goods of the parish accrues to the religious house, one must expect that some other person is the recipient of the part which does not accrue to the religious house. But no such other party is mentioned as sharing the ownership of the temporal goods in the type of union under discussion. The priest exercising the care of souls receives a reasonable income, it is true, but this income is received from the religious superior and not directly from the goods of the benefice. Hence, the meaning of the word *particeps* in the context of canon 1425, § 1 must be understood in the sense that the religious house acquires the temporal goods of the parish. Added strength is given to this conclusion by the use of the word *fit* indicating that there is a change of substance in the thing under discussion. In a former draft of canon 1425, § 1 made in 1916, the word *erit* was used. In the final draft, however, *fit* was substituted for *erit* to emphasize the fact that there was an actual transfer of the ownership of the temporal goods of the benefice in favor of the religious house.[145]

A union *ad temporalia tantum quod attinet,* therefore, has the following juridical effects:

(1) The religious house becomes the recipient of the dominion of the temporal goods of the parish.

(2) The religious superior must present a priest of the secular clergy to the local ordinary who appoints him to the benefice.

(3) The priest of the secular clergy who exercises the care of souls must be assigned a reasonable amount of income to afford him an appropriate sustenance.[146]

The solemnities necessary in order to effect a union *ad temporalia tantum quod attinet* are the same as those prescribed for the *pleno*

[144] ". . . si omnes beneficii fructus distributionibus constent . . ."—canon 1356, § 3. "*Fructus*" here designates the endowment itself or the goods of the benefice.

[145] Delgado, *De Relationibus inter Parochum Religiosum et eius Superiores Regulares* (Rio de Janeiro: Editôra Vozes Limitada, 1943), pp. 34, 35.

[146] Canon 1425, § 1; Cocchi, *Commentarium,* VI, 214.

iure effected union.[147] Nowhere is the consent of the parishioners required if an innovation is to be effected in the status of benefices. However, since the change affects them, and since they may have reason to oppose the transfer of the temporalities to the religious house, they or their representatives should be given a hearing. This was maintained by canonists under the former discipline, and according to the decisions of the Sacred Congregation of the Council.[148]

It seems that the bishop could appose a condition to this contract by defining the amount of income which is to be reserved for the sustenance of the secular priest who is to exercise the care of souls. That unions of this type are rare, if not entirely non-existent, is attested by Nebreda, who says that he does not know of any parish incorporated to a religious community *ad temporalia tantum quod attinet*.[149]

Another type of union of parishes to religious institutes is mentioned by authors. In it the parish is united not to a religious house, but to a religious institute, while it still remains a secular parish.[150] In this case the temporalities of the parish do not become subject to the dominion of the religious institute as in the case of a union *ad temporalia tantum quod attinet* nor does the parish become a religious parish as in the case of a *pleno iure* effected union. The pastor is not the religious house, but a member of the religious community. The parish, however, remains secular, and is in every respect under the supervision and direction of the local ordinary as other parishes in his diocese. The procedure followed in a contract whereby a parish is so assigned to religious is similar to that followed in a *pleno iure* effected union.[151] First, the boundaries of the parish are agreed upon by the local ordinary and the religious superior. Next, the conditions binding the contractants are clearly specified. These con-

[147] Cf. *supra*, pp. 127, 128.

[148] Wernz, *Ius Decretalium*, II, n. 272; Cocchi, *Commentarium*, VI, 226.

[149] Nebreda, "De Loci Ordinariorum Iuribus circa Pia Legata Donationesve tum Religiosis tum Eorum Ecclesiis etiam Paroecialibus facta"—*CpR*, VII (1926), 330.

[150] Coronata, *Institutiones*, I, n. 469; Augustine, *Commentary*, II, 515; *The Canonical and Civil Status of Catholic Parishes in the United States*, p. 82.

[151] Cf. *supra*, pp. 127, 128.

ditions will be dictated by the circumstances which brought about the formulation of the contract.

The parish is assigned to the care of the religious congregation by an indult of the Holy See. The method of tenure is mutually agreed upon by the local ordinary and the competent religious superior, the Supreme Moderator with the consent of his council.[152] This type of contract is often executed in large cities and in dioceses where the secular clergy is not sufficiently numerous to administer to the spiritual needs of all the faithful.

The following is an example of such contracts:

This contract made on the...........day of...........19........ by and between His Excellency........................ Bishop of.................... and the Very Reverend...................., Superior General of.................... attest:
1. That His Excellency.................... Bishop of.................... for himself and his successors in office, and with the consent of his Consultors, and after having received a decree from The Sacred Congregation of the Council, grants in perpetuity to the aforesaid religious congregation of .... the parish of Saint .... whose limits are....................
2. The Superior General of the.................... for himself and his successors, hereby agrees to administer the aforesaid parish in matters both spiritual and temporal in accord with the ecclesiastical laws, by providing a sufficient number of priests to meet the actual and future needs of this parish.
3. The Superior General of the aforesaid congregation agrees to erect or cause to be erected, with revenues of the parish, such buildings as a school, church, parochial residence when the need arises, subject always to the approval of the Bishop of the Diocese of....................
4. The priests of the aforesaid congregation appointed as parish priests or assistants in this parish shall enjoy the same rights and privileges, and shall be subject to the same obligations as obtain in the case of other parish priests and assistants in the aforesaid Diocese of...............
5. The Superior General of the aforesaid congregation for himself and his successors agrees to conform to canon 456 of the Code of Canon Law for the appointment of the pastor of this parish, to canon 454,

[152] *Normae of 1901*, n. 271.

§ 5, for his removal, and to canon 476, § 4, for the appointment of his assistants.

The signature and seal of the bishop are placed upon the document followed by the signature and seal of the religious superior. Sometimes there are four additional signatures of witnesses, two for each of the contracting parties. These extra witnesses are not necessary except for additional solemnity, but it is advisable to provide them to guarantee means of proof of the signatures of both contractors. At the foot of the page, or on an additional page, the indult from the Holy See is appended, or an express reference to it is made in the following manner:

In virtue of Indult n.................... of the Sacred Congregation of the Council we grant to the congregation of..................the aforesaid parish of........................... according to the above written contract.

(Signed)..

Bishop of..

Duplicates of the document are made and each of the contractors receives a signed and sealed copy. If the local ordinary keeps the original indult in the diocesan archives, the religious receive an exact copy of it. If the religious keep the original, an exact copy is made for the diocesan archives.[158]

As in the case of the *pleno iure* effected union, the religious superior submits a copy of the contract to the Sacred Congregation of Religious, in which copy he states also the reasons for accepting the parish, and indicates that he has acted with the consent (if the constitutions so demand; otherwise the advice) of the chapter or council. The local ordinary also submits a copy of the proposed contract to the Sacred Congregation of the Council, in which copy he outlines his reasons for the transfer and indicates that the consent of the board of diocesan consultors and other interested parties has been sought. Generally the reasons asserted are the needs of the faithful and the insufficient number of secular priests to minister to the faithful. Here is an example of such a petition:

[158] Dooley, "The Juridical Status of Parishes of Religious: Another View"—*The Jurist*, III (1943), 124-125.

BEATISSIME PATER,

Episcopus..................., ad pedes Sanctitatis Vestrae provolutus, quo aptius bono animarum fidelium paroeciae.................. loci .... providere valeat, attenta cleri saecularis diocesani paucitate, de consensu consultorum dioecesanorum, humillime petit facultatem, qua concredere possit in perpetuum praedictam paroeciam Congregationi.......................... ad normam iuris et consuetudinis diocesanae nec non peculiaris conventionis inter ipsum Episcopum et Superiores eiusdem Congregationis die.................. 19........ initam.

The reply of the Sacred Congregation is appended to the petition:

SACRA CONGREGATIO CONCILII, attentis expositis ab Episcopo.................. eidem benigne tribuit facultates iuxta preces. ceterisque servatis de iure servandis.

Datum Romae, die.................. 19........

(Signed)..Praefectus

....Secretarius.

The bishop keeps this indult attached to his copy of the petition in the diocesan archives, and forwards to the religious superior an exact copy of both, impressed with the episcopal seal, and carrying also the notation *Concordat cum originali,* together with the bishop's signature.

The same procedure is followed when the contract states that the religious congregation has accepted the care of the parish for a stated term of years. In that event the term of duration of the contract is specifically stated in article 1.[154]

In the case of temporary contracts the following clause may also be added:

It is agreed between the contracting parties that the terms of this contract may be modified by either party with the intervention of the Holy See as required by ecclesiastical law, provided that due notice of the intention to make such modification is communicated to the other party six months before the modification becomes effective.

The antecedent period of required notice may be longer than six months. This is the period decreed by the II Plenary Council of

[154] *Supra,* p. 153.

Baltimore (1866) as the minimum necessary to enable the local ordinary to make adequate provision for the continuance of pious works in his diocese.[155] In a contract such as the one outlined above, the six months' notice clause is not incorporated to indicate an assertion of the unqualified right of either party, or of any intention to abandon the contract conditioned by the mere fact that a six months' notice is given. It rather indicates that the contractants are aware that time may bring about conditions which demand that certain modifications be made. In that event both parties would be alloted a reasonable amount of time to prepare themselves for such modifications. Since the contract was made subject to the approval of the Holy See, only the Holy See would be competent to permit its dissolution. Modifications in the contract, however, could be made by the mutual agreement of the contracting parties, provided that no matter was touched which, according to Canon Law, demanded the approval of the Holy See.

The Decrees of the IV Provincial Council of Portland (1932) allow for a provision whereby the relinquishment of a pious work is permitted by mutual agreement after notification. The length of time in the notification to be given is to be specified in the contract. However, the subject matter of the contract referred to in the decrees concerns the undertaking of the work of teaching in parochial schools, for which no permission of the Holy See is necessary.[156]

Apostolic nuncios, internuncios, and delegates have the faculties to grant to local ordinaries in particular cases or for a limited time permission to place religious priests in charge of parishes when this is deemed necessary because of the dearth of diocesan priests.[157] This

[155] *Concilii Plenarii Baltimorensis II Acta et Decreta*, n. 407.

[156] Decretum 29: "Instituto religioso schola paroecialis ne comittatur neve subtrahatur sine approbatione Ordinarii loci in scriptis data. Et Ordinarius et institutum religiosum pacto bilaterali scripto conveniant de tempore quo ad mutuam de cessatione a munere docendi in scholis paroecialibus praemonitionem praestandam teneantur."—*Acta et Decreta Concilii Provincialis Portlandensis in Oregon Quarti, Portlandiae in Ecclesia Metropolitana Celebrati diebus VIII, IX, X Septembris MCMXXXII*, p. 41.

[157] N. 48: "Concedendi in casibus particularibus vel ad tempus, Ordinariis dioecesanis facultatem praeficiendi paroeciis religiosis in defectu sacerdotum saecularium, de consensu tamen Superiorum, et cum clausula ut saltem duo

faculty has also been conceded to missionary bishops by the Sacred Congregation for the Propagation of the Faith.[158]

This faculty does not militate against the opinion espoused above,[159] which declared that contracts for the services of members of religious congregations could be entered into without the permission of the Holy See, even though the fulfillment of the contract would demand the absence of a religious from the religious house beyond six months. That agreement concerns a contract whereby a religious renders *assistance* in a secular parish when there is a dearth of diocesan priests. The faculty conceded to the apostolic delegates, nuncios and internuncios is granted in order that they may permit bishops to *place* religious priests in *charge* of parishes.[160] The fact that two other religious, at the very least, must live with the acting pastor is an indication also that these priests are not placed in the parish to assist diocesan priests living in the same rectory. This faculty seems to be a dispensation not from the prescript of canon 606, § 2, but from canon 1411, 1°, which states that secular benefices pertain only to the secular clergy.

ARTICLE 4. JURIDICAL EFFECTS OF THE ASSIGNMENT OF PARISHES TO RELIGIOUS CONGREGATIONS

When the Code speaks of parishes entrusted to religious in any way whatsoever, it uses the general term, and describes them as parishes *religiosis concreditae*.[161]

alii religiosi cum parocho cohabitent, servatisque in reliquis sacrorum canonum dispositionibus."—*Index Facultatum Quas, pro Locis Missionis suae, Nuntiis, Internuntiis, et Delegatis Apostolicis penes Civitates seu Nationes, post Codicem Iuris Canonici Publicationem Tribuere SSmus Dominus Noster Decrevit, Ceteris Abrogatis.* (Contained in Vermeersch-Creusen, *Epitome*, I, n. 813.)

158 S. C. de Prop. Fide, 9 dec. 1920—*AAS*, XIII (1921), 18.

159 *Supra*, pp. 102 et seq.

160 ". . . *praeficiendi* paroeciis religiosis. . . ."—*Supra*, p. 156.

161 Canons 472, § 2; 475, § 1. Reilly (*The Visitation of Religious*, p. 133, fn. 1) argues against the view that there is a complete cleavage between the terms, *paroecia pleno iure unita* and *paroecia religiosis concredita*. He maintains that the phrase *paroecia religiosis concredita* refers to any parish under the spiritual care of religious, whether *pleno iure unita* or not, saving the case of a

Besides the *pleno iure* effected union and the union *ad temporalia tantum quod attinet,* there is another possible relationship between a parish and a religious congregation, by means of which the parish is entrusted to the religious priests in order that they may assume the care of souls. By this assignment the parish is not incorporated with the religious house in any way. This has sometimes been called a union *quoad spiritualia tantum quod attinet.*[162] This relationship has been described as "a mere concession in trust, which entirely abstracts from the more generous rights accruing through full or partial incorporation, by granting to the religious house or institute no further rights than those enjoyed by the superior in presenting or approving a priest of his own religious community as the prospective appointee and his subsequent right, concurrent with that of the local ordinary, in removing that religious from his post of duty."[163]

The parish in this case cannot be called a religious parish, since this term is restricted to a parish incorporated with a religious house by means of a *pleno iure* effected union.[164] The parish remains secular, and the religious in charge of souls is not a vicar but has the title of pastor. This is evident since there is no moral person in whom there vests the title of pastor.[165] The pastor is nevertheless removable at the will of the local ordinary or of the competent

union *ad temporalia tantum quod attinet.* That the latter union is excluded is clear from a comparison of canon 456 with canon 1425, § 1; cf. also Coronata, *Institutiones,* I, n. 472; Wernz-Vidal, *Ius Canonicum,* III, n. 415; Augustine, *The Canonical and Civil Status of Catholic Parishes in the United States,* pp. 188-189.

162 Reilly, *The Visitation of Religious,* p. 132.

163 Bastnagel, *The Appointment of Parochial Adjutants and Assistants,* The Catholic University of America Canon Law Studies, n. 58 (Washington, D. C.: The Catholic University of America, 1930), p. 159.

164 Canon 1425, § 2.

165 Coronata (*Institutiones,* I, n. 472, p. 555, fn. 1)—"De paroecia pleno iure unita loquuntur cc. 452; 471; 1423 [5!], § 2; de paroecia precario vel alio modo religiosis concredita c. 454, § 5. Differentia in hoc est quod in priori casu parochus est persona moralis; in altero vero casu est persona ipsa physica religiosa. . . ."

superior, each of whom has the obligation of advising the other of his action in this case.[166]

It has been noted above that many authors contend that where a parish is united to a religious house by a *pleno iure* union, the necessity for a formal talking possession of the parish by the religious vicar cannot be urged since the actual pastor is the moral person of the religious house.[167] However, in the present case, since the religious is a true pastor and not the vicar of the habitual pastor, there is no reason to exclude him from the obligation of taking possession of the parish as other pastors are obliged to do by canon 461.

As in the case of religious vicar, the religious pastor of a secular parish assigned to the care of the religious is subject to the visitation of the local ordinary as is also the parish itself. However, the religious pastor is always free, even in this situation, from the visitation of the local ordinary in matters pertaining to his religious observance. If there is established a religious house in conjunction with the parish, and the superior of the house is distinct from the pastor, matters of religious observance are within the province of the religious superior.[168]

It may be remarked here that in the opinion of canonists, the old law prescribing that a religious functioning as pastor could not undertake the administration of a parish alone has been abolished. Formerly, the pastor had to have at least one companion residing in the rectory with him and co-operating in the administration of the parish but the Code is silent on this point. Hence, the presumption is conceived by authors to exist that this law is no longer binding.[169]

[166] Canon 454, § 5, refers to all pastors pertaining to religious communities and makes them, "ratione personae, amovibiles ad nutum."

[167] Cf. *supra*, p. 130.

[168] Canon 631, § 1.

[169] Wernz-Vidal, *Ius Canonicum*, III, n. 416; Coronata, *Institutiones*, I, n. 635; Vermeersch-Creusen, *Epitome*, I, n. 730. However, when religious are assigned temporarily as pastors because of the dearth of diocesan clergy and in virtue of the special faculties granted to Nuncios, Internuncios, and Apostolic Delegates, the obligation is still binding that at least two other religious reside in the house with the religious pastor—cf. *supra*, p. 156.

The religious pastor of the secular parish assigned to religious is bound to the same obligations as secular pastors; to the law of residence, to attendance at diocesan and deanery conferences; and to all the other obligations imposed upon pastors in general in canons 460-470; 471, § 1 and § 4.[170]

Regarding the administration of temporal goods, the same problems do not arise as those which present themselves when the parish is incorporated to the religious house. However, the following points of possible conflict and the solution to be adopted may be noted: Whatever is given to the pastor for the purpose of divine worship becomes the property of the parish as in other secular parishes. Mass stipends, salaries, stole fees and whatever sort of income which would become the property of the secular pastor, become the property of the religious congregation to which the religious pastor belongs. However, gifts which are unequivocally given to him for his personal estate are added to his patrimony if the constitutions of his institute permit this.[171] Since the parish is a secular benefice, the local ordinary has the identical right of supervision over the temporal goods of the parish as he does in the rest of his diocese. Pious foundations are also subject to the local ordinary.[172]

The religious pastor may collect alms for the benefit of his parishioners, for the parochial schools and other pious foundations connected with the parish. These alms are to be distributed according to his own prudent judgment under the supervision of the religious superior. The collection, retention, and administration of alms intended for the ornamentation, conservation, and building of the church pertains to the local ordinary. In the case where the religious is pastor, this power will in all probability be delegated to him by the local ordinary. Such, at least, is the prudent suggestion of many authors.[173] The wording of canon 630, § 4 seems to attribute to the local ordinary in the case of a secular parish ruled over by a religious pastor the same jurisdiction as the religious

[170] Cf. *supra*, p. 135.

[171] Creusen, *Religious Men and Women in the Code*, n. 324.

[172] Canons 1545-1549; cf. Maroto, "Annotationes," *CpR*, VII (1926), 440.

[173] Wernz-Vidal, *Ius Canonicum*, III, n. 416; Vermeersch-Creusen, *Epitome*, I, n. 730; Schaefer, *De Religiosis*, n. 501.

superior has in the case where both the parish and the church are religious. This would seem to indicate by analogy, direct and exclusive right of administration. However, the religious house is the actual pastor in the case of a parish incorporated with a religious house, whereas in the case under discussion the bishop is not the pastor. It would seem, then, to be the normal and less vexatious procedure to permit the religious to act in this matter as secular pastors do, that is, to administer the property under the supervision of the local ordinary.[174] Such a stipulation should be made when the contract assigning the parish to the care of the religious is executed.

[174] Canon 1519; Coronata, *Institutiones*, I, n. 635; Melo, *De Exemptione Regularium*, p. 90; Augustine, *Commentary*, IV, 361.

CHAPTER XII

TERMINATION AND RESCISSION OF CONTRACTS

THERE are a number of methods by which a contract may be discharged. The most obvious and most common method is that of performance. Once a contract has been validly formulated, law and justice require the precise fulfillment of all its obligations according to the terms agreed upon. Discharge by performance is the method ordinarily contemplated by the contracting parties. However, before the time determined for the fulfillment of the contract, or before the contract has run its course, it may be extinguished in other ways. It may be abrogated by agreement through the mutual consent of the parties, provided that the rights of other parties affected by the contract are safeguarded. It may be extinguished by operation of law, or its invalidity declared because of violation of statute. Its non-performance may be excused when performance is rendered impossible by an act of God or an act of the other contracting party.[1] Hence, it is generally stated that a contract may be discharged by performance, agreement, impossibility of performance in certain cases, operation of law and breach.[2]

If there is not at least a substantial performance of contract when due, or if there is no performance at all, there is a breach of contract, unless some lack of performance was brought about by the other party's fault, or performance was waived or released by subsequent contracts. "A breach of contract is any action or omission of one party to a contract by which the other party is hindered or disturbed in the enjoyment of some property or privilege, to which by virtue of the contract he has become entitled."[3] The party guilty of breach of contract can neither sue upon the contract nor successfully defend against a suit for damages.

Canon Law has no difficulty in accepting the Anglo-American

[1]Williston, *The Law of Contracts,* III, 1793.

[2] U. S. v. Golden (C. C. A. N. M.), 34 F (2d) 367, 373.

[3] Williston, *The Law of Contracts,* III, 1796.

category of the methods in which a contract may be discharged. All of these methods were known even to the older canonists who classified them in the following manner: (1) Discharge by the actual fulfillment of the terms of the contract corresponds to the Anglo-American method of discharge by performance. (2) Abrogation of the contract by mutual consent is known in Anglo-American law as abrogation by agreement. (3) Rescission by the sentence of a competent judge corresponds to the Anglo-American method of extinguishing a contract by operation of law. (4) Impossibility of the fulfillment of the terms of a contract has its counterpart in Anglo-American law when a contract's non-performance is excused for the reason that performance is rendered impossible. (5) *Praescriptio* is known in Anglo-American law as limitation of actions.[4]

Canon Law concedes, in addition, the extraordinary remedy of *restitutio in integrum,* which is available to minors and moral persons. Even if the civil law does not allow a remedy of this type, since it is sanctioned as a method of discharging a contract in the Code of Canon Law, the remedy is available in ecclesiastical courts.[5] Its admission as an available remedy for the rescission of a contract even in those cases in which the civil law does not recognize the remedy is in accord with the general provision concerning the acceptance of the civil legislation on contracts, as stated in canon 1529.

The concession of this action is not recognized for juristic personalities by American law. Although it is admitted that the aims of religious corporations are of a higher order than those of other corporations, their status according to the civil law is on the same level with that of other societies. They are subject to the same restrictions and are endowed with substantially the same rights and subject to the same liabilities as private corporations.[6] Even in the face of this denial of civil recognition of the right of moral ecclesiastical persons to use the remedy of *restitutio in integrum,* its availability to them must be asserted, since it is guaranteed them by the Code.

[4] Wernz, *Ius Decretalium,* III, n. 249.

[5] Canons 1687-1689.

[6] Zollmann, *American Church Law,* n. 126.

Article 1. Duration of Contracts in General

The duration of a contract is generally specified in the articles of the contract itself. The termination of a contract, although usually determined according to the passage of a period of time, may also be stipulated as contingent upon the occurrence of a particular event. For example, a parish may be delivered to the care of a religious congregation by contract for ten years, one hundred years, or perpetually. The articles of contract may, however, base the termination of the contract upon some local contingency, so that the parish would be under the care of the religious congregation "as long as the parish is mainly Negro." [7] A contract expressly stipulating that it is to continue for a particular length of time or until the happening of a particular event, if it is not subsequently rescinded or terminated by mutual agreement, remains in force and terminates in accordance with its terms, and not sooner.[8]

In cases where the wording is vague as to provision limiting the duration of the contract, the law furnishes certain rules for the construction of contracts.[9] The intent of the court is to ascertain by an application of the rules of construction to the langauge used, the manner and extent to which the parties intended to be bound.[10] A contract, therefore, is construed according to the intention of the parties themselves and the manifestation of their intention by words, acts or relations in which the agreement is expressed, or from which it is implied. All the existing laws and customs pertaining to the subject matter of the contract must be investigated, as well as the necessary incidental rights, unless these are expressly excluded by the articles of contract.[11]

The usual custom of the locality affecting a particular type of contract must in a case of patent ambiguity be considered if no

[7] Dooley, "The Juridical Status of the Parishes of Religious: Another View"—*The Jurist*, III (1943), 123.

[8] Scheel v. Harr, App. 80 P. (2d) 1035.

[9] Woolridge v. Wolf, 149 N. E. 685, 254 Mass. 728.

[10] Lovell v. Commonwealth Thread Co., 172 N. E. 77, 272 Mass. 138.

[11] Williston, *The Law of Contracts*, II, 602.

specific article providing for the norms of interpretation was written into the contract, or no specific statute provides for its interpretation. For example, custom has given a specific connotation to the phrase, "Week-end work." It could not be held that the phrase, "as long as this parish is mainly Negro," is implied in all contracts when such parishes are delivered to the care of religious. However, if the work of the congregation which accepted the parish is exclusively concerned with Negroes, such an intention could be construed to be contained implicitly in the contract.[12]

A. *Computation of Time in Contracts*

As a general principle, in virtue of canon 33, § 2, the civil law is to be followed in the computation of time in contracts. The civil law recognizes the terms of contract as the determinant in contractual matters—not only regarding the duration of the contract, but also regarding the computation of time in the contract. This recognition is in accord with the legal principle based on the natural law that contracts are recognized as receiving their legal sanction from the agreement of the parties.[13] Canon Law assumes that the computation for determining contractual obligations follows the civil law, unless the contractants agree to some other mode of reckoning.[14]

It is disputed whether the prescription in canon 33, § 2, concerning the adoption of the civil law provisions in the reckoning of time for contracts is general, or whether it refers only to the hours of the day. Van Hove explicitly states that the norm in canon 33, § 2, is

[12] An application of the rule whereby custom affected the duration of a contract is evidenced in the decision of a court that the offer to pay a monthly sum for playing baseball was restricted to monthly payment for the baseball season only, in view of previous negotiations between the parties for a season contract and the usual custom followed in this type of contract.—Pfiester v. Western Union Telegraph Co., 118 N. E. 407, 282 Ill. 69. Ann. Cas. (1918) 738 reversing 203 Ill. App. 435.

[13] "Contractus ex conventione legem accipere dinoscuntur."—Reg. 85, R. J., in VI°.

[14] "Quod attinet ad tempus urgendi contractuum obligationes, servetur, nisi aliter expressa pactione conventum fuerit, praescriptum iuris civilis in territorio vigentis."—Canon 33, § 2.

general, and is therefore not restricted to the choice of the reckoning of hours only.[15]

Dubé contends that the exception refers to the reckoning of the hours only, and is not to be extended to other periods of time. He argues this point from the position of this regulation after canon 33, § 1, which treats of the computation of hours exclusively. If this modification had been intended to affect all units of time, he insists that it would have found its logical position within or immediately following canon 31, in which the general norms for the reckoning of time are prescribed. Further, canon 33, § 2, uses the singular *praescriptum iuris civilis,* which indicates that the canon intends to modify only this one particular choice of units of time, namely the hours. The question is not of great practical importance, since the contracting parties are free to express the duration of the contract and the computation of time in general when they enter into the agreement.[16]

The opinion as expressed by Dubé, which limits the choice of time to the hours of the day, seems to be the more acceptable one. The general adoption of the civil law of each territory in contractual matters indicates the desire of the legislator to conform as much as possible to the civil law in order to avoid conflicts. The only exceptions to this general provision are those stated in the various canons of the Code. By restricting the choice of time, the conformity desired by canon 1529 is made easier of fulfillment.

Another question concerned with the computation of time in regard to contracts arises out of the interpretation of the phrase, *nisi aliter expressa pactione conventum fuerit.* It has been held that, if the civil law forbids the choice of a time-reckoning in contractual matters, and demands that the computation as established

[15] Van Hove, *Commentarium Lovaniense in Codicem Iuris Canonici,* Vol. I, Tomus III, *De Consuetudine—De Temporis Supputatione* (Mechliniae: Dessain, 1933), n. 279, 3. Hereinafter cited *De Temporis Supputatione.*

[16] Cf. Dubé, *The General Principles for the Reckoning of Time in Canon Law,* The Catholic University of America Canon Law Studies, n. 144 (Washington, D. C.: The Catholic University of America Press, 1941), p. 118. Hereinafter cited Dubé, *The Reckoning of Time in Canon Law.*

by the civil law be followed, the contractants must follow this prescription of the civil law.[17]

The more common opinion of canonists admits that the choice of a time-reckoning at variance with that prescribed by civil law would be admissible even in this case, since canon 1529 admits the prescriptions of civil law in contracts only in so far as they have been enacted as Canon Law. The prescription of Canon Law which permits the contractants to choose by an express agreement a computation of time differing from that imposed by the civil law seems to be guaranteed by the restrictive clause of canon 1529. Hence, the faculty granted in canon 33, § 2, is held to take precedence over a contrary ruling of civil law.[18]

The latter opinion is more consonant with the wording of canon 1529. The legislator has explicitly intervened in regard to the choice by an express agreement of a time-reckoning on the part of the contractants. Since the Code specifies that the contracting parties have this faculty, the refusal on the part of the civil law to permit its exercise would seem to constitute an unacceptable provision of civil law.

Finally, a difference of opinion concerning the interpretation of the words *urgendi contractuum obligationes,* in canon 33, § 2, is evident. Some authors have declared that these words should be given a wide rather than a restrictive interpretation. According to this theory, all contractual obligations contemplated by canon 1529 should be included. The faculty to choose an acceptable reckoning of time, or, in default of an explicit choice, the adoption of the civil law method of reckoning, would comprehend the time for bringing an action as well as the time appointed for the performance of contracts.[19]

Other canonists restrict the choice of a time-reckoning to the matter of demanding the fulfillment of the obligations of contract. In the absence of a specific choice on the part of the contractants,

[17] Van Hove, *De Temporis Supputatione,* n. 279, 3.

[18] Michiels, *Normae Generales Iuris Canonici,* II, 134; Ojetti, *Commentarium,* I, 200; Vermeersch-Creusen, *Epitome,* I, n. 114; Maroto, *Institutiones,* I, n. 255; Dubé, *The Reckoning of Time in Canon Law,* p. 119.

[19] Wernz-Vidal, *Ius Canonicum,* I, n. 246; Van Hove, *De Temporis Supputatione,* n. 279, 3, note 4.

the civil law determines the time for demanding the fulfillment of contracts. In all other cases, the civil law computation of time holds to the exclusion of a choice on the part of the contractants.[20] Dubé remarks that a restriction of the meaning of *urgere* in the phrase under discussion would make it synonymous with *exigere*. He admits that such a restrictive meaning is found in the Code in canons 24, 336, § 1, 2251, 2347 and 1686. The latter canon allows an *exceptio metus vel doli* if and when the execution of a contract is urged.[21]

It seems that the same restrictive interpretation could be applied with reference to the matter of demanding the fulfillment of the obligations of contract, and thus it would exclude the determination of other contractual obligations. The time for the performance of contracts would then be determined by the civil law. The canonical justification for limiting the favor conceded in permitting the choice of a time-reckoning consists in the fact that the general adoption of the civil law in contractual matters is favored by the Code in order to forestall conflicts of law wherever possible.

B. *Duration of Implied Contracts*

In the formulation of contracts it is most desirable, in order to avert future litigation, that the articles of contract be specific in expressing the intent of the contracting parties as to every element of the contract. Circumstances of time and duration of contract must be particularly attended to and minutely stated in order that security of commitments may be established without risk. In business relations men are careful to stipulate exactly the extent of their duties and the duration of their business relationships. Prudence demands the same degree of caution in all contractual relationships. When there is an absence of explicit time provisions and disputes later arise, the court must look to the implications of the contract itself. It may be comparatively easy from the wording of the contract or from the actions of the parties to determine what implicit provisions

[20] Toso, *Ad Codicem Iuris Canonici Commentaria Minora* (5 vols., Romae: Jus Pontificium, 1920-1927), I, 104. Hereinafter cited *Commentaria Minora;* Blat, *Commentarium*, I, 120.

[21] Dubé, *The Reckoning of Time in Canon Law*, p. 121.

in respect to the time element were intended by the contractants. Since the contract acquires legal sanction from the agreement of the parties,[22] the principles for the interpretation of laws are applicable when the extent and significance of its terms remain to be determined.

The following legal principles may be adduced as being in striking conformity with those of Canon Law, and acceptable by the ecclesiastical court. The words of the contract are taken in their legal meaning if they have one. If the words have no legal meaning, their customary use must be ascertained, or the sense as indicated by the actions of the parties in pursuance of contract, and as illustrated by their subsequent agreements in reference to the nature and performance of their obligations.[23]

In contracts between ecclesiastical parties, these principles are to be adopted according to the general provision of canon 1529. In regard to the construction and interpretation of contracts, there is a mutual acceptance of the rules by both Canon Law and civil law, since the same principles are proposed by both. In the application of the legal meaning of the matter of contract, canonical institutes such as parishes and religious houses will be interpreted according to their meaning in the Code. Other terms applying to temporal institutes such as sale will derive their legal meaning from the definition accorded them by the civil law.

In elaboration of this assertion, the basic principles of interpretation of both Canon Law and civil law may be adduced. The principles of interpretation as contained in canons 17-20 are in striking conformity with the legal principles followed by the civil law.[24] The legal meaning of the words of the contract must be ascertained by comparison with the other terms of the contract.[25]

Certain principles are given for the inevitable *lacunae* which may result either from an oversight on the part of the contractants, or which may be brought about by developments subsequent to the making of the contract. In the absence of explicit or implicit legislation covering the disputed point, the governing norm is to be sought

[22] Reg. 85, R. J., in VI°; cf. *supra*, p. 165.

[23] Williston, *The Law of Contracts*, II, n. 602.

[24] Cf. *supra*.

[25] Cf. Canon 18.

in prescripts regulating similar matters. The general principles of law combined with canonical equity afford a further norm. Finally, the usage (*stylus*) and customary practice of the Roman Curia and the teachings of expert canonists are resorted to in order to bring about a clarification of the meaning of the terms of contract.[26]

If the terms of a contract are not specifically stated as to periods of time, the contract is open to construction by a court, unless the duration intended is evident from other clauses in the contract. It is not sufficient to place the construction on isolated phrases in order to determine the termination of a contract, but individual provisions must be construed with the contract as a whole.[27] Thus, the duration of a contract may be dependent on the fulfillment of some future event or condition.[28] A contract may terminate also by reason of the termination of its principal clauses. A subsidiary provision in a contract becomes inoperative when the main purpose of the contract terminates.[29]

An article providing that a six months' notification be given before a modification of contract is made by either party would not be construed as militating against the duration of the contract, either perpetual or temporary, as stated in another article of the contract. It can only be considered as an admission that circumstances may arise which will demand readjustments in the original agreement. By the insertion of this article a certain period of time is conceded to the parties to prepare themselves for the readjustment, or to show cause why the modification of the contract is unnecessary. This conclusion follows from a comparison of this clause with the other clauses in the contract where perpetuity or specific duration of contract are stated.[30]

An expression which, standing alone, would generally indicate perpetuity in a contract, may where it appears in a contract limited

[26] Canon 20.

[27] Home Acre v. Swenson-Dibble Land Co., 192 N. W. 42, 179 Wis. 556; Cf. Canon 18.

[28] Cf. *supra*, p. 164.

[29] Hetherington v. Williams Firth Co., 98 N. E. 797, 212 Mass. 257; cf. "Accessorium naturam sequi congruit principalis."—Reg. 42, R. J., in VI°.

[30] Cf. *supra*, p. 156.

as to duration be construed with reference to the limit of duration of the contract, unless a contrary intent is clearly manifest.[81] This conclusion is based on the comparison of the clauses of the contract in their text and context, and offers the same interpretation as that provided for by canon 18.

It may be asserted that no generic rule can be indicated concerning the perpetuity or transitory nature of implied contracts. The duration of the contract may be deduced, however, from construction which seeks to ascertain primarily the intent of the contractants as manifested by their words, acts or relation.[82] The purpose or object which the contract seeks to obtain is a salient feature in the ascertainment of the intent of the parties, but the reasons or motives which induced the parties to contract are not necessarily included in the construction thereof.[83] However, the "whereas" clauses in a written contract setting forth the reasons or inducements for formulating the contract are often indicative of the true intention of the parties.[84] These rules of construction are acceptable to ecclesiastical courts, and their adoption is consonant with the general canonization of civil law in canon 1529.

Paramount, therefore, is the necessity of ascertaining the intention of the contractants at the time they entered into the contract. Historical circumstances may give an indication of what the parties intended, and these circumstances would have to be investigated when there was no written contract and the contractants were no longer living. Since the construction of the contracts under discussion in this dissertation is within the province of the ecclesiastical court, the usual forms of evidence admissible in contentious trials would also be valuable in determining the intent of the parties when no witnesses were available. These instruments may be public or private.[85]

Public ecclesiastical documents are enumerated, but not exhaustively, in canon 1813, § 2. Civil documents recognized as public

[81] Hopedale Machinery Co. v. Entwistle, 133 Mass. 442.

[82] Williston, *The Law of Contracts*, II, n. 602.

[83] Brennan v. Monson, 50 P. (2d) 534, 97 Colo. 448.

[84] U. S. Fidelity & Guaranty Co. v. Sellers, 225 S. W. 26, 160 Ark. 599.

[85] Canon 1812.

by the civil law are also admissible as evidence before ecclesiastical tribunals.[36] Public documents either ecclesiastical or civil have the presumption (*praesumptio iuris*) of genuineness in their favor.[37] Civil documents admissible as evidence in ecclesiastical trials are of a nature and kind similar to public ecclesiastical instruments. They include documents attested as true by public notaries, the acts of civil judicial procedure and official acts of civil magistrates.[38]

Regarding contracts by which a parish is assigned to a religious congregation in the United States, perpetuity may be argued from the fact that the Code desires stability in the assignment of parishes.[39] It is true that in view of his characteristic personal status the individual religious in the care of souls is removable at the will of the bishop or of the religious superior, but there is no reason to deny to the pastor in title, namely the moral person of the religious community, that stability which is enjoyed by pastors in general. After the declaration of the Pontifical Commission for the Interpretation of the Code on September 26, 1921, in response to the question submitted by the Apostolic Delegate, the status of parishes in the United States as true parishes in the canonical sense of the term cannot be denied.[40]

In view of the fact that the normal status of parishes demands that the pastor be a permanent appointee, this usual mode of action would enjoy the presumption of the law in contracts in which no specific time limits had been set and in which the duration of the contract cannot be deduced from the action of the parties.[41] So insistent

[36] Canon 1813, § 2.

[37] Canon 1814.

[38] Vermeersch-Creusen, *Epitome,* III, n. 200.

[39] Canon 454, § 1.

[40] Cf. Letter of the Apostolic Delegate, U. S., 10 nov. 1922—Bouscaren, *The Canon Law Digest* (2 vols., Milwaukee: The Bruce Publishing Co., 1934-1943), I, 149; Hannan, "The Juridical Status of the Parishes of Religious," *The Jurist* I (1941), 332.

[41] Concerning the stability of tenure of parishes in general, Coronata states: "Status normalis reipublicae ecclesiasticae per se requirit erectionem seu constitutionem paroeciarum inamovabilium; amovibiles permittuntur pro casibus anormalibus et magnae difficultatis."—*Institutiones,* I, n. 470, 2°, note 1.

is the Code upon this point that all new parishes automatically become irremovable, unless the bishop, after having heard the diocesan consultors, feels compelled by special circumstances to declare them movable.[42] By this enactment especially the Code evidences its favor for the perpetuity of the parochial office.[43]

Article 2. Abrogation by Agreement

Mutual rescission of contract or rescission by agreement has been defined as "the discharge of both parties from the obligation of a contract assumed to be legally binding by a new agreement made by them subsequently to the original contract and before performance thereof is due." [44] In the agreement to abrogate a contract, a new contract is virtually entered into. All the elements of a new contract are present. There is a meeting of minds by the contracting parties, i.e., the original contractants; a subject matter that is physically and morally possible; a valid consent is given by both parties; and a reason involving a consideration is present in the new act. The reason for the mutual repudiation of the former contract will almost certainly be determined as the utility of the two parties.[45]

Although the civil law does not regard the rescission of a contract as a new contract, it does regard it as a new agreement.[46] It seems then that the qualities of this new agreement are subject to the same limitations as those which are indicated for the general law concerning contracts. As has been noted above, the following points concerning the formulation of contracts are acceptable by both Canon Law and civil law. (1) The actions must be physically and morally possible. (2) The objects must be actually existing or existent in the future. (3) The subject matter of the contract must be the possession of at least one of the contractants. (4) The promise must be validly assented to and the consent must be a true

[42] Canon 454, § 3.

[43] Vermeersch-Creusen, *Epitome*, I, n. 496.

[44] Edwards v. Muri, 237 P. 209, 211, 73 Mont. 339.

[45] Cf. *supra*, pp. 66-67.

[46] Edwards v. Muri, 237 P. 209, 211, 73 Mont. 339.

consent externally manifested in some way. (5) The consent must be deliberate and not vitiated substantially by error, fear or fraud.[47]

It seems that the same solemnities will have to be observed in the abrogation of a contract as were demanded for the formulation of the original contract. If the original contract was in writing in compliance with a prescript of Canon Law, the agreement abrogating the contract seems by implication likewise to demand a written instrument. Although this view indicates the more prudent method to be followed in the abrogation of contracts, it cannot be deemed to be mandatory unless the provisions of Canon Law provide for such a course of action. The necessity for a written instrument in the abrogation of a contract seems to follow from the fact that the regulation demanding written contracts for certain matters is determined by the subject matter of the contract. However, American law does not demand a written instrument for the revocation of a contract, and in the absence of canonical provisions to the contrary, a written instrument could not be urged.[48]

Since the new agreement to abrogate the contract is based upon the former contract, and the subject matter remains the same, it seems that the restrictions which were demanded by Canon Law for the formulation of the original contract are also imposed for its abrogation. Canon Law, for example, demands that the consent of the diocesan consultors or of the council of a religious congregation be obtained before certain contracts may be executed. If such consent is demanded by the Code or by the constitutions of the religious congregation, then a consent from the same bodies must be obtained for the revocation of the contract with reference to which the consent was originally given. Similarly, if the permission of the Holy See intervened for the formulation of the original contract, the same agency must be invoked for its repudiation. In the assignment of a particular parish to a religious congregation, this permission had to be obtained before the contract could have a valid effect.[49] By the abrogation of the contract a transfer of the original assign-

[47] Cf. *supra*, pp. 65-67.

[48] Cf. Statute of Frauds—Williston, *The Law of Contracts*, I, 449, 450.

[49] Cf. *supra*, pp. 153-155.

ment is implied, and such transfers may not be made without the permission of the Holy See.[50]

Even under the civil law concept of rescission, it is the parties who are recognized as capable of rescinding the contract. Now, those whose consent is required by Canon Law are parties to the contract, even though not appearing by name on the face of the contract.[51] Thus, diocesan consultors or the members of the council of the religious superior may be regarded as parties to the contract if their consent is required for the making of the contract. Further, by its intervention in a contract in order to grant a dispensation which is needed for establishing the articles of the contract, the Holy See becomes an assenter to the contract, although it may not be strictly considered a party thereto. However, Canon Law implicitly requires the consent of the Holy See for the abrogation of a contract which was approved by that authority. Therefore the Holy See has the same right as the parties to rescind the contract, and the necessity for the Holy See's intervention thus constitutes an exception to the civil law on contracts, as adopted by the general provision of canon 1529.

ARTICLE 3. INVALIDITY OF CONTRACTS

The scope of Canon Law's adoption of the civil law concerning contracts includes the recognition by the ecclesiastical court of the invalidity of a contract in the eyes of the civil law because of the failure of the contracts to comply with the acceptable provisions of the civil law.[52] The ecclesiastical court would in such a case examine the arguments proposed for impugning the validity of the contract, and decide whether the necessary elements for validity were present. On the basis of this examination of the civil law, the

[50] Canon 1422.

[51] The parties to a contract may mutually agree to rescind the agreement, and a contrary stipulation in the contract would not militate against the power of the parties to rescind it.—Alexander Hamilton Institute v. Hart, 129 N. W. 481, 180 Wis. 90. The right to rescind is restricted to the parties or to those delegated by them to act.—Johnson v. Reed, 9 Mass. 78, 6 Am. D. 36.

[52] Cf. *supra*, pp. 58-61.

court's decision would rest, and the declaration of nullity would be given.[53]

Even though the provisions of the civil law are accorded cognizance in contractual matters, the concept itself of invalidity is a moral notion, which is exclusively within the competence of canonical interpretation. Canonists have raised many questions concerning the force of invalidating laws, and it is admittedly a question which is "involved, difficult, and confusing."[54] It is not within the scope of the present discussion to dwell at length on the controverted points, but the notion of invalidating laws must be examined if one is to ascertain their effects on contracts.[55]

Invalidating laws are divided into those which directly invalidate the juridical act and those which do so indirectly inasmuch as they demand certain solemnities as conditions for the validity of the act. The solemnities may be intrinsic to the act itself, for example, the form of celebrating marriage as prescribed by canon 1094; or they may be extrinsic to the act, for example, the necessity of obtaining the permission of the of the Holy See in order to effect certain alienations.[56]

Rescindibility has a meaning differing from that of invalidity, since it is applicable to an act which, although possessing all the essentials for validity, can be revoked by the competent judge because of some extrinsic circumstance, such as fear which induced a party to enter into a contract, or the great loss consequent upon it.[57] There are, however, invalidating laws which closely resemble laws which permit only rescissory actions. These invalidating laws are the ones which require a judicial decision to make their invalidity effective. Two stages are present in the latter type of invalidating laws. One

[53] Canons 1679-1683.

[54] D'Annibale, *Summula Theologiae Moralis* (5. ed., 3 vols., Romae, 1908), I, 211.

[55] For a thorough discussion of this matter the reader is referred to the following series of articles appearing in *The Jurist*, III (1943): Roelker, "The Concept of Invalidating Laws," pp. 32-63; "The Power to Enact Invalidating Laws," pp. 231-245; "The Interpretation of Invalidating Laws," pp. 364-403; "The Effect of Invalidating Laws," pp. 550-566.

[56] Canons 534, § 1; 1532, § 1; Vermeersch-Creusen, *Epitome*, I, n. 76.

[57] Vermeersch-Creusen, *Epitome*, I, n. 76.

stage establishes their invalidity, and the other applies the judicial sentence of invalidity.[58] Roelker [59] points out that acts contrary to such invalidating laws are considered as valid until the judicial decision is given. He states that non-penal laws so ordering a judge to invalidate an act contrary to them should be considered rescissory laws.

The fact of the existence of invalidating laws in both Canon Law and civil law is not disputed.[60] With the canonization, in canon 1529, of civil law regarding contracts, invalidating laws of the civil code which do not contravene the divine positive or natural law or the prescripts of Canon Law must be held to be valid in the ecclesiastical forum.

Canon 11, speaking for canonical enactments, declares that invalidating laws may be couched in express or equivalent terms.[61] Some canonists contend that the formalities or solemnities required by some laws constitute the precise ambit of the word, *aequivalenter*, in this canon.[62] Others maintain that even a law assigning formalities or solemnities to an act must contain a clause which expressly invalidates the act when they have been omitted.[63]

Roelker, discussing both opinions, asserts that any kind of equivalent invalidation is within the scope of canon 11. Included in this sphere would be all laws which demand formalities or solemnities for their validity without any express reference to invalidity as an effect of their omission. The same writer continues:

> "There is no doubt that a rigid interpretation of the formalities required by law must lead one to maintain the absolute necessity

[58] Michiels, *Normae Generales Iuris Canonici*, I, 269.

[59] "The Effect of Invalidating Laws."—*The Jurist*, III (1943), 554.

[60] Roelker, "The Concept of Invalidating Laws."—*The Jurist*, III (1943), 38.

[61] "Irritantes aut inhabilitantes eae tantum leges habendae sunt, quibus aut actum esse nullum aut inhabilem esse personam *expresse* vel *aequivalenter* statuitur."—Canon 11. (Italics inserted by the writer.)

[62] Cance, *Le Code de Droit Canonique* (4. ed., 3 vols., Paris: Librarie Le Coffre, 1930), I, 48; Cocchi, *Commentarium*, I, 88-89; Coronata, *Institutiones*, I, n. 21; Vermeersch-Creusen, *Epitome*, I, n. 76.

[63] Van Hove, *De Legibus Ecclesiasticis*, n. 168; Toso, *Commentaria Minora*, I, 48.

> of complying with these formalities in order to act validly. In demanding certain formalities, the legislator is understood to expect a compliance with these formalities. Anything short of complete compliance with the law is insufficient for validity. Since invalidity of the act is not stipulated as a penalty for the transgression of the law, such invalidity would occur even if, through ignorance or error, the formalities were omitted in whole or in part."[64]

Under this view, and always in practice *ad cautelam,* the ecclesiastical court must, therefore, take cognizance of the possibility of invalidity of contract resulting from the failure to meet the necessary requirements prescribed by Canon Law. Consequently, failure of the bishop to obtain the consent of his diocesan consultors in order to enter into a contract when this consent is required by law invalidates the contract.[65] The absence of a canonical reason invalidates the union, the transfer, the division or the dismemberment of a benefice by the local ordinary.[66] The canonical cause required for the division and dismemberment of parishes is limited to the difficulty which would otherwise be undergone by the faithful in attending the parish church, or to the fact that the parishioners are so numerous that their spiritual needs cannot be provided for even by the employment of additional assistant priests.[67]

The failure on the part of the religious superior to obtain the consent of his council in those matters in which the Code or the constitutions of the congregation demand consent would nullify a contract.[68]

For the erection of a religious house which demands papal approbation, the local ordinary must manifest his consent in writing.[69] Many canonists maintain that, even in those cases where the permission of the Holy See is not required, the local ordinary's consent

[64] Roelker, "The Interpretation of Invalidating Laws."—*The Jurist,* III (1943), 392-393.

[65] Canons 105, 1°; 1532, § 1; 1541, § 2; 1542, § 2, 2° cf. *supra,* p. 86.

[66] Canon 1428, § 2.

[67] Canon 1427, § 2; 476, § 1.

[68] Cf. *supra,* p. 121.

[69] Canon 497, § 1.

must nevertheless be given in writing.[70] Larraona contends that the lack of writing affects the validity of the act. He adduces the following arguments:

(1) The context of canon 497, § 1, indicates this necessity in the case of permission for the erection of houses which need papal permission. The consent given for the erection of other houses is the identical consent.

(2) Written consent is required for the opening or construction of a dependent edifice separated from the religious house. Therefore the same consent should be required for the independent house of which the other units are only a part.[71]

(3) Written consent is required for the erection of lay associations,[72] for the aggregation of associations to confraternities,[73] and for the erection of a church or of a public oratory.[74] Larraona argues that the erection of a religious house is a matter at least equal in importance to the other matters, and therefore a written permission is required for its erection also.[75]

Most of the authors hold that, since the Code does not expressly demand a manifestation in writing of this permission of the local ordinary, the necessity for a written document cannot be urged. It is commendable to have a written permission, so that proof of the validity of the foundation may be more easily proved should any necessity arise, but, in the absence of a specific precept, the obligation cannot be said to be of such a nature that the validity of the foundation would be vitiated by its absence.[76]

The Statute of Frauds which is substantially in force in all the

[70] Pejška, *Ius Canonicum Religiosorum*, p. 52; Oesterle, *Praelectiones Iuris Canonici*, I, 246; Larraona, "Commentarium Codicis,"—*CpR*, I (1920), 112-114.

[71] Cf. Canon 497, § 3.

[72] Canon 686, § 3.

[73] Canon 723, § 2.

[74] Canons 1162, § 1; 1191, § 1.

[75] Larraona, *loc. cit.*

[76] Schaefer, *De Religiosis*, n. 80; De Meester, *Compendium*, I, n. 391; Coronata, *Institutiones*, I, n. 523; Fanfani, *De Iure Religiosorum*, n. 21; Flanagan, *The Canonical Erection of Religious Houses*, p. 56.

American States requires certan contracts to be in writing. These contracts fall into the following general categories:

(1) Contracts for the transfer of any interest in real property except by leases for short periods determined by the statutes of various States.

(2) Contracts which cannot be performed within one year from their date.

(3) Contracts of executors or administrators guaranteeing the payment of the debt of a decedent out of their own estate.

(4) Contracts promising to answer for the debt, default, or miscarriage of another.

(5) Contracts made in consideration of marriage.

(6) Contracts for the sale of chattels above a certain value unless the buyer accepts part of the goods sold or pays a portion of the purchase money.[77]

(7) Wills. These too come under the Statute of Frauds. Nuncupative wills are permitted only to soldiers and sailors under stringent conditions.[78] The writing required by the Statute of Frauds need not be a formal contract, but even a mere memorandum disclosing the terms of the agreement and signed by the parties suffices.[79]

Furthermore, the following formalities prescribed by civil law must be observed in various cases. Deeds conveying the whole title must follow a specific form [80] and be acknowledged by a notary.[81] Corporations must sign according to their by-laws and offer seal.[82] Negotiable instruments, to be negotiable, must comply with definite formalities, though they are valid without them against the original

[77] The value for the sale of chattels stipulated in the Uniform Sales Act is $500, but some States have changed this sum in the adoption of the Uniform Sales Act.—Cf. Bays, *Business Law* (New York, Macmillan Co., 1919), p. 132.

[78] Williston, *The Law of Contracts*, I, 449, 450.

[79] Williston, *The Law of Contracts*, I, 449.

[80] Williston, *The Law of Contracts*, I, 4, 139.

[81] 18 C. J. 193.

[82] Williston, *op. cit.*, II, 1138.

maker.[83] Agents must indicate their principal to escape personal liability.[84]

Failure to set down in writing the terms of agreements comprehended by the Statute of Frauds or failure to comply with the formalities necessary for a valid instrument by the declaration of civil law would invalidate the contract, and this invalidity could be alleged in a suit before an ecclesiastical court in accordance with the general principle of the acceptance of the civil law on contracts.

Article 4. The Rescission of Contracts

The authority to rescind a contract in American law is based on the premise that the enforcement of contracts entered into under certain conditions is inequitable. The reasons for which a contract may be rescinded by a court of equity are the following: (1) Where fraud has been practiced in the formulation of the contract. (2) Where undue influence has been exercised by one party over the other. (3) Where the parties have entered into the contract under a mutual mistake.[85]

These are the same general classifications which permit rescissory actions in Canon Law. However, Canon Law has specific legislation on these points.[86]. By providing special statutes concerning the elements which allow a rescissory action, the Code has indicated its desire to withdraw the matter of the recission of contracts from the province of the civil law. This is not to imply that the principles followed by Anglo-American law differ substantially from those accepted by Canon Law. As has been indicated, conformity exists as to the reasons for which a rescissory action may be sought. However, in view of the special legislation on the elements permitting a rescissory action, the explicit provisions contained in the Code are to be followed in preference to the civil law when there is a question of the rescission of contract. This conclusion is in accordance with

[83] Williston, *The Law of Contracts,* II, 1135-1139.

[84] Hall v. Crandall, 29 Cal. 567, 89 Am. D. 64.

[85] Williston, *The Law of Contracts,* III, 1987.

[86] Canons 103 and 104.

the provision of canon 1529, which adopts the civil law on contracts unless the canons provide otherwise.

Canon Law does not invalidate acts performed under the influence of grave fear or deceit, but rather affirms their validity.[87] However, as in American law, for reasons of equity the legislator declares that these acts may be deprived of all juridical efficacy. The law affords certain media by means of which an equitable solution of an evident inequity may be effected. These means are called rescissory actions. A rescissory action affirms the right to petition the competent judge to deprive an act of its valid force even though it is not, in the strict terminology of the law, an invalid act. Rescissory actions are made available for the sake of remedying the evil effects of acts or contracts placed under the influence of fear, deceit or error even in cases in which these factors do not invalidate the act or contract as affecting its substance or as amounting to and involving a *conditio sine qua non.*[88]

The definition of fear accepted by canonists is that stated by Ulpian (+228): "a confusion or perturbation of the mind by present or future danger." [89] It is, therefore, an eliciting reaction upon one's will as deriving from one's irascible sensibilities in reference to the evil from which one flees.[90] An act performed under the influence of fear does not take away the voluntariness of the act. Fear does not impede the objective and deliberate judgment of reason. It does not deprive one of the fullness of choice, but rather leaves freedom intact. The knowledge of the end remains in the intellect, and that end is wished for along with the necessary means to attain it. One acting through fear actually makes a selection through a free choice of what seems at the time to be the lesser of two evils. Fear confines and restricts choice, but it does not take away the freedom to choose. The choice is indeed a free one, but it is also a reluctant one, to which the victim would not accede if fear were absent. From the point of view that the freedom of choice is thus circumscribed,

[87] Canon 103, § 2.

[88] Canon 103, § 2; 104.

[89] "Instantis vel futuri periculi causa mentis trepidatio."—D. (4.2) 1.

[90] Cf. Roberti, *De Delictis et Poenis* (1 vol. in 2, Romae: Libraria Pontificii Instituti Utriusque Iuris, 1930-1938), Vol. I, Pars I, 151.

the voluntariness of the action is modified to the extent that the object of the will is modified and thus is called involuntary under a certain aspect (*involuntarium secundum quid*). What is lacking in the act performed under the influence of fear is not liberty but spontaniety.[91]

The type of fear postulated for the concession of a rescissory action must have certain qualities: it must be grave and it must be unjustly inflicted.[92] The gravity of fear necessary to permit a rescissory action evidently excludes a minor degree of fear (*metus levis*), but a relatively grave fear (i. e., a fear that is grave in reference to the person acting and under the circumstances present, though not resulting from a situation which would normally engender that high degree of fear) is sufficient.[93]

Another condition necessary for the type of fear which allows the right to a rescissory action is that it be unjustly threatened. Such would be the fear that is excited by private authority, that is, by one not entitled to threaten in order to gain consent to the contract. It is also unjustly threatened when there is a lack of proportion between the greatness of the evil threatened and the reason for which it was threatened. For example, in the way of contrast, a superior may threaten a subject with reasonable penalties in order to gain his consent, or for the purpose of urging the subject to perform something which it is within the superior's power to command.

In order to permit a rescissory action, a third condition must be verified, namely, that the fear threatened be the result of an external agency (*ab extrinseco*). This is evident from the word, *incusso*, used in canon 103, § 2.[94] Fear resulting from a cause internal to the person, such as sickness, or from some externally neces-

[91] Cf. Wernz-Vidal, *Ius Canonicum*, III, n. 103; Augustine, *Commentary*, II, 31-32; McCoy, *Force and Fear in Relation to Delictual Imputability*, The Catholic University of America Canon Law Studies, n. 200 (Washington, D. C.: The Catholic University of America Press, 1944), p. 77.

[92] Canon 103, § 2.

[93] Pirhing, Lib. I, tit. 40, n. 48; Schmalzgrueber, Lib. I, tit. 40, nn. 5, 6; Wernz, *Ius Decretalium*, V, n. 530; Vermeersch-Creusen, *Epitome*, III, n. 111; Coronata, *Institutiones*, I, n. 150.

[94] Augustine, *Commentary*, II, 31.

sary cause or natural phenomenon, such as an earthquake, the emergence of which is independent of a free human agent, is fear from within (*ab intrinseco*), and accordingly does not constitute a sufficient reason for warranting a rescissory action. Fear of the latter type arises, as it were, from necessity, and hence cannot be likened to fear which results from threats made for the precise purpose of obtaining consent.[95]

A fourth quality of the type of fear necessary to permit a rescissory action is that it be unjust considered in itself (*quoad substantiam*). This quality is verified when the threat concerns an injury to the agent or someone closely connected with him, and is inflicted without a just cause or is in no way deserved. The more common opinion of canonists is that fear must be unjust *quoad substantiam*, resulting from a threat made with the precise purpose of forcing consent to the contract, if the option of a rescissory action is to arise.[96]

Coronata[97] contends that an act resulting from fear which is unjust only in the manner in which it was produced (*quoad modum*) is also sufficient to allow a rescissory action. Other canonists[98] hold that one who acts under the influence of fear produced *quoad modum* cannot be said to act from fear at all as far as the option of a judicial rescissory action is the point of consideration.

The general law of the Code allows the option of a rescissory action also to him who in a contract was victimized through deceit.[99] Deceit is connivance to cheat another, with the result that it causes him to suffer injury. It may consist of hiding the truth, of telling a lie, or of some machination employing both words and deeds.[100]

95 Wernz, *Ius Decretalium,* V, n. 530; Wernz-Vidal, *Ius Canonicum,* VII, nn. 106-109; Augustine, *Commentary,* II, 31.

96 Lega, *Praelectiones de Iudiciis Ecclesiasticis* (4 vols., Romae, 1896-1901), I, n. 262; Vermeersch-Creusen, *Epitome,* III, n. 111; Augustine, *Commentary,* II, 31.

97 *Institutiones,* I, n. 150.

98 Lega, *Praelectiones de Iudiciis Ecclesiasticis,* I, n. 262; Vermeersch-Creusen, *Epitome,* III, n. 111.

99 Canon 103, § 2; 1684, § 1.

100 Ulpian gives Labeo's definition of deceit (*dolus*) as "calliditas, fallacia, machinatio ad circumveniendum, fallendum, decipiendum alterum adhibita."—D (4.3) 1.

The method employed is immaterial, provided that the evil intention of deceiving the other party to the contract is present. The distinction between deceit (*dolus*) as the voluntary cause of deception and fraud (*fraus*) as the involuntary cause does not seem to be accepted in Canon Law.[101] It must be ascertained whether the deceit which was practiced stands as a cause of the other party's action. If the deceit was only concomitant, and not the impulsive cause of the act, the rescissory action cannot be invoked.[102]

Deceit must be proved, since no one is presumed evil. The proof of deceit is based on various conjectures: (1) The qualities of the persons involved constitute a factor which furnishes an indication as to their general unreliability and their aptitude to practice deceit. (2) The circumstances surrounding the act may on examination show whether it was legally performed without deception or whether the rights of a third party were prejudiced. (3) The manner in which the act itself was performed may give further indications of the intent to deceive; if, for example, the contract concerns some matter which is normally dealt with openly, but on this occasion the agreement was arrived at secretly. (4) Grave loss suffered by one party may be an evident indication that the injured party was deceived as to the nature of the contract.[103]

Finally, a rescissory action is granted by the general law of the Code in the case of error. Error is a state of mind in which a false judgment is made concerning a certain thing.[104] This judicial action is granted in those cases in which the error does not affect the validity of the act, as it does when it concerns the substance of the contract itself, or is equivalent to a *conditio sine qua non*.[105] For instance, an error affecting the validity of the act would occur in the case in which one of the parties thought the contract concerned a parish, and the other had in mind a contract involving the school connected with the parish and accordingly excluded the parish from the contract. On the other hand, the error which allows a rescissory

[101] Toso, *Commentaria Minora*, II, 50.

[102] Augustine, *Commentary*, II, 33.

[103] Wernz, *Ius Decretalium*, V, n. 520.

[104] Cf. Coronata, *Institutiones*, I, n. 152.

[105] Canon 104.

action is a simple error, that is, one which does not affect the substance of the contract, one which does not amount to a *conditio sine qua non* of the contract, and one which is not brought about by means of the deceit of the other party to the contract.[106]

A further condition for the potential rescissory effect inherent in contracts made under error is that grave damage is suffered in consequence of the error. Grave damage is considered to be involved when it amounts to more than one half the full amount of the contract. The option of a judicial action for rescinding a contract which was based on simple error is limited to a two years duration of time.[107]

The Sacred Congregation of the Council is competent to take cognizance of disputes directly concerning parishes and ecclesiastical goods which arise as a result of contracts between bishops and religious congregations. This Sacred Congregation will adjudicate controversies in the disciplinary sphere, but judicial matters are referred by it to the competent tribunal.[108] Questions, however, which are purely disciplinary, and thus involve persons rather than the matter of the contract, are, according to canon 251, § 2, within the competence of the Sacred Congregation of Religious. It has been stated above, for instance, that in matters concerning the removal of the religious pastor, the proper Congregation for recourse on the part of the religious superior or also of religious pastor is the Sacred Congregation of Religious.[109]

Both of the Sacred Congregations, whose competence has just been indicated, refer judicial matters to the competent tribunal.[110] Because of the dignity of the moral persons involved in a contract between a diocese and a religious congregation, these cases are reserved to the Tribunals of the Holy See, and cannot be introduced

[106] Vermeersch-Creusen, *Epitome,* III, n. 113.

[107] Canon 1684, § 2.

[108] Canon 250, § 2, § 5.

[109] Cf. *supra,* p. 139. "Quare ad eam [S. Congregationem negotiis religiosorum sodalium praepositam] privative spectant omnes quaestiones quae familiam religiosam aut sodales religiosos attingunt, etiam si cum non religiosis, v. g., episcopis, convertuntur."—Vermeersch-Creusen, *Epitome,* I, n. 327.

[110] Canon 250, § 5; 251, § 2.

before any ecclesiastical court of inferior jurisdiction.[111] These Tribunals are two in number, the Sacred Roman Rota and the Apostolic *Signatura,* the former tribunal being the competent forum of first instance.[112]

If the judicial suit can be averted by means of an amicable settlement (*compositio*),[113] which is equivalent to a judicial sentence or a *res iudicata,*[114] the Sacred Congregation of the Council is competent to effect this settlement.[115] Canon 1927 forbids this mode of settlement in matters pertaining to benefices, when the litigation concerns the title of the benefice itself, unless legitimate authority sanctions the compromise. In cases concerning temporal ecclesiastical goods, a settlement may be made, but the formalities of law incident to the alienation of ecclesiastical goods must be observed. Since such a settlement is clearly a contract with proper consideration, the civil law statutes of the place where the extra-judicial settlement takes place must be followed in so far as they do not contravene the divine positive or natural law or the prescriptions of Canon Law.[116] In demanding that the civil law statutes be observed in this settlement the Code manifests a consistency of attitude in recognizing that the civil law of the territory has been canonized in regard to contracts, as has already been asserted in canon 1529.

Article 5. Extraordinary Remedies

In addition to judicial actions for the declaration of nullity and the rescission of contracts, and the extra-judicial settlement by arbitration (*compositio*), Canon Law allows two extraordinary remedies for the protection of contractual rights. One is allowed by way of an exception to a judicial suit brought by an opponent. By this means the suit may be excluded because of the plaintiff's failure to protect his rights within the time allotted by law. This is known as

[111] Canon 1557, § 2, 2°.

[112] Canon 1599, § 2.

[113] Canon 1928.

[114] Vermeersch-Creusen, *Epitome,* III, n. 225.

[115] Canon 250, § 2.

[116] Canon 1926.

praescriptio.[117] The other is an equitable remedy to correct a harm done, and it is called *restitutio in integrum*.[118]

A. *Limitation of Actions*

Canon Law uses the general term *praescriptio* to describe both a means for the acquisition of rights or of property and a method of attaining freedom from certain obligations. American Law distinguishes these two phases by applying the terms, adverse possession or prescription, to indicate the method of acquiring title, and the term, limitation of actions, to indicate the method of defense against a judicial action. Limitation of actions is primarily a matter of procedural law affecting the right to sue.[119]

The notion of limitation of actions is based upon the fact that men are expected to be vigilant in the protection of their rights. If one party claims the right to institute an action against another, this right must be asserted within a reasonable period of time, while the evidence is still rather easily available; while the parties and witnesses still remember the circumstances of the agreement.[120] Accordingly, law decrees that if an action is not instituted before the passage of a stated period of time named in the law, the defendant may plead that neglect as a defense to the proceeding. In this case the defendant has no obligation of disputing the merits of the controversy.

Canon Law has adopted the civil law of the respective nations regarding the limitation of actions concerning contentious cases, with the exceptions, however, as stated in canons 1509-1512.[121] Further exceptions are made to this general rule for contentious actions, in which exceptions definite periods of time are specified in Canon Law

[117] Canons 1508-1512; 1701.

[118] Canons 1687-1689.

[119] Martin, *Adverse Possession, Prescription and Limitation of Actions. The Canonical "Praescriptio,"* The Catholic University of America Canon Law Studies, n. 202 (Washington, D. C.: The Catholic University of America Press, 1944), n. 4. Hereinafter cited *Adverse Possession.*

[120] Cf. Martin, *Adverse Possession,* nn. 1, 2, 247.

[121] Canon 1508.

for the limitation of actions. For example, a time limit of two years is stated for the beginning of an action to rescind a contract because of damage greater than half the value of the original contract resulting from the error of one of the contractants.[122]

Canon 1511, § 2, provides that actions for the recovery of immovable property, precious movables and rights pertaining to an ecclesiastical moral person may be brought at any time within thirty years from the time such action accrues, whether they be personal or real actions. Therefore, in the case of contracts involving bishops, as representing the moral person of the diocese, and religious congregations, which are also ecclesiastical moral persons, the civil law statute of limitations is not followed. Since both contractants have the status of moral persons, at least thirty years would have to run before either could allege that the right to bring judicial action had been forfeited. This concession gives both parties an advantage in regard to the time limit which other persons do not enjoy, since they must follow the statute of limitation of actions as prescribed by the civil law. In the American States, the time for the limitation of actions varies from State to State, and even within the same State according to the type of liability involved, but all the periods prescribed by civil statutes in the States of this country are shorter than thirty years.[123]

B. *Restitutio in Integrum*

The classic definition of *restitutio in integrum* is the following: It is an extraordinary remedy of law by which a person who has been gravely damaged by an invalid but rescissible act or transaction may, because of natural equity, be returned, through the ministry of a competent judge, to that status in which he was before being damaged.[124]

[122] Canon 1684; cf. *supra*, p. 186. Exceptions to the general rule of canon 1508 are stated in canons 1684, § 2; 1688, § 2; 1695, § 2; 1698, § 2; and 1893; cf. Martin, *Adverse Possession*, nn. 164, 189.

[123] Cf. Martin, *Adverse Possession*, pp. 140-146.

[124] Reiffenstuel, Lib. I, tit. 41, n. 3. The words "by a valid but rescissible act" have, in canon 1687, § 2, been added to Reiffenstuel's definition.—Cf. Feeney, *Restitutio in Integrum*, The Catholic University of America Canon Law

This remedy is one which is accorded principally to minors, although it is also available to adults under certain conditions.[125] Since moral persons are accorded the status of minors before the law of the Code, it is available to them also. Indeed, canon 1687, § 1, explicitly includes them as being entitled to this remedy.[126] *Restitutio in integrum* is not a privilege or an action, although it has an obvious relationship to rescissory actions.[127] It is a concession of the legislator to remedy inequities which cannot be corrected by the available judicial actions, namely, a declaration of nullity or a rescissory action. The latter is available only when the amount of damage suffered through simple error by the petitioner is clearly stated as one in excess of one half the amount of the original contract.[128] Canon 1687, § 1, merely states that *restitutio in integrum* is available to prevent a grave damage. The determination of the extent of the prerequisite damage is left to the discretion of the judge.[129]

Restitutio in integrum is not intended to be a substitute for other actions which can be introduced for the protection of contractual rights. If, therefore, the contract is invalid, it must be attacked on the score of nullity.[130] If error, fear, or deceit vitiate the contract, the rescissory actions given for the correction of these defects are to be used.[131] However, it may happen that the nullity of an act is not obvious, or that it cannot be proved. In this case the *restitutio in integrum* may be sought subordinately to the principal action.[132]

Three essential conditions are required for the use of *restitutio*

Studies, n. 129 (Washington, D. C.: The Catholic University of America Press, 1941), p. 49; cf. also, Lega, *De Iudiciis Ecclesiasticis,* I, n. 269.

125 Canon 1687, § 2.

126 ". . . "minorum iure fruentibus . . . suppetit remedium extraordinarium restitutionis in integrum."

127 Feeney, *Restitutio in Integrum,* p. 50.

128 Canon 1684, § 2; cf. *supra,* p. 186.

129 Roberti, *De Processibus* (2 vols., Romae: Apud Aedes Facultatis Iuridicae ad S. Apollinaris, 1926), I, n. 388.

130 Canon 1680, § 1.

131 Canon 1684.

132 Noval, *Commentarium Codicis Iuris Canonici, Liber IV, De Processibus, Pars I, De Iudiciis* (Augustae Taurinorum: Marietti, 1920), n. 343.

in integrum: (1) Grave damage must be suffered by the one seeking the remedy. (2) The contract must be a valid but rescissible one. (3) A worthy cause for the application of the remedy must be present.[183] To these a fourth condition may be added, namely, that a legal remedy at least equally effective cannot be sought.[184]

Since both parties to the contracts under discussion, the bishop representing the diocese and the religious superior representing the religious congregation, enjoy the rights of minors, the remedy of *restitutio in integrum* is available to each against the other, provided that the conditions outlined above are fulfilled. The worthy cause in the case of a moral person is predicated on its inability to protect itself because of its complete reliance on its administrators. In order to avail itself of the remedy, the moral person must prove through its representatives that a grave damage was incurred from a valid but rescissible act, and that no other legal remedy which is equally effective is available.

A moral person which has entered into a valid contract of alienation for which a just price has been realized, but has by means of this contract unreasonably or excessively prejudiced its rights or patrimony, can seek the *restitutio in integrum*. It is true that an action for recovery of damages may also be sought against the careless or incautious administrator, but this is often impossible, or at least in vain, when the administrator is a religious superior. Further, by rescinding the contract entirely, the *restitutio in integrum* not only restores the equivalent of the right sacrificed but also the right itself.[185] When the damage has been brought about by the acceptance of a contract for service, which is often the case in contracts between bishops and religious congregations, then a prosecution of the offending administrator, even if compensation is recovered from him, will not remedy every aspect of the inequality resulting from his administration.

In order to afford full protection to moral persons, the remedy of the *restitutio in integrum* is made available to the successors in

[183] Canon 1687, § 1; cf. Feeney, *Restitutio in Integrum*, pp. 49-53.

[184] Vermeersch-Creusen, *Epitome*, III, n. 118.

[185] Feeney, *Restitutio in Integrum*, p. 60.

office of those who have been guilty of maladministration as well as to the latter, since this remedy is conceded, not because of the person involved, but primarily because of the damage suffered.[186] In any event, when given to the moral person, which never dies, the remedy is of its nature perpetual, subject, however, to extinction according to the norms of limitation of actions.[187]

186 Lega, *Commentarius in Iudicia Ecclesiastica iuxta Codicem Iuris Canonici,* curante Victorio Bartoccetti (3 vols., Romae: Anonima Libraria Cattolica Italiana, 1938-1941), I, 434.

187 Cf. *supra,* p. 188.

CONCLUSIONS

1. Since there is no exception regarding the matter in the Code, it is held that the acceptable provisions of civil law apply in contractual relations between bishops and religious congregations.

2. The fundamental notions of contract are very similiar in both Canon and civil law. In the definition of contract the same elements are evident, the Canon Law notion of "*causa*" being a counterpart of the civil law notion of "consideration."

3. The assertion that the religious superior is competent to renounce the use of the right to a church or a public oratory as accorded in the law to every house of a clerical institute, does not seem to be juridically sound.

4. In a contract for the service of its members, the religious congregation could permit an individual religious to remain separated from the body of his community without recurring to the Holy See for permission, provided that the member was engaged in the works of the religious ministry.

5. A *pleno iure* effected union of a parish with a religious house does not necessarily imply that the church as well as the parish is of a religious status.

6. The common law regarding the taking possession of the parochial benefice applies to the parochial vicar in the same sense as it does to other pastors.

7. In the *pleno iure* effected union of a parish with a religious house as well as in the union *ad temporalia tantum quod attinet* the religious house becomes the recipient of the dominion of the temporal goods of the parish.

8. The approval of the Holy See is necessary for contracts involving either a temporal or a perpetual assignment of parishes to religious congregations.

9. In an implied contract assigning a parish to a religious congregation, the presumption of perpetuity is consonant with the legislation of the Code on parishes and pastors.

10. Arbitration concerning disputes arising out of contracts relative to the assignment of parishes by bishops to religious congregations is to be effected by the Sacred Congregation of the Council.

11. Judicial actions, and the extraordinary remedy of *restitutio in integrum* before the competent ecclesiastical tribunal are available to both contractants, the bishop, representing the diocese, and the religious congregation.

12. Neither of the two can profit by way of legal prescription against the other's right of judicial action until thirty years have elapsed since the right to such action accrued.

APPENDIX

1. Permission to Erect a Religious House

Contract between the Diocese of .... and the Congregation of ....

1. The Most Reverend N. N., Bishop of ...., having duly consulted the Diocesan Consultors, does hereby authorize and permit the said Congregation of ...., to establish a religious house in the city of .... in the aforementioned Diocese of ....

2. This foundation is subject to the general laws of the Code of Canon Law and to the Plenary, Provincial and Diocesan laws which are or will be in force in the said Diocese of ....

3. The scope and purpose of the said house are as follows:
   (a) it will be a house of residence for priests and brothers of the Congregation of ....
   (b) it will be a house of residence for the mission bands of the said congregation whose members may be assigned to give missions, retreats, etc. in various parishes and dioceses.
   (c) it will serve as a house of residence for student priests of the said congregation who may attend lectures at the nearby University of ....

4. The Congregation of .... agrees to engage in no further activities in the Diocese of .... without the express permission of the Most Reverend Bishop of the said diocese.

5. No parish or care of souls is attached to the house as such.

6. The land and buildings of the said house are exclusively the property of the Congregation of .... The latter congregation assumes all public and private responsibility henceforth for this property.

7. The Congregation of .... hereby acknowledges that it bears all financial responsibility of whatever kind for this house, as well as all claims and all contracts incident thereto.

8. The said congregation agrees to remove from residence in the said house any and every member whose presence in the diocese is lawfully objected to by the Most Reverend Bishop of .... Witnessed this............day of ...., 19............

Attest: (Seal of diocese) (Signed) ....
Bishop of ....

(Signature of Witnesses) (Signed) ....

(Seal of the congregation) Provincial Superior of the Congregation of ....

2. Contracts Concerning Parishes

CONTRACTUS

Illmum. et Revmum. Episcopum ...., inter et Adm. Revum. Superiorem Generalem Congregationis .... in Statibus Foederatis Americae Septentrionalis constitutae initus, relate ad Ecclesiam Sti. .... in urbe ....

Ut saluti spirituali fidelium in urbe .... commorantium faciliori ac tutiori consuleretur ratione et ut opus religionis promoveretur, Revmus. Episcopus .... opportunum censuit Ecclesiam paroecialem Sti. .... intra limites comitis ...., nuncupatam, Patribus Congregationis .... Provinciae Americanae concedere his sub conditionibus:

1. Beneplacitum Apostolicum ad hoc obtineatur;
2. Rector praedictae ecclesiae est praesentandus a Superiore Regulari iuxta Congregationis .... constitutiones, et instituendus ab Ordinario loci;
3. Rector ecclesiae eiusque adiutores in iis quae curam animarum ac Sacramentorum attingunt, subsunt ordinationibus ac mandatis Ordinarii loci;
4. Integra manent iura ac privilegia Regularium quoad internam familiae religiosae disciplinam;
5. At subsunt iis omnibus quae Leo Papa XIII disposuit in Constitutione "Romanos Pontifices" quoad Regulares quibus cura animarum est concessa, et normis in Codice Iuris Canonici praescriptis, necnou Conciliorum Plenariorum et Synodorum Provinciae ac Dioeceseos Constitutionibus;
6. Patres Congregationis .... praedictam ecclesiam deserere nequeunt, invito loci Ordinario, nisi saltem sex menses elapsi fuerint a tempore quo de hac intentione Ordinarium loci certiorem fecerint. (Conc. Balt. II, n. 407).

7. Hoc in casu, bona ecclesiae, donis et oblationibus fidelium acquisita, ad diocesim cedunt, iis exceptis, quae intuitu congregationis religiosae fuerint a fidelibus oblata. (Const. "Romanos Pontifices").

8. Quoad scholas catholicas praedictae ecclesiae, exceptis excipiendis, pacta supra allata serventur.

Lectum et acceptatum ab infrascriptis die .... mensis ...., 19....... in Cancellaria Dioeceseos ....

Testes: (Sigillum dioeceseos) (Signed) ....

.... Episcopus ....

(Sigillum congregationis) (Signed) ....

....

Superior ....

HIS EXCELLENCY, THE MOST REVEREND ....,
BISHOP OF .... AND
THE VERY REVEREND ...., SUPERIOR GENERAL OF THE CONGREGATION OF ....

1. The Most Reverend ...., Bishop of ...., admits the Congregation of .... into the Diocese of ...., and gives to the said congregation [*in perpetuum* or for .... years] the present corporate limits of the city of ...., in the State of ...., [if the contract is made *in perpetuum,* the words "and deeds to it the present church property of that city" are added].

2. The Superior General of the Congregation of ...., subject to the approval of the Holy See, for himself and his successors in office, hereby agrees to administer the territory designated in accordance with the law of the Church, by providing a sufficient number of priests to meet the present and future needs thereof subject to the approval of the Most Reverend Bishop of ....

3. The Most Reverend Bishop of .... gives the aforesaid congregation pastoral jurisdiction until such time as the establishment of a new parish or parishes becomes necessary, over all that territory now constituting the parish of St. ...., namely:

(Here the parish boundaries are outlined).

4. The Fathers of the Congregation of .... appointed to the office of pastor or assistant priests in the aforementioned parish shall enjoy the same rights and privileges and be subject to the same

duties as obtain for other pastors and assistant priests in the Diocese of .... according to the norms of the Code of Canon Law.

5. The appointment and removal of pastors and assistant priests shall conform to the requirements of the Code of Canon Law.

6. The Superior General of the aforementioned congregation agrees to erect or cause to be erected, with revenues of the parish, such buildings as may be needed from time to time, subject always to the approval of the Most Reverend Bishop of the Diocese of ....

7. The diocese does not obligate itself to subsidize or contribute to the support of the aforesaid parishes or missions established or to be established within the territory granted to the congregation.

8. This contract shall be effective on and after the .... day of................, 19.........

Attest: (Seal of the Diocese) (Signed) ....

(Signature of Witnesses) Bishop of ....

(Seal of the Congregation) (Signed) ....

Superior General of ....

3. Contract For Service of Sisters in Parochial Schools

This contract between the Sisters of ...., represented by Reverend Mother Provincial ...., and the Diocese of ...., represented by the Most Reverend ...., Bishop of ...., and the Reverend ...., pastor of St. .... Church, witnesses:

1. That the Sisters of .... agree to assume the teaching and conduct of St. .... grammar school in the city of .... at the beginning of the scholastic year in September, 19........; that the Sisters of .... will supply (number) teaching Sisters; that in the event of sufficient increased enrollment in future years, the Reverend Mother Provincial will endeavor to supply the needed number of additional teachers.

2. The Diocese of .... guarantees that the pastor of St. .... Church will pay the teaching Sisters the usual stipend of $........ per month for ten months or $........ per year, payable monthly.

3. The pastor of St. .... Church agrees to furnish adequate living quarters for the Sisters in .... Convent. Heat, light, upkeep, and repairs will be the concern of the pastor of St. .... Church.

4. Since the teaching Sisters, if they were in a separate convent, would be under necessity to bear the expense of their own table out of the salaries they receive, according to the custom of this diocese, the teaching Sisters will remit out of their annual salary $........ per Sister to the Superioress of St. .... Convent.

5. Should the Sisters of .... find it practicable to send an additional teacher who might instruct pupils in Music to the Convent outside the regular school hours, income derived therefrom would be the entire possession of the Sisters, less the board charge indicated in the preceding paragraph.

6. The Sisters of .... and the Most Reverend Bishop of .... mutually agree, that should either party to this contract desire to sever this contractual relationship, six months notice of such severance will be given.

(Signed) ....
Bishop of ....
(Signed) ....
Pastor of ....
(Signed) ....
Provincial of the Sisters of ......

4. Contract For Service of Teachers in High School

The following contract to go into effect on .... day of ...., 19........, is hereby entered into between the Diocese of .... and its .... High School, represented by the Most Reverend ...., Bishop of ...., on the one hand; and the Congregation of ...., represented by the Very Reverend ...., Provincial, on the other hand:

1. The Fathers of the Congregation of .... hereby agree to provide the said .... High School, for its present and future needs, with a sufficient number of competent Professors to teach all grades of the said High School; all these Professors to belong to the Congregation of ....; it being expressly stipulated that no other teachers, especially lay teachers, may be engaged as Professors in the said school.

2. The Very Reverend Provincial Superior of the Congregation of .... will have the right to appoint, remove, and replace the Professors; but the Most Reverend Bishop of ...., reserves to himself for any special case or emergency the right of removal when this may seem to him to be advisable; in which case previous notice must be given to the Very Reverend Provincial Superior by the Bishop.

3. The Diocese of .... hereby binds itself to provide a faculty house at its own expense for the use of the Fathers; also to provide light, water, fuel, and necessary but not expensive nor superfluous furniture; to pay the wages of the school janitors.

4. The Diocese of .... will not be held responsible for any expenses incurred by the Fathers for their maintenance, clothing, medicine, medical attention, travel, and other personal needs.

5. The Very Reverend Provincial Superior has the right to appoint one of the Fathers of the Congregation of .... as the local Superior of the School; the said Superior of the School will not be obliged to teach.

6. An immutable salary of $........ for said Superior and for each Father to cover twelve months' service, and payable in ten equal installments, will be given by the Diocese of ....to the aforesaid Provincial Superior or his local representative.

7. By mutual agreement, and after six months notice in writing, the contracting parties may altar or annul, in whole or in part, this contract, excepting the salary clause.

Signed and sealed this .... day of .... in the year of Our Lord, 19.........

Witnesses: (Seal of the diocese) (Signed) ....

Bishop of ....

(two) (Seal of the congregation) (Signed) ....

Provincial of ....

5. General Form of Contract Suitable For School, Hospital, Home, Orphanage, or Social Work

This agreement or contract made and entered into this .... day of .... in the year of Our Lord, 19........ between the Diocese of ...., party of the first part, and the Congregation of ...., party of the second part, witnesseth:

Whereas, the party of the first part is the owner of the property at (Here designate the property)

1. The said party of the first part agrees to grant to the said party of the second part the free use of the said property at .... in the city of ...., State of ...., as long as the party of the second part continues to be engaged in the work of (Here designate the type of work demanded)

2. The said party of the first part agrees to pay both the taxes and the insurance premium of the said property.

3. Furthermore, the said party of the first part agrees to pay for the necessary painting and the necessary repairs on the above mentioned property.

4. The said party of the first part shall not be held responsible except for those things herein stated.

5. The party of the first part further agrees to appropriate the sum of $........ towards the expense of heating and lighting the above mentioned property, each year for .... years beginning with the taking of possession of the above mentioned property by the party of the second part; the party of the second part agrees that after the abovementioned .... years the party of the first part will not be responsible for heating and lighting, but that the party of the second part assumes full responsibility for the expense of heating and lighting the property above mentioned.

6. The party of the second part agrees to supply a number of (Fathers, Sisters, Brothers) sufficient to conduct the work of .... according to the judgment of the party of the first part. These (Fathers, Sisters, Brothers) shall be appointed, removed or replaced by the (Very Reverend Provincial, Reverend Mother) of the Congregation of .... Should any (Father, Sister, Brother) become incapacitated by age, sickness, or accident, or in any other way unsuited, in the judgment of the party of the first part, for the work of .... it will be in the power of the party of the first part to discontinue (his, her) services, upon which (he, she) will be transferred from the community attached to the work of ....

7. The said party of the first part shall be the judge of the number of (Fathers, Sisters, Brothers) required for the proper conduct of the said work of .... and shall have the right of approval of those (Fathers, Sisters, Brothers) appointed by the party of the second part.

8. The party of the second part agrees that said premises shall not be occupied nor be permitted to be occupied otherwise than as a dwelling for members of the party of the second part engaged in the work of the said ....

IN WITNESS WHEREOF, the parties to these presents have hereunto set their hand and seals, the day and year first above written.

Attest: (Seal of Diocese) (Signed) ....

(Signatures of witness) Bishop of ....

(Seal of the Congregation) (Signed) ....

Superior of ....

BIBLIOGRAPHY

Canon Law Sources

Acta Apostolicae Sedis, Commentarium Officiale, Romae, 1909—

Acta et Decreta Concilii Plenarii Baltimorensis III, Baltimorae, 1886.

Acta et Decreta Concilii Provincialis Portlandensis in Oregon Quarti, Portlandiae in Ecclesia Metropolitana Celebrati diebus VIII, IX, X, Septembris MCMXXXII.

Acta et Decreta Sacrorum Conciliorum Recentiorium, Collectio Lacensis, 7 vols., Friburgi Brisgoviae, 1870-1890.

Acta Sanctae Sedis, 41 vols., Romae, 1865-1908.

Bruns, H. T., *Canones Apostolorum et Conciliorum Veterum Saeculorum IV-VII*, 2 vols., Berolini, 1839.

Bullarii Romani Continuatio Summorum Pontificum, 19 vols., Prati, 1756-1883.

Bullarum Diplomatum et Privilegiorum Sanctorum Romanorum Pontificum Taurinensis Editio, 25 vols., Augustae Taurinensis, 1857-1872.

Canones et Decreta Sacrosancti Oecumenici Concilii Tridentini, Romae 1904.

Codex Iuris Canonici Pii X Pontificis Maximi iussu digestus Benedicti Papae XV auctoritate promulgatus praefatione Fontium Annotatione et Indice Analytico-Alphabetico ab Emo Petro Card. Gasparri auctus, Romae: Typis Polyglottis Vaticanis, 1917. Reimpressio, 1934.

Codices Gregorianus, Hermogenianus, Theodosianus, edidit Gustavus Haenel, prostant Bonnae: Apud Adolphum Marcum, 1942.

Codicis Iuris Canonici Fontes cura Emi Petri Card. Gasparri editi, 9 vols., Romae (postea Civitate Vaticana): Typis Polyglottis Vaticanis, 1923-1939. (Vols. VII-IX ed. cura et studio Emi Iustiniani Card. Serédi.)

Collectanea in Usum Secretariae Sacrae Congregationis Episcoporum et Regularium, cura A. Bizzarri Archiepiscopi Phillipensis Secretarii edita, Romae: Ex Typographia Polyglotta, S. C. de Propaganda Fide, 1885.

Collectanea S. Congregationis de Propaganda Fide, 2 vols., Romae: Typographia Polyglotta, S. C. de Propaganda Fide, 1907.

Concilii Plenarii Baltimorensis II Acta et Decreta, 2. ed., Baltimorae, 1894.

Corpus Iuris Canonici, Pars I, *Decretum Magistri Gratiani*, ed. Lipsiensis secunda post Aemilii Ludovici Richteri curas ad librorum manu scriptorum et editionis Romanae fidem recognovit et adnotatione critica instruxit Aemilius Friedberg, Lipsiae, 1879. Editio anastatice repetita, Lipsiae, 1922.

Corpus Iuris Canonici, Pars II, *Decretalium Collectiones*, ed. Lipsiensis secunda, post Aemilii Ludovici Richteri curas instruxit Aemilius Friedberg, Lipsiae, 1881. Editio anastatice repetita, Lipsiae, 1922.

Corpus Iuris Civilis, 3 vols., Vol. I, ed. stereotypa quinta decima, *Institutiones*, quas recognovit Paulus Krueger, *Digesta* quae recognovit Theodorus Mommsen, retractavit Paulus Krueger, Berolini: Apud Weidmannos, 1928.

Corpus Iuris Civilis, 3 vols., Vol. II, ed. stereotypa nona, *Codex Iustinianus*, quem recognovit et retractavit Paulus Krueger, Berolini: Apud Weidmannos, 1915.

Corpus Iuris Civilis, 3 vols., Vol. III, ed. stereotypa quinta, *Novellae*, quas recognovit Rudolfus Schoell, absolvit Guglielmus Kroll, Berolini: Apud Weidmannos, 1928.

Decretales Gregorii Papae IX, suae integritati una cum glossis restituatae cum privilegio Gregorii XIII, Pont. Max. et aliorum Principum, Romae, 1582.

Decretum Gratiani, emendatum et notationibus illustratum una cum glossis restitutum cum privilegio Gregorii XIII, Pont. Max. et aliorum Principum, Romae, 1582.

Index Facultatum quas, pro Locis Missionis suae, Nuntiis, Internuntiis, et Delegatis Apostolicis penes Civitates seu Nationes, post Codicem Iuris Canonici Publicationem Tribuere SSmus Dominus Noster Decrevit, Ceteris Abrogatis.

Liber Sextus Decretalium D. Bonifatii Papae VIII, suae integritati cum Clementinis et Extravagantibus, earumque Glossis restitutis, Romae, 1582.

Mansi, J. D., *Sacrorum Conciliorum Nova et Amplissima Collectio*, 53 vols. in 60, Vols. 1-31, Florentiae, Venetiis, Parisiis, 1759-1798; Vols. 31b-53, Parisiis, Leipzig, Arnhem, 1901-1927.

Normae secundum quas S. Cong. Episcoporum et Regularium procedere solet in approbandis novis institutis votorum simplicium, Romae: Typis S. C. de Propaganda Fide, 1901.

Normae secundum quas S. Congregatio de Religiosis in novis congregationibus approbandis procedere solet, Romae: Typis Polyglottis Vaticanis, 1922.

Potthast, A., *Regesta Pontificum Romanorum inde ab anno post Christum natum* 1198 *ad annum* 1304, 2 vols., *Berolini*, 1874-1875.

Regesta Pontificum Romanorum ab condita Ecclesia ad annum post Christum natum 1198, *edidit Philippus Jaffé*, ed. secunda correctam et auctam auspiciis Guglielmi Wattenbach curaverunt, F. Kaltenbrunner, P. Ewald, S. Löwenfeld, 2 vols. in 1, Lipsiae, 1885-1888.

Sacrae Rotae Romanae Decisiones Recentiores, Pars I, Francofurti, 1623; Pars II, Aurelii, 1623; Partes III-XIX, Romae, 1645-1703.

Sacrae Rotae Romanae Decisiones coram Molines, 5 vols., Romae, 1728.

Schroeder, Henry J., *Canons and Decrees of the Council of Trent*, St. Louis: B. Herder Book Co., 1941.

Thesaurus Resolutionum Sacrae Congregationis Concilii, 167 vols., Romae, 1718-1908.

Civil Law Sources

Alabama, Code of, St. Paul: West Publishing Co., 1941.

Arizona Code, compiled by Henry D. Ross, Alfred C. Lockwood, and Archibald G. McAlister, Indianapolis: Bobbs-Merrill Co., 1940.

Arkansas, A Digest of the Statutes, by Walter L. Pope, Helms Publishing Co., 1937.

Colorado Statutes Annotated 1935, compiled under the supervision of A. H. Michie, C. W. Sublett and R. R. Rusmisel, Denver: Robinson Printing Co., 1936.

Connecticut, The General Statutes of, Revision of 1930, published by authority of the State Secretary, 1930.

Delaware, Revised Code of 1935, Wilmington: Star Publishing Co., 1936.

District of Columbia, The Code of the, Washington, D. C., 1930.

Florida Statutes, 1941 [no editor, no publisher], 1943.

Georgia, Code of, Annotated 1943, compiled by H. S. Strazier, Orville A. Park and H. B. Skillman, Atlanta: Harrison Publishing Co., 1943.

Idaho Annotated Code of 1932, compiled by T. Bailey Lee, C. Ben Ross, and Fred E. Lukens, Indianapolis: Bobbs-Merrill Co., 1932.

Illinois Revised Statutes, 1945, compiled and edited under Smith-Hurd Classification, Chicago: Burdette Smith Co., 1945.

Indiana Annotated Statutes, edited by Harrison Burnon, revised by Benj. F. Watson, Indianapolis: Bobbs-Merrill Co., 1934.

Iowa Code of 1939, edited by V. G. Whitney, Des Moines, 1939.

Kansas, General Statutes of 1935, edited by Franklin Corrick, Topeka: W. C. Austin, 1936.

Kentucky Revised Statutes 1944, edited by Robert K. Cullen and L. C. Turner, published by Kentucky Statute Revision Commission, 1944.

Louisiana, Civil Code of the State of, Revision of 1870, 2 vols., 2 ed. by Benj. W. Dart, 1945.

Maine, The Revised Statutes of the State of, Augusta: Kennebec Journal Press, 1945.

Maryland, The Annotated Code of the Public General Laws of, 2 vols., edited by Horace E. Flack, Baltimore, 1939.

Massachusetts, Tercentenary Edition of the General Laws of the Commonwealth of, edited by William E. Dorman and Henry Wiggin, Boston, 1932.

Michigan, The Compiled Laws of the State of, 1929, edited by William B. Brucker, Oscar K. Riopelle and John Kaminski, Lansing, 1930.

Minnesota, Mason's Statutes, 1927, St. Paul, 1927.

Mississippi Code Annotated, 1942, 8 vols., edited by Greek I. Rice and George H. Ethridge, Atlanta: Harrison Co., 1943.

Missouri, Statutes of the State of, 1939, revised by Phil M. Donnelly et alii, Jefferson City: Millard Printing Co., 1940.

Montana, The Revised Code of, 1935, edited by H. K. Anderson and Carl McFarland, Great Falls: Tribune Printing and Supply Co., 1936.

Nebraska, Revised Statutes of 1943, edited by 1943 Statute Commission, Lincoln, 1944.

Nevada Compiled Laws, 1929, compiled and annotated by Curtis Hillyer, San Francisco, 1930.

New Hampshire, Laws of the State of, 1901, Concord, 1901.

New Hampshire, The Revised Laws of the State of, edited by Thomas Marble and Maryland H. Morse, Concord: Rumford Press, 1942.

New Jersey, Revised Statutes of, 1937, 4 vols., edited by Statute Commission, 1938.

New Mexico Statutes of 1941, 6 vols., edited by Charles R. Brice, Herbert Girhart, and Edward P. Chase, Indianapolis: Bobbs-Merrill Co., 1942.

New York, Cahill's Consolidated Laws of, 2 ed., edited by Basil Jones, Chicago, 1930.

North Carolina Code of 1931, edited by A. Hewson Michie and Beirne Skedman, Charlottesville, 1931.

North Dakota Revised Code of 1943, edited by Code Revision Committee, Fargo: Knight Printing Co., 1944.

Ohio, Throckmorton's Code, 1940, edited by William E. Baldwin, Cleveland: Banks-Baldwin Co., 1940.

Oklahoma Statutes, 1941, St. Paul: West Publishing Co., 1942.

Oregon Compiled Laws Annotated, edited under supervision of the Supreme Court of Oregon, San Francisco: Bancroft, Whitney Co., 1940.

Pennsylvania, Purdon's Statutes of 1936, St. Paul: West Publishing Co., 1936.

Rhode Island General Laws of 1938, edited by L. W. Cappelli, Providence: Thompson and Thompson, 1939.

South Carolina Code of Laws, 1942, edited by Code Commission, Clinton: Jacobs Press, 1943.

Tennessee, The Code of, 1932, edited by Samuel C. Williams, Robert T. Shannon and George Harsh, Kingsport, 1932.

Texas Complete Statutes, 1928, Kansas City, 1928.

Utah Code Annotated 1943, Chicago: Callaghan & Co., 1943.

Vermont, The Public Laws of, 1933, Montpelier: Capitol City Press, 1934.

Virginia, The Code of, 1942, editorial supervision of A. Hewson Michie, Charles W. Sublett and Beirne Skedman, Charlottsville: Michie Co., 1942.

Washington, Pierce's Code of the State of, annotated by Frank Pierce, Seattle: Frank Pierce, 1944.

Wisconsin Statutes, 1943, edited by E. E. Brossard, Racine: Former Co., 1944.

Wyoming Revised Statutes, 1931, edited by William Courtright, Cheyenne, 1931.

Authors

Amos, Sheldon, *Roman Civil Law,* London, 1883.

Augustine, Charles, *A Commentary on the New Code of Canon Law,* 8 vols., St. Louis: B. Herder Book Co., Vol. II, 4 ed., 1923, Vol. III, 4 ed., 1929, Vol. VI, 2 ed., 1923.

Augustine, Charles, *The Canonical and Civil Status of Catholic Parishes in the United States,* St. Louis: B. Herder Book Co., 1926.

Augustine, Charles, *The Rights and Duties of Ordinaries*, St. Louis: B. Herder Book Co., 1924.

Ayrinhac, H. A., *Administrative Legislation in the New Code of Canon Law*, New York: Longmans, Green & Co., 1930.

Balmes, Hilaire, *Les Religieux a Voeux Simples d'apres le Code*, Paray-le-Monial, 1921.

Barbosa, Augustinus, *Iuris Ecclesiastici Libri Tres*, Lugduni, 1650.

Barbosa, Augustinus, *Pastoralis Sollicitudo seu de Officio et Potestate Episcopi Descriptio*, 3 partes in 2 vols., Lugduni, 1656.

Bastnagel, Clement, *The Appointment of Parochial Adjutants and Assistants*, The Catholic University of America Canon Law Studies, n. 58, Washington, D. C.: The Catholic University of America, 1930.

Battandier, Albert, *Guide Canonique pour les Constitutions des Instituts a Voeux Simples*, 6. ed., Paris, 1923.

Bays, Alfred, *Business Law*, New York: Macmillan Co., 1919.

Benedictus XIV, *De Synodo Dioecesana*, 3 vols., Romae, 1788.

Beste, Udalricus, *Introductio in Codicem*, Collegeville, Minn.: St. John's Abbey Press, 1938.

Biederlack, J.—Führich, M., *De Religiosis*, Oeniponte, 1919.

Blackstone, William, *Commentaries on the Law of England*, 12. ed., 4 vols., Dublin, 1775.

Blat, Albertus, *Commentarium Textus Codicis Iuris Canonici*, 5 vols., Romae, 1919-1927.

Bouix, D., *Tractatus de Jure Regularium*, 2 vols., Parisiis, 1857.

Bouscaren, T. Lincoln, *The Canon Law Digest*, 2 vols., Milwaukee: The Bruce Publishing Co., 1934-1943.

Brown, Brendan, *The Canonical Juristic Personality with Reference to its Status in the United States of America*, The Catholic University of America Canon Law Studies, n. 39, Washington, D. C.: The Catholic University of America, 1927.

Buckler, W. H., *Contract in Roman Law*, London, 1895.

Cance, Adrien, *Le Code de Droit Canonique*, 4 ed., 3 vols., Paris: Librairie le Coffre, 1930.

Chelodi, Ioannes, *Ius de Personis iuxta Codicem Iuris Canonici*, ed. altera a Sac. Ernesto Bertagnolli recognita et aucta, Tridenti: Libr. Edit. Tridentum, 1927.

Clancy, Patrick, *The Local Religious Superior*, The Catholic University of America Canon Law Studies, n. 175, Washington, D. C.: The Catholic University of America Press, 1943.

Cocchi, Guidus, *Commentarium in Codicem Iuris Canonici ad Usum Scholarum*, 5 vols. in 8, Taurinorum Augustae: Officina Libraria Marietti, 1920-1930.

Coronata, Mattheus Conte a, *Institutiones Iuris Canonici ad Usum Utriusque Cleri et Scholarum*, 5 vols., Taurini: Ex Officina Libraria Marietti, 1933-1939, Vols. I-II, 2. ed., 1939, Vols. III-V, 1933-1936.

Creusen, Joseph—Ellis, Adam C.—Garesché, Edward F., *Religious Men and Women in the Code*, 4. English ed., Milwaukee: Bruce Publishing Co., 1940.

D'Annibale, *Summula Theologiae Moralis,* 5. ed., 3 vols., Romae, 1908.

Delgado, Conrado, *De Relationibus Inter Parochum Religiosum et eius Superiores Regulares,* Rio de Janeiro: Editora Vozes Limitada, 1943.

De Luca, Ioannes B., *Theatrum Veritatis et Justitiae,* 15 vols. in 8, Coloniae Agrippinae, 1706.

De Meester, Alphonsus, *Juris Canonici et Juris Canonico-Civilis Compendium,* 3 vols. in 4, Brugis, 1921-1928.

Dignan, Joseph, *A History of the Legal Incorporation of Catholic Church Property in the United States (1784-1932),* Washington, D. C.: The Catholic University of America, 1933.

Downs, John, *The Concept of Clerical Immunity,* The Catholic University of America Canon Law Studies, n. 126, Washington, D. C.: The Catholic University of America Press, 1941.

Doheny, William J., *Practical Problems in Church Finance,* Milwaukee: The Bruce Publishing Co., 1941.

Dubé, Arthur J., *The General Prinicples for the Reckoning of Time in Canon Law,* The Catholic University of America Canon Law Studies, n. 144, Washington, D. C.: The Catholic University of America Press, 1941.

Fagnanus, Prosper, *Commentaria in Quinque Libros Decretalium,* Venetiis, 1709.

Fanfani, Ludovicus, *De Iure Religiosorum ad Normam Codicis Iuris Canonici,* 2. ed., Taurini-Romae: Ex Officina Libraria Marietti, 1925.

Feeney, Thomas, *Restitutio in Integrum,* The Catholic University of America Canon Law Studies, n. 129, Washington, D. C.: The Catholic University of America Press, 1941.

Ferraris, Lucius, *Prompta Bibliotheca Canonica, Iuridica, Moralis, Theologica necnon Ascetica, Polemica, Rubricistica, et Historica,* 8 vols., Romae 1885-1892; *Supplementum,* ed. Ianuarius Bucceroni, Romae, 1899.

Flanagan, Bernard, *The Canonical Erection of Religious Houses,* The Catholic University of America Canon Law Studies, n. 179, Washington, D. C.: The Catholic University of America Press, 1943.

Gaius, *Institutiones,* ed. Johannes Baviera, in *Fontes Iuris Romani Antejustiniani,* Florentiae, 1909.

Gibalini, Joseph, *De Universa Rerum Humanarum Negotiatione,* 2 vols., Lugduni, 1863.

Girard, Paul F., *Manuel Elementaire de Droit Romain,* Paris, 1924.

——, *Textes de Droit Romain,* Paris, 1923.

Goyeneche, S., *Iuris Canonici Summa Principia,* Pars. II, *De Religiosis,* Romae: Tip. Pol. "Cuore di Maria," 1938.

Hannan, Jerome, *The Canon Law of Wills,* The Catholic University of America Canon Law Studies, n. 86, Washington, D. C.: The Catholic University of America, 1934.

Heston, Edward, *The Alienation of Church Property in the United States,* The Catholic University of America Canon Law Studies, n. 132, Washington, D. C.: The Catholic University of America Press, 1941.

Hinschius, Paulus, *Decretales Pseudo-Isidorianae et Capitula Angilramni*, Lipsiae, 1863.

Hostiensis, Cardinalis (Henricus de Segusio), *Commentaria in Quinque Libros Decretalium*, 5 vols. in 3, Venetiis, 1581.

——, *Summa Aurea*, Lugduni, 1568.

Kent, James, *Commentaries on American Law*, 4 vols., New York, 1848.

Leage, R. W., *Roman Private Law*, second edition by C. H. Ziegler, London: Macmillan & Co., 1937. Reprinted, 1942.

Lega, Michael, *Commentarius in Iudicia Ecclesiastica iuxta Codicem Iuris Canonici*, curante Victorio Bartoccetti, 3 vols., Romae: Anonima Libraria Cattolica Italiana, 1938-1941.

Lega, Michael, *Praelectiones de Iudiciis Ecclesiasticis*, 4 vols., Romae, 1896-1901.

Leitner, Martin, *Handbuch des katolishen Kirchenrechts auf Grund des neuen Kodex*, 5 vols., Vol. I, 2. ed., Regensburg: Kösel & Pustet, 1921.

Leurenius, Petrus, *Forum Ecclesiasticum*, 5 vols., Venetiis, 1729.

Maroto, Phillipus, *Institutiones Iuris Canonici*, 2 vols., Madrid, 1918-1919.

Martin, Thomas Owen, *Adverse Possession, Prescription and Limitation of Actions. The Canonical "Praescriptio,"* The Catholic University of America Canon Law Studies, n. 202, Washington, D. C.: The Catholic University of America Press, 1944.

McCoy, Alan, *Force and Fear in Relation to Delictual Imputability*, The Catholic University of America Canon Law Studies, n. 200, Washington, D. C.: The Catholic University of America Press, 1944.

McManus, James, *The Administration of Temporal Goods in Religious Institutes*, The Catholic University of America Canon Law Studies, n. 109, Washington, D. C.: The Catholic University of America, 1937.

Melo, Antonius, *De Exemptione Regularium*, The Catholic University of America Canon Law Studies, n. 12, Washington, D. C.: The Catholic University of America, 1921.

Merkelbach, Henricus, *Summa Theologia Moralis*, 3 vols., Parisiis: Typis Desclée de Brouwer et Soc., 1931-1933.

Michiels, Gommarus, *Normae Generales Iuris Canonici*, 2 vols., Lublin: Universitas Catholica, 1929.

Muirhead, J., *The Institutes of Gaius and the Rules of Ulpian*, Edinburgh, 1904.

Noval, Joseph, *Commentarium Codicis Iuris Canonici*, Liber IV, *De Processibus*, Pars. I, *De Iudiciis*, Augustae Taurinorum: Marietti, 1920.

O'Brien, Joseph, *The Exemption of Religious in Church Law*, Milwaukee: Bruce, 1943.

Oesterle, Gerardus, *Praelectiones Iuris Canonici*, Romae, 1931.

Ojetti, Benedictus, *Commentarium in Codicem Iuris Canonici*, 4 vols., Romae, 1927-1931.

——, *Synopsis Rerum Moralium et Iuris Pontificii*, 3. ed., 4 vols., Romae, 1909-1914.

Ottaviani, Alaphridus, *Institutiones Iuris Publici Ecclesiastici*, 2. ed., 2 vols., Civitate Vaticana: Typis Polyglottis Vaticanis, 1935-1936.

Papi, Hector, *The Government of Religious Communities,* New York, 1919.

——, *Religious in Church Law,* New York, 1924.

Pejška, Joseph, *Ius Canonicum Religiosorum,* 3. ed., Friburgi Brisgoviae: B. Herder, 1927.

Petra, Vincentius, *Commentaria ad Constitutiones Apostolicas,* 5 vols. in 4, Venetiis, 1729.

Pirhing, Ernricus, *Jus Canonicum Nova Methodo Explicatum,* 5 vols. in 4, Dilingae, 1674-1678.

Poste, Edward, *Gaii Institutionum Iuris Civilis Comentarii Quatuor,* 2. ed., Oxford, 1875.

Prümmer, Dominicus, *Manuale Iuris Canonici in Usum Scholarum,* 3. ed., Friburgi Brisgoviae: B. Herder, 1922.

Raus, J. B., *De Sacrae Obedientiae Virtute et Voto,* Lugduni: Typis Emmanuel Vitte, 1923.

——, *Institutiones Canonicae iuxta Novum Codicem Iuris,* 2. ed., Lugduni: Typis Emmanuel Vitte, 1931.

Reiffenstuel, Anacletus, *Jus Canonicum Universum, editio novissima cui accessit Tractatus de Regulis Iuris,* 6 vols., Romae, 1831-1834.

Reilly, Thomas, *The Visitation of Religious,* The Catholic University of America Canon Law Studies, n. 120, Washington, D. C.: The Catholic University of America, 1938.

Restatement of the Law of Contracts, 2 vols., St. Paul: American Law Institute, 1932.

Roberti, Franciscus, *De Delictis et Poenis,* 1 vol. in 2, Romae: Libraria Pontificii Instituti Utriusque Iuris, 1930-1938.

——, *De Processibus,* 2 vols., Romae: Apud Aedes Facultatis Iuridicae and S. Apollinaris, 1926.

Robinson, William, *Elementary Law,* Boston, 1910.

Roelker, Edward, *Principles of Privilege According to the Code of Canon Law,* Catholic University of America Canon Law Studies, n. 35, Washington, D. C.: The Catholic University of America, 1926.

Schaefer, Timotheus, *Compendium de Religiosis ad Normam Codicis Iuris Canonici,* Münster i. W.: Ex Officina Libraria Aschendorff, 1931.

Schmalzgrueber, Franciscus, *Ius Ecclesiasticum Universum,* 5 vols. in 12, Romae, 1843-1845.

Schroeder, Henry, *Disciplinary Decrees of the General Councils,* St. Louis: B. Herder, 1937.

Stephens, Serjeant, *New Commentaries on the Law of England,* 6. ed., 4 vols., London, 1868.

Suarez, Franciscus, *Opera Omnia,* ed. nova a Carolo Berton, 28 vols., Parisiis: Apud Ludovicum Vivès, 1856-1861.

Thomas Aquinas, St., *Summa Theologica,* emendata a De Rubeis, Billuart et aliorum Notis Selectis Ornata, 6 vols., Taurini: Marietti, 1937.

Toso, Albertus, *Ad Codicem Iuris Canonici Commentaria Minora,* 5 vols., Romae: Jus Pontificium, 1920-1927.

U. S. Statutes at Large, XXX, 55th Congress 1897-1899, Washington, 1899.

Van Hove, A., *Commentarium Lovaniense in Codicem Iuris Canonici,* Vol. I, Tomus II, *De Legibus Ecclesiasticis,* Mechliniae: Dessain, 1930; Vol. I, Tomus III, *De Consuetudine-De Temporis Supputatione,* Mechliniae: Dessain, 1933.

Vecchiotti, Septimus, *Institutiones Canonicae,* 16. ed., 3 vols., Taurini, 1875.

Vermeersch, A., *Theologiæ Moralis, Principia, Responsa, Consilia,* 4 vols., Romae: Università Gregoriana, 1922-1924.

Vermeersch, A.—Creusen, J., *Epitome Iuris Canonici cum Commentariis ad Scholas et ad Usum Privatum,* 3 vols., Vol. I, ed. quarta, 1929, Vol. II, ed. tertia, 1927, Vol. III, ed. tertia, 1928, Mechliniae-Romae: H. Dessain.

Vromant, G., *De Bonis Ecclesiae Temporalibus ad Usum Utriusque Cleri, praesertim Missionariorum et Religiosorum,* Louvain: Desbarax, 1927.

Wernz, Franciscus X., *Ius Decretalium ad Usum Praelectionum in Scholis Textus Canonici sive Iuris Decretalium,* 2. ed., 6 vols., Romae-Prati, 1906-1913.

Wernz, F.—Vidal P., *Ius Canonicum ad Codicis Normam Exactum,* 7 vols. in 8, Romae: Apud Aedes Universitatis Gregorianae, 1923-1938.

Williston, Samuel, *The Law of Contracts,* 4 vols., New York, 1920.

Woywod, S., *A Practical Commentary on the Code of Canon Law,* 7. ed., revised by Callistus Smith, 2 vols., 1943, New York: Joseph F. Wagner.

Zollmann, Carl, *American Church Law,* St. Paul: West Publishing Co., 1933.

ARTICLES

Bastnagel, Clement, "Status of Religious Oratory after Waiver of Right to Public Oratory"—*The Jurist,* IV (1944), 151-158.

Boudinhon, A., "An Nullus semper sit Actus Superioris non Petito Consilio"—*Jus Pontificium,* VIII (1928), 28-35.

Couly, A., "Les Biens Temporels de L'Eglise"—*Le Canoniste Contemperain,* XLV (1922), 14-25.

"Decisions and Decrees"—*The Jurist,* I (1941), 163-168.

Doheny, William, "Church Finance and Problems of Alienation"—*The Jurist,* I (1941), 97-107.

Dooley, Eugene A., "The Juridical Status of the Parishes of Religious: Another View"—*The Jurist,* III. (1943), 117-128.

Ellis, Adam, "Triginta Millia Libellarum seu Francorum"—*Periodica,* XXVII (1938), 348-353.

Goyeneche, S., "Consultationes"—*CpR,* III (1922), 215-216; 329-337; VI (1925), 357-360; 484-486; X (1929), 39-44, 177-183.

Hannan, Jerome D., "The Juridical Status of the Parishes of Religious"—*The Jurist,* I (1941), 329-335.

Larraona, Arcadius, "Annotationes"—*CpR,* II (1921), 183-185.

——, "Consultationes"—*CpR,* V (1924), 217-225.

——, "Commentarium Codicis"—*CpR,* I (1920), 112-114; 134-139; 171-177; II (1921), 201-210; 275-287; III (1922), 45-53; IV (1923), 39-46; 134-139; V (1924), 324-334; 417-436; VII (1926), 30-36; VIII (1927), 441-448; X (1929), 33-42; XII (1931), 244-252; 353-359; 435-442; XIII (1932), 24-35; 92-99; 184-195; XIV (1933), 38-44; 169-182; 252-256.

Maroto, Phillipus, "Annotationes"—*CpR,* I (1920), 166-171; V (1924), 122-134; VII (1926), 435-442.

Nebreda, Eulogius, "De Loci Ordinariorum Iuribus circa Pia Legata Donationesve tum Religiosis tum Eorum Ecclesiis etiam Paroecialibus facta"—*CpR,* VII (1926), 107-118; 191-198; 261-271; 317-333.

Ojetti, Benedictus, "In Canonem 105 Codicis J. C."—*Jus Pontificium,* VII (1927), 13-25.

Piontek, Cyril, "A Gentleman's Agreement"—*The Jurist,* III (1943), 284-305.

Roelker, Edward, "The Concept of Invalidating Laws,"—*The Jurist,* III (1943), 32-63.

——, "The Power to Enact Invalidating Laws,"—*The Jurist,* III (1943), 231-257.

——, 'The Interpretation of Invalidating Laws,"—*The Jurist,* III (1943), 364-403.

——, "The Effect of Invalidating Laws,"—*The Jurist,* III (1943), 550-566.

Vermeersch, Arthurus, "De commoratione extra propriam religionis domum,"—*Periodica,* X (1922), 36-37.

Periodicals

American Ecclesiastical Review, The, Philadelphia, 1889-1943, Baltimore, 1944-

Analecta Juris Pontificii, 26 vols., Romae, 1855-1869; Parisiis, 1872-1891.

Apollinaris, Romae, 1928-

Canoniste Contemperain, Le, 45 vols., Paris, 1878-1922.

Commentarium pro Religiosis, Romae, 1920; ab anno 1935: *Commentarium pro Religiosis et Missionariis.*

Homiletic and Pastoral Review, The, New York, 1900-

Jurist, The, Washington, D. C., 1941-

Jus Pontificium, Romae, 1921-

Periodica de Re Canonica et Morali utili praesertim Religiosis et Missionariis, Brugis, 1905-1927.

Periodica de Re Morali, Canonica, Liturgica, Brugis, 1928-1936; Romae, 1937-

ABBREVIATIONS

AAS—Acta Apostolicae Sedis.
AER—American Ecclesiastical Review.
Am. D.—American Decisions.
Am. R.—American Reports.
Am. S. R.—American State Report.
Analecta J. P.—Analecta Juris Pontificii.
Ann. Cas.—American and English Annotated Cases.
App. D. C.—District of Columbia Appeals.
Ark.—Arkansas Reports.
ASS—Acta Sanctae Sedis.
Atl.—Atlantic Reporter.
Barb. (N. Y.)—Barbour's New York Supreme Court Reports.
Cal.—California Reports.
Cal. App.—California Appeals.
C. C. A.—U. S. Circuit Court of Appeals Report.
Civ. App.—Civil Appeals.
C. J.— Corpus Juris.
Coll. Lac.—Collectio Lacensis.
Colo.—Colorado Reports.
Comm. App.—Common Appeals.
Conn.—Connecticut Reports.
CpR—Commentarium pro Religiosis.
F.—Federal Reporter.
Fontes—Codicis Iuris Canonici Fontes cura—Gasparri editi.
Ga.—Georgia Appeals
Gill & J.—Gill and Johnson's Reports (Maryland).
Hill (N. Y.)—Hill's New York Reports.
Hun—Hun's New York Supreme Court Reports.
Iowa—Iowa Reports.
Ill.—Illinois Reports.
Ill. App.—Illinois Appelate Court Reports.
Ind. App.—Indiana Appeals.
JE—Jaffé-Ewald.
JK—Jaffé-Kaltenbrunner.
JL—Jaffé-Löwenfeld.
Kan.—Kansas Reports.
L. Ed.—Lawyer's Edition Supreme Court Reports.
La.—Louisiana Reports.
La. App.—Louisiana Appeals.
L.R.A.—Lawyers' Reports Annotated.

Mansi—*Sacrorum Conciliorum Nova et Amplissima Collectio.*
Mass.—Massachusetts Reports.
Md.—Maryland Reports.
Mich.—Michigan Reports.
Minn.—Minnesota Reports.
Mo.—Missouri Reports.
Mo. App.—Missouri Appeals Reports.
Mont.—Montana Reports.
N. C.—North Carolina Reports.
N. E.—Northeastern Reporter.
N. M.—New Mexico Reports.
N. W.—Northwestern Reporter.
N. Y. S.—New York Supplement.
N. Y. Super.—New York Superior Court Reports.
Ohio App.—Ohio Appeals.
Okla.—Oklahoma Territorial Reports.
P.—Pacific Reporter.
Pa.—Pennsylvania State Reports.
Pen. & W. (Pa.)—Penrose and Watts Pennsylvania Reports.
Periodica—*Periodica de Re Canonica et Morali utili praesertim Religiosis et Missionariis.*
Pont. Comm. Intr.—Pontifica Commissio Interpretationis.
Potthast—*Regesta Pontificium Romanorum.*
R. I.—Rhode Island Reports.
S. C. C.—Sacra Congregatio Concilii.
S. C. de Relig.—Sacra Congregatio de Religiosis.
S. C. Ep. et Reg.—Sacra Congregatio Episcoporum et Regularium.
S. Ct.—Supreme Court Reporter of Decisions of United States Supreme Court.
S. E.—Southeastern Reporter.
So.—Southern Reporter.
S. R. R.—Sacra Romana Rota.
S. W.—Southwestern Reporter.
Tex.—Texas Reports.
U. S.—United States Reports.
Utah—Utah Reports.
Wall.—Wallace United States Supreme Court Reports.
Wash.—Washington State Reports.
Wis.—Wisconsin Reports.
W. W. Harr. (Del.)—W. W. Harrington (Delaware) Reports.

A. M. D. G.

ALPHABETICAL INDEX

BIOGRAPHICAL NOTE

TIMOTHY LYNCH was born in Hoboken, New Jersey, on August 15, 1915. He received his elementary education at Saint Paul of the Cross Parochial School, Jersey City, New Jersey, and was graduated in June, 1928. In September of the same year he entered the preparatory seminary of the Missionary Servants of the Most Holy Trinity, Saint Joseph's Preparatory College, Holy Trinity, Alabama, and completed the course of studies in June, 1932. He entered the novitiate of the Missionary Servants of the Most Holy Trinity at Holy Trinity, Alabama, where he made his religious profession on June 11, 1933. He continued his studies at Saint Joseph's College, Holy Trinity, Alabama. From the year 1935 until 1937, he was Instructor at St. Augustine's Military Academy, Rio Piedras, Puerto Rico. His philosophical and theological studies were made at the Catholic University of America and at Carmelite College, Washington, D. C., where he was ordained to the priesthood on May 29, 1943. In September, 1943, he entered the School of Canon Law of the Catholic University of America, where he received the Baccalaureate Degree in Canon Law in May, 1944, and the Licentiate Degree in Canon Law in May, 1945.

CANON LAW STUDIES *

1. Freriks, Rev. Celestine A., C.PP.S., J.C.D., Religious Congregations in Their External Relations, 121 pp., 1916.
2. Gallihier, Rev. Daniel M., O.P., J.C.D., Canonical Elections, 117 pp., 1917.
3. Borkowski, Rev. Aurelius L., O.F.M., J.C.D., De Confraternitatibus Ecclesiasticis, 136 pp., 1918.
4. Castillo, Rev. Cayo, J.C.D., Disertacion Historico-Canonica sobre la Potestad del Cabildo en Sede Vacante o Impedida del Vicario Capitular, 99 pp., 1919 (1918).
5. Kubelbeck, Rev. William J., S.T.B., J.C.D., The Sacred Penitentiaria and Its Relation to Faculties of Ordinaries and Priests, 129 pp., 1918.
6. Petrovits, Rev. Joseph, J.C., S.T.D., J.C.D., The New Church Law on Matrimony, X-461 pp., 1919.
7. Hickey, Rev. John J., S.T.B., J.C.D., Irregularities and Simple Impediments in the New Code of Canon Law, 100 pp., 1920.
8. Klekotka, Rev. Peter J., S.T.B., J.C.D., Diocesan Consultors, 179 pp., 1920.
9. Wanenmacher, Rev. Francis, J.C.D., The Evidence in Ecclesiastical Procedure Affecting the Marriage Bond, 1920 (Printed 1935).
10. Golden, Rev. Henry Francis, J.C.D., Parochial Benefices in the New Code, IV-119 pp., 1921 (Printed 1925).
11. Koudelka, Rev. Charles J., J.C.D., Pastors, Their Rights and Duties According to the New Code of Canon Law, 211 pp., 1921.
12. Melo, Rev. Antonius, O.F.M., J.C.D., De Exemptione Regularium, X-188 pp., 1921.
13. Schaaf, Rev. Valentine Theodore, O.F.M., S.T.B., J.C.D., The Cloister, X-180 pp., 1921.
14. Burke, Rev. Thomas Joseph, S.T.D., J.C.D., Competence in Ecclesiastical Tribunals, IV-117 pp., 1922.
15. Leech, Rev. George Leo, J.C.D., A Comparative Study of the Constitution "Apostolicae Sedis" and the "Codex Juris Canonici," 179 pp., 1922.
16. Motry, Rev. Hubert Louis, S.T.D., J.C.D., Diocesan Faculties According to the Code of Canon Law, II-167 pp., 1922.
17. Murphy, Rev. George Lawrence, J.C.D., Delinquencies and Penalties in the Administration and the Reception of the Sacraments, IV-121 pp., 1923.
18. O'Reilly, Rev. John Anthony, S.T.B., J.C.D., Ecclesiastical Sepulture in the New Code of Canon Law, II-129 pp., 1923.

* From nn. 1-100 inclusive only nn. 25 and 57 are still obtainable.
From n. 101 onward all numbers are available except the following: nn. 101-118 inclusive, and also n. 122.

19. Michalicka, Rev. Wenceslas Cyrill, O.S.B., J.C.D., Judicial Procedure in Dismissal of Clerical Exempt Religious, 107 pp., 1923.
20. Dargin, Rev. Edward Vincent, S.T.B., J.C.D., Reserved Cases According to the Code of Canon Law, IV-103 pp., 1924.
21. Godfrey, Rev. John A., S.T.B., J.C.D., The Right of Patronage According to the Code of Canon Law, 153 pp., 1924.
22. Hagedorn, Rev. Francis Edward, J.C.D., General Legislation on Indulgences, II-154 pp., 1924.
23. King, Rev. James Ignatius, J.C.D., The Administration of the Sacraments to Dying Non-Catholics, V-141 pp., 1924.
24. Winslow, Rev. Francis Joseph, O.F.M., J.C.D., Vicars and Prefects Apostolic, IV-149 pp., 1924.
25. Correa, Rev. Jose Servelion, S.T.L., J.C.D., La Potestad Legislativa de la Iglesia Catolica, IV-127 pp., 1925.
26. Dugan, Rev. Henry Francis, A.M., J.C.D., The Judiciary Department of the Diocesan Curia, 87 pp., 1925.
27. Keller, Rev. Charles Frederick, S.T.B., J.C.D., Mass Stipends, 167 pp., 1925.
28. Paschang, Rev. John Linus, J.C.D., The Sacramentals According to the Code of Canon Law, 129 pp., 1925.
29. Piontek, Rev. Cyrillus, O.F.M., S.T.B., J.C.D., De Indulto Exclaustrationis necnon Saecularizationis, XIII-289 pp., 1925.
30. Kearney, Rev. Richard Joseph, S.T.B., J.C.D., Sponsors at Baptism According to the Code of Canon Law, IV-127 pp., 1925.
31. Bartlett, Rev. Chester Joseph, A.M., LL.B., J.C.D., The Tenure of Parochial Property in the United States of America, V-108 pp., 1926.
32. Kilker, Rev. Adrian Jerome, J.C.D., Extreme Unction, V-425 pp., 1926.
33. McCormick, Rev. Robert Emmett, J.C.D., Confessors of Religious, VIII-266 pp., 1926.
34. Miller, Rev. Newton Thomas, J.C.D., Founded Masses According to the Code of Canon Law, VII-93 pp., 1926.
35. Roelker, Rev. Edward G., S.T.D., J.C.D., Principles of Privilege According to the Code of Canon Law, XI-166 pp., 1926.
36. Bakalarczyk, Rev. Richardus, M.I.C., J.U.D., De Novitiatu, VIII-208 pp., 1927.
37. Pizzuti, Rev. Lawrence, O.F.M., J.U.L., De Parochis Religiosis, 1927. (Not Printed.)
38. Bliley, Rev. Nicholas Martin, O.S.B., J.C.D., Altars According to the Code of Canon Law, XIX-132 pp., 1927.
39. Brown, Mr. Brendan Francis, A.B., LL.M., J.U.D., The Canonical Juristic Personality with Special Reference to its Status in the United States of America, V-212 pp., 1927.
40. Cavanaugh, Rev. William Thomas, C.P., J.U.D., The Reservation of the Blessed Sacrament, VIII-101 pp., 1927.

41. Doheny, Rev. William J., C.S.C., A.B., J.U.D., Church Property: Modes of Acquisition, X-118 pp., 1927.
42. Feldhaus, Rev. Aloysius H., C.PP.S., J.C.D., Oratories, IX-141 pp., 1927.
43. Kelly, Rev. James Patrick, A.B., J.C.D., The Jurisdiction of the Simple Confessor, X-208 pp., 1927.
44. Neuberger, Rev. Nicholas J., J.C.D., Canon 6 or the Relation of the Codex Juris Canonici to the Preceding Legislation, V-95 pp., 1927.
45. O'Keefe, Rev. Gerald Michael, J.C.D., Matrimonial Dispensations, Powers of Bishops, Priests, and Confessors, VIII-232 pp., 1927.
46. Quigley, Rev. Joseph A. M., A.B., J.C.D., Condemned Societies, 139 pp., 1927.
47. Zaplotnik, Rev. Johannes Leo, J.C.D., De Vicariis Foraneis, X-142 pp., 1927.
48. Duskie, Rev. John Aloysius, A.B., J.C.D., The Canonical Status of the Orientals in the United States, VIII-196 pp., 1928.
49. Hyland, Rev. Francis Edward, J.C.D., Excommunication, Its Nature, Historical Development and Effects, VIII-181 pp., 1928.
50. Reinmann, Rev. Gerald Joseph, O.M.C., J.C.D., The Third Order Secular of Saint Francis, 201 pp., 1928.
51. Schenk, Rev. Francis J., J.C.D., The Matrimonial Impediments of Mixed Religion and Disparity of Cult, XVI-318 pp., 1929.
52. Coady, Rev. John Joseph, S.T.D., J.U.D., A.M., The Appointment of Pastors, VIII-150 pp., 1929.
53. Kay, Rev. Thomas Henry, J.C.D., Competence in Matrimonial Procedure, VIII-164 pp., 1929.
54. Turner, Rev. Sidney Joseph, C.P., J.U.D., The Vow of Poverty, XLIX-217 pp., 1929.
55. Kearney, Rev. Raymond A., A.B., S.T.D., J.C.D., The Principles of Delegation, VII-149 pp., 1929.
56. Conran, Rev. Edward James, A.B., J.C.D., The Interdict, V-163 pp., 1930.
57. O'Neill, Rev. William H., J.C.D., Papal Rescripts of Favor, VII-218 pp., 1930.
58. Bastnagel, Rev. Clement Vincent, J.U.D., The Appointment of Parochial Adjutants and Assistants, XV-257 pp., 1930.
59. Ferry, Rev. William A., A.B., J.C.D., Stole Fees, V-136 pp., 1930.
60. Costello, Rev. John Michael, A.B., J.C.D., Domicile and Quasi-Domicile, VII-201 pp., 1930.
61. Kremer, Rev. Michael Nicholas, A.B., S.T.B., J.C.D., Church Support in the United States, VI-136 pp., 1930.
62. Angulo, Rev. Luis, C.M., J.C.D., Legislation de la Iglesia sobre la intencion en la application de la Santa Misa, VII-104 pp., 1931.
63. Frey, Rev. Wolfgang Norbert, O.S.B., A.B., J.C.D., The Act of Religious Profession, VIII-174 pp., 1931.

64. Roberts, Rev. James Brendan, A.B., J.C.D., The Banns of Marriage, XIV-140 pp., 1931.
65. Ryder, Rev. Raymond Aloysius, A.B., J.C.D., Simony, IX-151 pp., 1931.
66. Campagna, Rev. Angelo, Ph.D., J.U.D., Il Vicario Generale del Vescovo, VII-205 pp., 1931.
67. Cox, Rev. Joseph Godfrey, A.B., J.C.D., The Administration of Seminaries, VI-124 pp., 1931.
68. Gregory, Rev. Donald J., J.U.D., The Pauline Privilege, XV-165 pp., 1931.
69. Donohue, Rev. John F., J.C.D., The Impediment of Crime, VII-110 pp., 1931.
70. Dooley, Rev. Eugene A., O.M.I., J.C.D., Church Law on Sacred Relics, IX-143 pp., 1931.
71. Orth, Rev. Clement Raymond, O.M.C., J.C.D., The Approbation of Religious Institutes, 171 pp., 1931.
72. Pernicone, Rev. Joseph M., A.B., J.C.D., The Ecclesiastical Prohibition of Books, XII-267 pp., 1932.
73. Clinton, Rev. Connell, A.B., J.C.D., The Paschal Precept, IX-108 pp., 1932.
74. Donnelly, Rev. Francis B., A.M., S.T.L., J.C.D., The Diocesan Synod, VIII-125 pp., 1932.
75. Torrente, Rev. Camilo, C.M.F., J.C.D., Las Procesiones Sagradas, V-145 pp., 1932.
76. Murphy, Rev. Edwin J., C.PP.S., J.C.D., Suspension Ex Informata Conscientia, XI-122 pp., 1932.
77. MacKenzie, Rev. Eric F., A.M., S.T.L., J.C.D., The Delict of Heresy in its Commission, Penalization, Absolution, VII-124 pp., 1932.
78. Lyons, Rev. Avitus E., S.T.B., J.C.D., The Collegiate Tribunal of First Instance, XI-147 pp., 1932.
79. Connolly, Rev. Thomas A., J.C.D., Appeals, XI-195, pp., 1932.
80. Sangmeister, Rev. Joseph V., A.B., J.C.D., Force and Fear as Precluding Matrimonial Consent, V-211 pp., 1932.
81. Jaeger, Rev. Leo A., A.B., J.C.D., The Administration of Vacant and Quasi-Vacant Episcopal Sees in the United States, IX-229 pp., 1932.
32. Rimlinger, Rev. Herbert T., J.C.D., Error Invalidating Matrimonial Consent, VII-79 pp., 1932.
83. Barrett, Rev. John D. M., S.S., J.C.D., A Comparative Study of the Third Plenary Council of Baltimore and the Code, IX-221 pp., 1932.
84. Carberry, Rev. John J., Ph.D., S.T.D., J.C.D., The Juridical Form of Marriage, X-177 pp., 1934.
85. Dolan, Rev. John L., A.B., J.C.D., The Defensor Vinculi, XII-157 pp., 1934.
86. Hannan, Rev. Jerome D., A.M., S.T.D., LL.B., J.C.D., The Canon Law of Wills, IX-517 pp., 1934.

87. Lemieux, Rev. Delise A., A.M., J.C.D., The Sentence in Ecclesiastical Procedure, IX-131 pp., 1934.
88. O'Rourke, Rev. James J., A.B., J.C.D., Parish Registers, VII-109 pp., 1934.
89. Timlin, Rev. Bartholomew, O.F.M., A.M., J.C.D., Conditional Matrimonial Consent, X-381 pp., 1934.
90. Wahl, Rev. Francis X., A.B., J.C.D., The Matrimonial Impediments of Consanguinity and Affinity, VI-125 pp., 1934.
91. White, Rev. Robert J., A.B., LL.B., S.T.B., J.C.D., Canonical Ante-Nuptial Promises and the Civil Law, VI-152 pp., 1934.
92. Herrera, Rev. Antonio Parra, O.C.D., J.C.D., Legislacion Ecclesiastica sobra el Ayuno y la Abstinencia, XI-191 pp., 1935.
93. Kennedy, Rev. Edwin J., J.C.D., The Special Matrimonial Process in Cases of Evident Nullity, X-165 pp., 1935.
94. Manning, Rev. John J., A.B., J.C.D., Presumption of Law in Matrimonial Procedure, XI-111 pp., 1935.
95. Moeder, Rev. John M., J.C.D., The Proper Bishop for Ordination and Dismissorial Letters, VII-135 pp., 1935.
96. O'Mara, Rev. William A., A.B., J.C.D., Canonical Causes for Matrimonial Dispensations, IX-155 pp., 1935.
97. Reilly, Rev. Peter, J.C.D., Residence of Pastors, IX-81 pp., 1935.
98. Smith, Rev. Mariner T., O.P., S.T.Lr., J.C.D., The Penal Law for Religious, VIII-169 pp., 1935.
99. Whalen, Rev. Donald W., A.M., J.C.D., The Value of Testimonial Evidence in Matrimonial Procedure, XIII-297 pp., 1935.
100. Cleary, Rev. Joseph F., J.C.D., Canonical Limitations on the Alienation of Church Property, VIII-141 pp., 1936.
101. Glynn, Rev. John C., J.C.D., The Promoter of Justice, XX-337 pp., 1936.
102. Brennan, Rev. James H., S.S., M.A., S.T.B., J.C.D., The Simple Convalidation of Marriage, VI-135 pp., 1937.
103. Brunini, Rev. Joseph Bernard, J.C.D., The Clerical Obligations of Canons 139 and 142, X-121 pp., 1937.
104. Connor, Rev. Maurice, A.B., J.C.D., The Administrative Removal of Pastors, VIII-159 pp., 1937.
105. Guilfoyle, Rev. Merlin Joseph, J.C.D., Custom, XI-144 pp., 1937.
106. Hughes, Rev. James Austin, A.B., A.M., J.C.D., Witnesses in Criminal Trials of Clerics, IX-140 pp., 1937.
107. Jansen, Rev. Raymond J., A.B., S.T.L., J.C.D., Canonical Provisions for Catechetical Instruction, VII-153 pp., 1937.
108. Kealy, Rev. John James, A.B., J.C.D., The Introductory Libellus in Church Court Procedure, XI-121 pp., 1937.
109. McManus, Rev. James Edward, C.SS.R., J.C.D., The Administration of Temporal Goods in Religious Institutes, XVI-196 pp., 1937.

110. Moriarty, Rev. Eugene James, J.C.D., Oaths in Ecclesiastical Courts, X-115 pp., 1937.
111. Rainer, Rev. Eligius George, C.SS.R., J.C.D., Suspension of Clerics, XVII-249 pp., 1937.
112. Reilly, Rev. Thomas F., C.SS.R., J.C.D., Visitation of Religious, VI-195 pp., 1938.
113. Moriarty, Rev. Francis E., C.SS.R., J.C.D., The Extraordinary Absolution from Censures, XV-334 pp., 1938.
114. Connolly, Rev. Nicholas P., J.C.D., The Canonical Erection of Parishes, X-132 pp., 1938.
115. Donovan, Rev. James Joseph, J.C.D., The Pastor's Obligation in Prenuptial Investigation, XII-322 pp., 1938.
116. Harrigan, Rev. Robert J., M.A., S.T.B., J.C.D., The Radical Sanation of Invalid Marriages, VIII-208 pp., 1938.
117. Boffa, Rev. Conrad Humbert, J.C.D., Canonical Provisions for Catholic Schools, VII-211 pp., 1939.
118. Parsons, Rev. Anscar John, O.M.Cap., J.C.D., Canonical Elections, XII-236 pp., 1939.
119. Reilly, Rev. Edward Michael, A.B., J.C.D., The General Norms of Dispensation, XII-156 pp., 1939.
120. Ryan, Rev. Gerald Aloysius, A.B., J.C.D., Principles of Episcopal Jurisdiction, XII-172 pp., 1939.
121. Burton, Rev. Francis James, C.S.C., A.B., J.C.D., A Commentary on Canon 1125, X-222 pp., 1940.
122. Miaskiewicz, Rev. Francis Sigismund, J.C.D., Supplied Jurisdiction According to Canon 209, XII-340 pp., 1940.
123. Rice, Rev. Patrick William, A.B., J.C.D., Proof of Death in Prenuptial Investigation, VIII-156 pp., 1940.
124. Anglin, Rev. Thomas Francis, M.S., J.C.D., The Eucharistic Fast, VIII-183 pp., 1941.
125. Coleman, Rev. John Jerome, J.C.D., The Minister of Confirmation, VI-153 pp., 1941.
126. Downs, Rev. John Emmanuel, A.B., J.C.D., The Concept of Clerical Immunity, XI-163 pp., 1941.
127. Esswein, Rev. Anthony Albert, J.C.D., Extrajudicial Penal Powers of Ecclesiastical Superiors, X-144 pp., 1941.
128. Farrell, Rev. Benjamin Francis, M.A., S.T.L., J.C.D., The Rights and Duties of the Local Ordinary Regarding Congregations of Women Religious of Pontifical Approval, V-195 pp., 1941.
129. Feeney, Rev. Thomas John, A.B., S.T.L., J.C.D., Restitutio in Integrum, VI-169 pp., 1941.
130. Findlay, Rev. Stephen William, O.S.B., A.B., J.C.D., Canonical Norms Governing the Deposition and Degradation of Clerics, XVII-279 pp., 1941.

131. Goodwine, Rev. John, A.B., S.T.L., J.C.D., The Right of the Church to Acquire Property, VIII-119 pp., 1941.
132. Heston, Rev. Edward Louis, C.S.C., Ph.D., S.T.D., J.C.D., The Alienation of Church Property in the United States, XII-222 pp., 1941.
133. Hogan, Rev. James John, A.B., S.T.L., J.C.D., Judicial Advocates and Procurators, XIII-200 pp., 1941.
134. Kealy, Rev. Thomas M., A.B., Litt.B., J.C.D., Dowry of Women Religious, IX-152 pp., 1941.
135. Keene, Rev. Michael James, O.S.B., J.C.D., Religious Ordinaries and Canon 198, V-164 pp., 1942.
136. Kerin, Rev. Charles A., S.S., M.A., S.T.B., J.C.D., The Privation of Christian Burial, XVI-279 pp., 1941.
137. Louis, Rev. William Francis, M.A., J.C.D., Diocesan Archives, X-101 pp., 1941.
138. McDevitt, Rev. Gilbert Joseph, A.B., J.C.D., Legitimacy and Legitimation, X-247 pp., 1941.
139. McDonough, Rev. Thomas Joseph, A.B., J.C.D., Apostolic Administrators, X-217 pp., 1941.
140. Meier, Rev. Carl Anthony, A.B., J.C.D., Penal Administrative Procedure Against Negligent Pastors, XI-240 pp., 1941.
141. Schmidt, Rev. John Rogg, A.B., J.C.D., The Principles of Authentic Interpretation in Canon 17 of the Code of Canon Law, XII-331 pp., 1941.
142. Slafkosky, Rev. Andrew Leonard, A.B., J.C.D., The Canonical Episcopal Visitation of the Diocese, X-197 pp., 1941.
143. Swoboda, Rev. Innocent Robert, O.F.M., J.C.D., Ignorance in Relation to the Imputability of Delicts, IX-271 pp., 1941.
144. Dubé, Rev. Arthur Joseph, A.B., J.C.D., The General Principles for the Reckoning of Time in Canon Law, VIII-299 pp., 1941.
145. McBride, Rev. James T., A.B., J.C.D., Incardination and Excardination of Seculars, XX-585 pp., 1941.
146. Król, Rev. John T., J.C.D., The Defendant in Ecclesiastical Trials, XII-207 pp., 1942.
147. Comyns, Rev. Joseph J., C.SS.R., A.B., J.C.D., Papal and Episcopal Administration of Church Property, XIV-155 pp., 1942.
148. Barry, Rev. Garrett Francis, O.M.I., J.C.D., Violation of the Cloister, XII-260 pp., 1942.
149. Boiduc, Rev. Gatien, C.S.V., A.B., S.T.L., J.C.D., Les Études dans les Religions Cléricales, VIII-155 pp., 1942.
150. Boyle, Rev. David John, M.A., J.C.D., The Juridic Effects of Moral Certitude on Pre-Nuptial Guarantees, XII-188 pp., 1942.
151. Canavan, Rev. Walter Joseph, M.A., Litt.D., J.C.D., The Profession of Faith, XII-143 pp., 1942.
152. Desrochers, Rev. Bruno, A.B., Ph.L., S.T.B., J.C.D., Le Premier Concile Plénier de Québec et le Code de Droit Canonique, XIV-186 pp., 1942.

153. Dillon, Rev. Robert Edward, A.B., J.C.D., Common Law Marriage, X-148 pp., 1942.
154. Dodwell, Rev. Edward John, Ph.D., S.T.B., J.C.D., The Time and Place for the Celebration of Marriage, X-156 pp., 1942.
155. Donnellan, Rev. Thomas Andrew, A.B., J.C.D., The Obligation of the Missa pro Populo, VII-131 pp., 1942.
156. Eltz, Rev. Louis Anthony, A.B., J.C.D., Cooperation in Crime, XII-208 pp., 1942.
157. Gass, Rev. Sylvester Francis, M.A., J.C.D., Ecclesiastical Pensions, XI-206 pp., 1942.
158. Guiniven, Rev. John Joseph, C.SS.R., J.C.D., The Precept of Hearing Mass, XIV-188 pp., 1942.
159. Gulczynski, Rev. John Theophilus, J.C.D., The Desecration and Violation of Churches, X-126 pp., 1942.
160. Hammill, Rev. John Leo, M.A., J.C.D., The Obligations of the Traveler According to Canon 14, VIII-204 pp., 1942.
161. Haydt, Rev. John Joseph, A.B., J.C.D., Reserved Benefices, XI-148 pp., 1942.
162. Huser, Rev. Roger John, O.F.M., A.B., J.C.D., The Crime of Abortion in Canon Law, XII-187 pp., 1942.
163. Kearney, Rev. Francis Patrick, A.B., S.T.L., J.C.D., The Principles of Canon 1127, X-162 pp., 1942.
164. Linahen, Rev. Leo James, S.T.L., J.C.D., De Absolutione Complicis in Peccato Turpi, V-114 pp., 1942.
165. McCloskey, Rev. Joseph Aloysius, A.B., J.C.D., The Subject of Ecclesiastical Law According to Canon 12, XVII-246 pp., 1942.
166. O'Neill, Rev. Francis Joseph, C.SS.R., J.C.D., The Dismissal of Religious in Temporary Vows, XIII-220 pp., 1942.
167. Prince, Rev. John Edward, A.B., S.T.B., J.C.D., The Diocesan Chancellor, X-136 pp., 1942.
168. Riesner, Rev. Albert Joseph, C.SS.R., J.C.D., Apostates and Fugitives from Religious Institutes, IX-168 pp., 1942.
169. Stenger, Rev. Joseph Bernard, J.C.D., The Mortgaging of Church Property, 186 pp., 1942.
170. Waldron, Rev. Joseph Francis, A.B., J.C.D., The Minister of Baptism, XII-197 pp., 1942.
171. Willett, Rev. Robert Albert, J.C.D., The Probative Value of Documents in Ecclesiastical Trials, X-124 pp., 1942.
172. Woeber, Rev. Edward Martin, M.A., J.C.D., The Interpellations, XII-161 pp., 1942.
173. Benko, Rev. Matthew Aloysius, O.S.B., M.A., J.C.D., The Abbot *Nullius*, XVI-148 pp., 1943.
174. Christ, Rev. Joseph James, M.A., S.T.L., J.C.D., Dispensation from Vindicative Penalties, XIV-285 pp., 1943.

175. Clancy, Rev. Patrick M. J., O.P., A.B., S.T.Lr., J.C.D., The Local Religious Superior, X-229 pp., 1943.
176. Clarke, Rev. Thomas James, J.C.D., Parish Societies, XII-147 pp., 1943.
177. Connolly, Rev. John Patrick, S.T.L., J.C.D., Synodal Examiners and Parish Priest Consultors, X-223 pp., 1943.
178. Drumm, Rev. William Martin, A.B., J.C.D., Hospital Chaplains, XII-175 pp., 1943.
179. Flanagan, Rev. Bernard Joseph, A.B., S.T.L., J.C.D., The Canonical Erection of Religious Houses, X-147 pp., 1943.
180. Kelleher, Rev. Stephen Joseph, A.B., S.T.B., J.C.D., Discussions with Non-Catholics: Canonical Legislation, X-93 pp., 1943.
181. Lewis, Rev. Gordian, C.P., J.C.D., Chapters in Religious Institutes, XII-169 pp., 1943.
182. Marx, Rev. Adolph, J.C.D., The Declaration of Nullity of Marriages Contracted Outside the Church, X-151 pp., 1943.
183. Matulenas, Rev. Raymond Anthony, O.S.B., A.B., J.C.D., Communication, a Source of Privileges, XII-225 pp., 1943.
184. O'Leary, Rev. Charles Gerard, C.SS.R., J.C.D., Religious Dismissed After Perpetual Profession, X-213 pp., 1943.
185. Power, Rev. Cornelius Michael, J.C.D., The Blessing of Cemeteries, XII-231 pp., 1943.
186. Shuhler, Rev. Ralph Vincent, O.S.A., J.C.D., Privileges of Religious to Absolve and Dispense, XII-195 pp., 1943.
187. Ziolkowski, Rev. Thaddeus Stanislaus, A.B., J.C.D., The Consecration and Blessing of Churches, XII-151 pp., 1943.
188. Heneghan, Rev. John Joseph, S.T.D., J.C.D., The Marriages of Unworthy Catholics: Canons 1065 and 1066, XVI-213 pp., 1944.
189. Carroll, Rev. Coleman Francis, M.A., S.T.L., J.C.L., Charitable Institutions.
190. Ciesluk, Rev. Joseph Edward, Ph.B., S.T.L., J.C.L., National Parishes in the United States.
191. Coburn, Rev. Vincent Paul, A.B., J.C.D., Marriages of Conscience, XII-172 pp., 1944.
192. Connors, Rev. Charles Paul, C.S.Sp., A.B., J.C.D., Extra-Judicial Procurators in the Code of Canon Law, X-94 pp., 1944.
193. Coyle, Rev. Paul Raymond, A.B., J.C.D., Judicial Exceptions, X-142 pp., 1944.
194. Fair, Rev. Bartholomew Francis, A.B., S.T.L., J.C.D., The Impediment of Abduction, XII-122 pp., 1944.
195. Gallagher, Rev. Thomas Raphael, O.P., A.B., S.T.Lr., J.C.D., The Examination of the Qualities of the Ordinand, X-166 pp., 1944.
196. Gannon, Rev. John Mark, S.T.L., J.C.D., The Interstices Required for the Promotion to Orders, XII-100 pp., 1944.

197. Goldsmith, Rev. J. William, B.C.S., S.T.L., J.C.D., The Competence of Church and State Over Marriages—Disputed Points, X-128 pp., 1944.
198. Goodwine, Rev. Joseph Gerard, A.B., S.T.B., J.C.D., The Reception of Converts, XIV-326 pp., 1944.
199. Kowalski, Rev. Romuald Eugene, O.F.M., A.B., J.C.D., Sustenance of Religious Houses of Regulars, X-174 pp., 1944.
200. McCoy, Rev. Alan Edward, O.F.M., J.C.D., Force and Fear in Relation to Delictual Imputability and Penal Responsibility, XII-160 pp., 1944.
201. McDevitt, Rev. Vincent John, Ph.B., S.T.L., J.C.L., Perjury.
202. Martin, Rev. Thomas Owen, Ph.D., S.T.D., J.C.D., Adverse Possession, Prescription and Limitation of Actions: The Canonical "Praescriptio," XX-208 pp., 1944.
203. Miklosovic, Rev. Paul John, A.B., J.C.L., Attempted Marriages and Their Consequent Juridic Effects.
204. Mundy, Rev. Thomas Maurice, A.B., S.T.L., J.C.D., The Union of Parishes, X-164 pp., 1944.
205. O'Dea, Rev. John Coyle, A.B., J.C.D., The Matrimonial Impediment of Nonage, VIII-126 pp., 1944.
206. Olalia, Rev. Alexander Ayson, S.T.L., J.C.D., A Comparative Study of the Christian Constitution of States and the Constitution of the Philippine Commonwealth, XII-136 pp., 1944.
207. Poisson, Rev. Pierre-Marie, C.S.C., A.B., Ph.L., Th.L., J.C.L., Droits Patrimoniaux des Maisons et des Eglises Religieuses.
208. Stadalnikas, Rev. Casimir Joseph, M.I.C., J.C.D., Reservation of Censures, X-141 pp., 1944.
209. Sullivan, Rev. Eugene Henry, S.T.L., J.C.D., Proof of the Reception of the Sacraments, X-165 pp., 1944.
210. Vaughan, Rev. William Edward, J.C.D., Constitutions for Diocesan Courts, X-210 pp., 1944.
211. Paro, Rev. Gino, S.T.D., J.C.L., The Right of Apostolic Legation.
212. Balzer, Rev. Ralph Francis, C.P., J.C.D., The Computation of Time in a Canonical Novitiate, X-227 pp., 1945.
213. Dougherty, Rev. John Whelan, A.B., S.T.L., J.C.L., De Inquisitione Speciali.
214. Dziob, Rev. Michael Walter, J.C.L., The Sacred Congregation for the Oriental Church.
215. Eidenschink, Rev. John Albert, O.S.B., B.A., J.C.D., The Election of Bishops in the Letters of Pope Gregory the Great, VIII-200 pp., 1945.
216. Gill, Rev. Nicholas, C.P., J.C.L., The Spiritual Prefect in Clerical Religious Houses of Study.
217. Hynes, Rev. Harry Gerard, S.T.L., J.C.D., The Privileges of Cardinals, XII-183 pp., 1945.
218. McDevitt, Rev. Gerald Vincent, S.T.L., J.C.D., The Renunciation of an Ecclesiastical Office, XIV-179 pp., 1945.

219. MANNING, REV. JOSEPH LEROY, J.C.D., The Free Conferral of Offices, VII-116 pp., 1945.
220. MEYER, REV. LOUIS G., O.S.B., A.B., S.T.B., J.C.D., Alms-gathering by Religious, XII-163 pp., 1945.
221. O'DONNELL, REV. CLETUS FRANCIS, M.A., J.C.L., The Marriage of Minors.
222. PRUNSKIS, REV. JOSEPH, J.C.D., Comparative Law, Ecclesiastical and Civil, in Lithuanian Concordat, X-161 pp., 1945.
223. SWEENEY, REV. FRANCIS PATRICK, C.SS.R., J.C.D., The Reduction of Clerics to the Lay State, X-199 pp., 1945.
224. VOGELPOHL, REV. HENRY JOHN, J.C.L., The Simple Impediments to Holy Orders.
225. BROCKHAUS, REV. THOMAS AQUINAS, O.S.B., J.C.L., Religious who are known as *Conversi*.
226. GRIESE, REV. ORVILLE NICHOLAS, S.T.D., J.C.L., Marriage and the Procreation of Offspring.
227. BOUDREAUX, REV. WARREN LOUIS, J.C.L., The *"ab acatholicis nati"* of Canon 1099, § 2.
228. BOWE, REV. THOMAS JOSEPH, A.B., J.C.L., Religious Superioresses.
229. DIEDERICHS, REV. MICHAEL FERDINAND, S.C.J., J.C.L., The Jurisdiction of the Latin Ordinaries over their Oriental Subjects.
230. DINGMAN, REV. MAURICE JOHN, A.B., S.T.L., J.C.L., The Plaintiff in Contentious Trials.
231. FRISON, REV. BASIL, C.M.F., M.MUS., J.C.L., The Retroactivity of Law.
232. GALVIN, REV. WILLIAM ANTHONY, M.A., J.C.L., The Administrative Transfer of Pastors.
233. GORACY, REV. JOSEPH C., J.C.L., The Diriment Matrimonial Impediment of Major Orders.
234. HALE, REV. JOSEPH FRANCIS, M.A., S.T.L., J.C.L., The Pastor of Burial.
235. HENRY, REV. JOSEPH ARTHUR, A.B., J.C.L., The Mass and Holy Communion: Interritual Law.
236. LINENBERGER, REV. HERBERT, C.PP.S., J.C.L., The False Denunciation of an Innocent Confessor.
237. LOWRY, REV. JAMES MARTIN, A.B., J.C.L., Dispensation from Private Vows.
238. LYNCH, REV. GEORGE EDWARD, A.B., S.T.L., J.C.L., Coadjutors and Auxiliaries of Bishops.
239. LYNCH, REV. TIMOTHY, M.S.SS.T., J.C.L., Contracts between Bishops and Religious Congregations.
240. MCCLUNN, REV. JUSTIN DAVID, A.B., S.T.L., J.C.L., Administrative Recourse.
241. MCGARVEY, REV. THOMAS JOSEPH, A.B., S.T.L., J.C.L., Bination.
242. MCGRATH, REV. JAMES, A.B., J.C.L., The Privilege of the Canon.
243. MARBACH, REV. JOSEPH FRANCIS, A.B., J.C.L., Marriage Legislation for the Catholics of the Oriental Rites in the United States and Canada.

244. SHIMKUS, REV. BERNARD ALOYSIUS, A.B., J.C.L., The Determination and Transfer of Rite.

245. SMITH, REV. VINCENT MICHAEL, A.B., S.T.L., J.C.L., Ignorance Affecting Matrimonial Consent.

246. WACHTRLE, REV. PAUL ANTHONY, A.B., J.C.L., The Baptism of the Children of Non-Catholics.

www.ingramcontent.com/pod-product-compliance
Lightning Source LLC
LaVergne TN
LVHW050249080826
844660LV00012B/616

* 9 7 8 0 8 1 3 2 2 4 1 9 0 *